The
Organic Garden
green
and easy

The
Organic Garden
green
and easy

Allan Shepherd

This paperback edition published in 2009 by Collins

Previously published as *The Organic Garden*
in 2007 by Collins,
an imprint of HarperCollins Publishers
77-85 Fulham Palace Road
Hammersmith, London W6 8JB

www.harpercollins.co.uk

Collins is a registered trademark of HarperCollins
Publishers Ltd

10 9 8 7 6 5 4 3 2 1

Text © 2007 Allan Shepherd (except pages 138-161 which
were written by and appear courtesy of Chloë Ward)
Photography © 2007 Cristian Barnett
Design and layout © 2007 HarperCollins Publishers Ltd

A catalogue record for this book is available from the
British Library.

Photographer: Cristian Barnett
Designers: Lisa Pettibone and Emma Ewbank
Editorial Director: Jenny Heller
Commissioning Editor: Alastair Laing

ISBN   978-0-00-729091-8

Colour reproduction by Colourscan, Singapore
Printed and bound in Italy by L.E.G.O.

Mixed Sources
Product group from well-managed
forests and other controlled sources
www.fsc.org Cert no. SW-COC-1806
© 1996 Forest Stewardship Council

FSC is a non-profit international organisation established to promote the
responsible management of the world's forests. Products carrying the FSC
label are independently certified to assure consumers that they come
from forests that are managed to meet the social, economic and
ecological needs of present and future generations.

Find out more about HarperCollins and the environment at
www.harpercollins.co.uk/green

Contents

Introduction

Picture the scene. I'm standing in a field halfway up a Welsh hillside knee-deep in slug-infested cabbages. As I bend down to pick another slimy gastropod off a brassica leaf I notice a tousled blond figure waving at me. Even with 30 metres between us I can see that my guest has four undone shirt buttons beneath the collar. It's not my lucky day. It's only my landlord, rock legend Robert Plant, come to pick up some basil. It can't get much more surreal than this, I think to myself, as I wander over to shake his hand, self-consciously wiping the slime trails off my fingers as I go. Here I am, organic market gardener and tenant farmer to the man who wrote 'Stairway to Heaven' and 'Whole Lotta Love'. I'm standing in his field, the sun is shining and right at that moment I'm having the time of my life. I am not worthy.

When I met Robert Plant ten years ago I was living out a good-life fantasy. A couple of friends and I farmed a rough bit of high-altitude sheep field, not at all what you'd imagine as a 'good' place to grow vegetables. We had a Rotavator that didn't work and a wonky-wheeled cliché of a car – a traditional French peasant's 2CV (apparently they were designed to carry so many dozens of eggs down a French farm track) – that broke down halfway through the season.

A hundred and one things that could go wrong did go wrong. We lost plants, money and one of our rabbit-catching cats. Not deceased, just debunked to a nearby farmhouse. By rights we shouldn't have survived more than a few weeks. But we did. And we actually managed to grow vegetables. Even with minimal experience we delivered a weekly box of vegetables to 50 families within a 30-kilometre radius.

My friends and I used to play a game we called fantasy farming. We'd see some neglected corner of a farm and plan grand schemes of orchards, organic smallholdings and market gardens. We were disillusioned with mainstream agriculture and thought we could do better. For a brief period in 1996, at Robert's place, we did.

We transformed a barren sheep field into a productive vegetable patch and enriched the lives of hundreds of people. Folks came to visit from all over Britain. Some came for a few hours. Others stayed for days. We had wonderful picnics of fresh salads and homemade elderflower wine. People brought musical instruments and played

> Some days, the sunny ones mainly, it was a bohemian rural idyll. We had discussions about politics as we dug. Friendships were made and one or two great romances forged.

Left The author with Sue Harper, who runs the organic cut flower business Sweet Loving Flowers, and her daughter Marly.

homemade songs (though never Robert, unfortunately). Our friend Kevin built a gardener's shed out of straw bales and lime plaster – one of the first of its type in Britain. We sat in it on rainy days dunking bakery doughnuts in tea.

Some days, the sunny ones mainly, it was a bohemian rural idyll. We had discussions about politics as we dug. Friendships were made and one or two great romances forged. There was plenty of heartache – and arguments too. It was the stuff of life.

The garden was even featured in the Lily Savage programme *Life Swaps* on BBC2. Jenny and Roxanne, the two women who started the garden and did most of the hard work setting it up, lived in an automated house of the future for a week while their swappees came to work on the field. My favourite line from the resulting TV programme came as one of the participants berated the vegetables: 'Why are you so slow?'

At the risk of sounding like someone who has never quite got over his first love, I haven't experienced the same feeling of contentment and connection to a piece of land since. Before I worked there I never imagined that gardening could bring together so many elements of life. Even when it rained, when the water soaked through our waterproofs to our skin, when the wind blew the clouds over us like dandelion seeds in a storm, it was still the best. And we got to sell basil to a rock god. Party on, dude.

Now go back another twelve years. It's 1984. I've never heard of Robert Plant. I'm on a bus back from Lincoln, having just experienced my first fast-food-induced food poisoning. I don't know why I'm ill. I'm an ignorant fourteen-year-old. A teenager obsessed by the Golden Arches. I'm fat and furious. I live in the middle of nowhere and every time I go near a city I have to get my fix. I'm part of the emerging culture of obesity. A trendsetter. Ahead of my time. I'm the only fatty in the village.

Despite my weight problem, I manage to garden a little vegetable plot with one of my friends. I keep the accounts. We buy seeds and fertiliser. We reap a huge harvest of vegetables, some of which we sell to the local shop. When we come to work out the accounts at the end of the season, the fertiliser has taken up most of the profit. It puts me off gardening. I go back to playing *Football Manager* on my Amstrad 464.

Then, somewhere between 1984 and 1996, I think I was abducted by organic-loving Led-Zeppelin-listening aliens.

If I can go organic, anyone can.

I own my own piece of land now. It's no Chelsea show garden but it's mine and I love it. I enter my garden and immediately want to slow down to the pace of a snail. I take it all

At night, when the garden is as quiet as a mouse, I like listening to the sound of ivy crack under the weight of snails, and watching bats swing in and out of the street light opposite, devouring moths with pendulum efficiency.

in. And see what thoughts are thrown up. More often than not the change of pace is inspiring.

When I look up through the wood behind my plot and see thousands of insects illuminated in the shafts of light that come through to the garden, I am reminded of how much life there is on planet Earth. They look like dust particles caught in a cinema projection, but they seem as wonderful as any image you might see on a silver screen. At night, when the garden is as quiet as a mouse, I like listening to the sound of ivy crack under the weight of snails, and watching bats swing in and out of the street light opposite, devouring moths with pendulum efficiency. During the day I watch spitfire house martins picking off daytime flyers.

It's the opposite of fast-paced veggie gardening. I'm in no hurry. I'm more interested in the wildlife in my garden. And creating a space that inspires me and my friends. Organic gardening is not just about growing food. It's also about creating beauty and biodiversity. This is what I tell myself, as I work my north-facing, damp, shady, slatey-soiled place, berating the vegetables for being too slow. It's good to eat food grown in your own garden but sometimes I get more out of just watching and listening.

To ease my regret at having lost out in the perfect garden lottery, I have developed a simple hierarchy of choice when it comes to buying fresh vegetables. I have a box of vegetables delivered every week. I supplement the box with a few things from an organic market stall and a local shop owned by an organic meat farmer. If all else fails I go to the supermarket.

As if this choice wasn't enough, my friends take pity on my shade-dwelling self and offer me vegetables from their own sun-kissed plots (which is a bit of a laugh anyway, living in Wales as we do). These vegetables always taste the best, perhaps because they are usually cooked or eaten raw straight from the plot. Despite my best teenage intentions I seem to have landed in community-spirited gardening nirvana.

As the adverts say, it doesn't stop there. We have a fantastically well-organised seed-swap group to keep favourite varieties of plants going, a wide selection of organic plots to visit and one of the UK's oldest Soil Association-approved vegetable plots, run by Roger MacLennan at The Centre for Alternative Technology. We have people selling organic cut flowers, others growing more salad than you can shake a stick at. Every other person seems to be a gardener. Frankly I feel inadequate.

And everyone wants to give you something or offer you some advice. It's as if organic gardeners in my area have gone through some sort of harmony realignment device and come out the other side wanting to help people. To be part of this community is uplifting and exciting.

But the truly amazing thing is that there's nothing particularly unusual about our scene. Go to almost any area of the country (and world) and you will find something similar going on. Frankly, my teenage self would be horrified by this slow food revolution. And none of it franchised! Just ordinary people coming together to make food important again.

Every which way you care to look there's some amazing activity going on in Britain: 300 organic box schemes, 250 farmers' markets, 1,000 community gardens, 59 city farms, 75 school farms, 500,000 volunteer gardeners, thousands of organic allotmenteers... the list goes on.

St Ann's Allotment Gardens in Nottingham, one of the biggest and oldest in the country, boasts a thriving list of community enterprises benefiting everyone from nursery-age children to the long-term unemployed. Ragman's Lane farm in Gloucestershire has taught generation after generation of organic gardeners. Ludlow has declared itself a Cittàslow centre for good living, creating in the town an atmosphere conducive to appreciating quality over speed in all aspects of life. In Cornwall the real Eden project is going on at Ken Fern's Plants for a Future in Lostwithiel. Here they're testing a new system of horticulture called perennial edible or forest gardening that could help us to garden successfully in conditions of climate change. In Totnes Martin Crawford of the Agroforestry Research Trust is doing the same. In Kent Iain Tolhurst is developing new ways to garden without recourse to artificial or animal-related by-products. Coventry has the Heritage Seed Library and Garden Organic (HDRA); Bristol, The Soil Association and the ethical bank, Triodos; London, Fresh and Wild organic food shops; Keighley, The Ecology Building Society. Every part of Britain has an emerging network of community-inspired organic businesses and volunteer organisations.

Why is all this happening? I think it's because people have rediscovered what it's like to be part of something. Whether it's a community or a local group or a movement. It's fun and it feels like you're doing something vitally important. It's bringing people together to combat loss of biodiversity, social injustice and, the biggest threat to our culture, global climate change.

If I was abducted by aliens, it happened metaphorically, one night in 1991 – the first time I visited The Centre for Alternative Technology, or CAT as it is generally known. In those days you arrived at CAT via a ten-minute walk up an unlit, unpaved driveway shaded by trees. I climbed the path with fifteen friends from Hull University (we were all volunteering for the weekend). When we emerged from the trees at the top of the drive we entered a starlit courtyard of stone buildings. It was the first time starlight took my breath away.

A small handmade wooden sign directed us to our billet for the weekend – an unpretentious little wooden hut I later found out was a reclaimed exhibit from the 1976 Ideal Home Show. It was called Tea Chest. There was no one around. It was like a fairytale house. I half expected a little hobgoblin to come out shaking a stick at me. We opened the door and right in front of us laid out on an old wooden table was a beautiful homemade cake with a little note attached to it. The note said: 'Help yourself.' Some people say how notes like 'I love you' or 'Will you marry me?' changed their lives. For me it was 'Help yourself'. With those two little words I was hooked. If this was organic living, count me in.

Visiting CAT for the first time was like pushing back the coats at the back of the wardrobe and stepping into Narnia. I couldn't believe such a place existed. Here were people who acted on their beliefs, not in a highminded fashion, but in a very practical down-to-earth way. They would show the world it was possible and preferable to live an organic lifestyle by doing it. By building houses with wood instead of concrete, by generating their own power using renewable energy, by growing their own organic food. Even by baking homemade cakes for complete strangers. Luxury items might have been scarce but they had plenty of passion and nerve. And they had community.

Through 70s' recession and 80s' economic miracle, the workers at CAT just carried on ploughing their own furrow. Showing that you didn't have to buy in to what the rest of the world had to offer. You could do something different. They weren't the only people to go against the prevailing wisdom. In the late 60s and early 70s organisations that have become household names were started in cramped offices all over Britain: Greenpeace, Friends of the Earth, The Soil Association, The Henry Doubleday Research Association (now Garden Organic).

But CAT has always been a little bit different. Out on a limb in Wales, hidden from view almost, it had the opportunity to test the alternatives without anyone really

Visiting CAT for the first time was like pushing back the coats at the back of the wardrobe and stepping into Narnia.

noticing. At least that was the intention. But even by 1976, within the first two years of its existence CAT attracted visitors. A trickle at first, then a steady stream of curious people, all wanting to know what was going on at the disused quarry in Machynlleth. Even TV execs became interested. They dispatched *Blue Peter* presenters and the *Why Don't You?* team to find out what you could do if you switched off your television set and did something less boring instead. Royalty came. First Prince Philip and then his son Charles. All the time CAT, or The Quarry as it became known, carried on doing what its founder Gerard Morgan Grenville set out to do – show that alternatives were not only possible but preferable.

And now the alternatives have come of age. The Soil Association represents the fastest-growing agricultural sector in Britain. Greenpeace and Friends of the Earth feature in just about every news broadcast. Garden Organic (HDRA) has the support of our leading garden horticulturalists. And CAT helps hundreds of thousands of people every year find practical, positive solutions to environmental problems.

The non-organic world is a place I will not go back to. Despite the CS Lewis analogy, I think the organic world is the more real. It is why I live.

When I was seventeen my A-level history teacher told me of a book that started 'come with me as we rush headlong towards the conclusion'. I can't remember the title of the book but the quote obviously made an impression on me because it's stuck in my head for nineteen years. I can't promise such a breathless experience as that, Mrs Hedley, if you're reading this, but I can say that this gardening book is unique.

This book goes beyond the realms of other organic gardening reference books by treating gardening as the starting point for a whole organic lifestyle. We show you how to garden organic and live organic. We believe you can't value organic living more highly than when you work a garden. Working a garden helps you appreciate why slow food is better than fast. Why home-grown is better than bought. And why seasonal is better than imported. A garden is like Google. A question answered with every hit.

CAT has three important words in its mission statement: to inspire, inform and enable. I hope *The Organic Garden* does just that too.

Left The visitor centre at CAT viewed from the hill behind, site of the wind turbine that provides some of the centre's electricity needs. The rest comes from water, solar energy and biofuel.

Ten principles of organic gardening

I want to start with a story – if you are sitting comfortably.

Once upon a time a contented shepherd called Elzéard Bouffier kept a flock of sheep alive on a hillside of wind-blown soil, in a corner of France almost lost and best forgotten. There were no trees on this land, nor were there any of the joys that trees would have brought with them. There were no springs of water and no streams. No plants. Or animals to eat them. And as there was nothing there to take pleasure or profit from, there were no people either. Apart, that is, from those who had to live there, who had no choice in the matter. And of these people most were as harsh and bitter as the wind that swept through the gaps in the walls of their blank stone houses.

Although he could have been easily discouraged by this landscape, Elzéard was not interested in the reality that was. Only with the reality that was yet to be. Content to be alone, not bitter or lonely in his isolation, longing for nothing, Elzéard spent his unoccupied hours planting acorns – wherever he found an empty desolate spot that deserved to be occupied by timber and leaves. With no wife or family to occupy his time, nor matters of important business to attend to, nor entertainment to distract him, with the years on his side, he realised he could plant a forest, and did so.

As the acorns grew into saplings and the saplings into trees, he noticed how the raindrops no longer ran along the surface of the compacted soil to puddle the hillside with damp craters. But instead ran down the leaves and the branches and the trunks of his oaks, into the soil, where the water stayed, until the earth could hold no more. Then it bubbled its way out again, through springs and into one of the many streams that now ran through the forest.

When the leaves fell he watched the worms and the ants break them up and drag them into the earth. He witnessed plants erupt from seeds he had not planted. He did not care how they had got there. Perhaps they had re-awakened from a deep slumber, or maybe they were fresh migrants arrested in flight from some other place and shackled to the earth by his trees. That they were there was the only thing that mattered, and that insects came to feed on their nectar and that

> When the leaves fell he watched the worms and the ants break them up and drag them into the earth. He witnessed plants erupt from seeds he had not planted.

birds came to feed on the insects. And that owls returned to hunt the mice that ate the seeds of the flowers. And that rabbits and deer came to eat the plants. And finally that humans returned in their tens of thousands to take pleasure in the amazing and mysterious natural phenomenon that was Elzéard Bouffier's forest.

The original version of *The Man Who Planted Trees* by Jean Giono is a golden cloth of literature compared to the tailored square of material I have presented above. I haven't really done it justice, so make it the next book you buy. What I will try to do in this book is give you the skills and ambition to have your own back garden Elzéard Bouffier moment. Not to plant a forest! Just to take a dead space and transform it into something living and wonderful. A good place for people, plants and animals.

One: create space

Space: as in, a place to be. Gardeners grow flowers and vegetables and fruit and herbs and trees and shrubs, but over all these things they create space.

They bring together disparate elements and make something whole and beautiful. They learn which combinations of plants and materials work well together and which don't. They appreciate how space can change the way we feel, defining our moods, inspiring and enchanting us. We know when we have stepped into a beautiful garden space. We can see how much love and work has been dedicated to it. We get an idea of what sort of person the gardener is. The gardener gives more time and attention to detail to a space than any other type of person. Unlike an interior designer who leaves when the job is finished, the gardener's job is never completely done and nor does a gardener want it to be. Though we rest between work, a garden space never sits still. Plants grow and die back, and have illnesses and unwelcome pest visitors. The garden space changes from day to day. We watch what's happening to our plants and tend to those which have succumbed to one of life's little mishaps. This is the joy of caring for a garden space.

Two: soil is everything

Before you plant a single thing, get your soil care right. Plants need nutrients from compost to grow strong and prosper. Some plants will grow on poor soils but the ones we demand to grow most often, the vegetables, the fruit and the cultivated flowers, need to eat a lot of food to grow. Chemical gardeners use artificial fertilisers to feed their plants. Organic gardeners use compost and other soil improvers.

Compost improves the structure of the soil, helping soils to retain water when plants need it most, and provides food for composting creatures. Healthy soils produce healthy plants less likely to be attacked by pests and disease.

One of the most striking displays at the CAT visitor centre is a simple row of vegetable beds, one next to the other, each one filled with a different quantity of slate, soil and compost. The first bed is made up entirely of slate waste. The second bed is just slate and soil. The third bed slate, soil and compost.

Plants grown in the first bed are always small and weedy, and are attacked readily by slugs and other pests. Plants grown in the second bed are only slightly better served by the soil than those in the first. Only in the third bed, the bed stacked high with soil and compost, are plants able to flourish as they should.

Three: grow a little food

Food grown at home is better for you and better for the planet. Raw food picked fresh from the plant is better for you than cooked. And there are always more foods to eat than we ever imagine.

When I moved to Wales I fell amongst inspirational people. Every single day of the year Roger MacLennan and his volunteers prepared for the whole of the CAT staff (and still do) enough salad for each of us to fill a large plate. Amongst the salads were leaves I had never tasted before and flowers I would never have thought you could eat. Each one of these plants was raised without a single chemical and with more or less no external energy required, by which I mean materials and resources brought in from beyond the garden. The compost was made on site. The wood for materials came from hedgerows around the garden. Even some of the tools were homemade. Amongst the rows of vegetables, Roger planted flowers to attract predator insects and around the edges he dug ponds for frogs to venture forth from and eat slugs. The food travelled approximately 200 metres to reach the table (at most!). And each day we sat together, talked and enjoyed what had been grown for us.

Four: don't garden alone

Wildlife is at the heart of your organic garden, so enlist the support of your garden allies. A true organic gardener assesses how to work with nature to get the most from their garden without having to be its constant guardian. The garden is more important to those species that occupy it full-time, so make a garden for those who always use it. If you do it right the pollinating insects will bring you flowers. The composting creatures will improve your soil. The predators will eat the pests. Garden for other species and they will garden for you.

Five: grow for ornament

Vegetable plots are only part of the story. Ornamental gardens can be organic, and edible and non-edible plants can be grown together in beautiful spaces. And beautiful spaces change lives. We are only beginning to understand how bad spaces ruin lives, but with each passing year there are fresh studies that reinforce the commonsense view that people with access to beautiful spaces are happier. Just as we see studies showing that young people perform better at school if they have access to healthy food, so we are beginning to see how people of all ages perform better in beautiful environments. In

Above *Verbena bonariensis* is highly attractive to insects.

Chicago, crime rates have fallen dramatically in areas where new parks have been created. It seems that people have more respect for each other and their local area when they are under less stress. And access to beautiful spaces reduces stress.

When I was twenty-six I met my friend and long-time collaborator Chloë Ward. Chloë is a true gardener, by which I mean it is her main occupation. Much of what I know about gardening I owe to her. Chloë is one of those rare people who can see beyond that which exists today to think about what might be possible in the future. Like Elzéard Bouffier, she plants for her own enjoyment but with an eye on what might be in the years to come. Many of the pictures you'll see in this book are taken at the Garden Organic (HDRA) gardens in Yalding, where she formerly worked as deputy head gardener. Chloë's particular mission is to grow edible plants in spaces that are designed not as vegetable gardens but as ornamental landscapes, mixing the ornamental and the edible. A fact borne out by her writing on food gardens in this book, including the section on the up-and-coming and relatively new technique known as forest gardening, a subject about which she is one of only a handful of people qualified to write on.

Six: value lies in the land

July 2006 saw two of the hottest days ever recorded in Britain. The beautiful damp, lush green Wales I know and love started to look like the Mediterranean. First, CAT gardener Roger MacLennan recorded the highest temperature in his garden in twenty years. Then the next day the record was broken. In 2006 the Welsh rain failed us. A temporary blip or a sign of things to come?

The question that concerns me most is how can we garden and live in an era of climate change without losing the peace, security and good living we enjoy today? As the government's chief advisor on the issue has already suggested, climate change is now a matter of national emergency. Perhaps we need to conjure up the spirit of that other great national gardening effort, the Dig for Victory campaign of the Second World War, to look forward to our better world. To rekindle a love of gardening in a time of global crisis would be a wonderful thing.

But what kind of gardening should we aspire to? In the future, will each of us need to garden for self-sufficiency and put our leisure pursuits to one side, just as millions of people did during the Second World War? Or is this a different kind of crisis, where it is more important to use our gardens as little centres for well-being and low-carbon lifestyles?

When I'm in my garden I buy less music, I rent fewer DVDs, I don't go out so much. I stay in, I dig, mend, make, plant, plan. I travel less. Use less electricity. Need no space heating. I invite people round and we party. It's all a way of cutting my carbon use.

I figure if I can build a good life for myself here, one that is continually refreshed by new experiences of my garden, landscape and home town, I don't need to travel or pursue carbon-costly activities. I'm trying to kick carbon addiction by creating a low-carbon lifestyle and my life is all the richer for it. I'm not saying I'm perfect, but my garden helps me keep within what the carbon experts say is a global fair share of carbon emissions – 2.6 tonnes of CO_2 per year, compared to a UK average of 10 tonnes – the amount of carbon every person in the world could produce each year without causing global climate change. I've long since given up on the idea of total self-sufficiency. CAT's Peter Harper once calculated the productivity of his garden. He weighed everything that came out of it – vegetables, fruit, garden waste, wood, the lot – for a year. He wanted to see in percentage terms how self-sufficient an average garden could be. He calculated that his garden could generate around 0.5 per cent of his annual space-heating demand in wood cuttings and about £140 worth of fruit and vegetables (at 1997 prices). After removing the cost of seeds and plants from this total, the economic value of his garden amounted to 0.9 per cent of total household expenditure. The true value of a garden lay not in its economic output, however, but 'in terms of entertainment, therapy, exercise, education, contribution to environmental quality, nutrition, convenience, gourmet delights and sheer connectedness with the Earth'. In other words, all things that are priceless.

Self-sufficiency is a grand ideal but it may not be what is needed during this period of global climate change. My friends Tom and Lisa Brown (pictured above left) have a smallholding and grow almost all their own foods, make endless amounts of honey, jams and chutneys, and generally lead what you might describe in the old cliché as 'The Good Life'. But they have a lifetime of learning under their belts and several acres of land in which to make their dream possible. The good life is a good life but it is also a full-time occupation. When I walk around Tom and Lisa's place I am struck by their absolute commitment to the value of land, and their place in the history of the land they now have stewardship over.

In this period of climatic instability we will need to care for our own little patches with equal passion. Bad weather erodes soil and weakens our plants. But if we know our land well we can help to do our bit to keep it strong and healthy. If we can guide our own gardens through the traumas that climate change may bring, we will have played our part.

Right A bee collects nectar from the flower of a leek.

Seven: plant for biodiversity

To keep a check on the villains in your garden, fill it up with lots of different species of plants. Gardens are healthier if they have a large variety of different species and plants are less likely to suffer from disease.

In the flatlands of Lincolnshire I lived amongst space that was more or less dead for nature. Field upon field of agricultural crops stretched out around my village. Every summer millions of black flies blew across the open hedgeless country into our gardens. Here they would rest upon our clothes on the line, so much so that we would have to wash them all over again. They fell between gaps in our window frames and filled up the aluminium corners like ground black pepper. They got into the roots of our hair and into the corners of our eyes. The worst job I could imagine in my childhood was mowing the lawn on a hot day, one hand on the sticky vibrating plastic handle of the hover mower, the other brushing away the sweat and the flies from my face.

And all beyond me I could see the flat, open, soulless fields filled with their single crops stretching out for miles and tractors showering chemicals over them. If you were a black fly where would you go? Beneficial insects like biodiversity and pests hate it.

Eight: make a social space

Make gardens for people as well as for plants and animals. Gardens are not just for wildlife or food production. They are social spaces too and need to be designed for humans.

As a gardener I'm most interested in atmosphere, purpose and technique – what a garden feels like to be in, what it will be used for and how I can make it work horticulturally. We need a garden to do different things for us. A garden space does not just cater for one emotion or for one person or activity. It must mean different things for us at different times. For me a garden is a foil to my ever-changing moods. It's a social space when I want it to be. A quiet space whenever I need it. A place to be active. A place to be still. A sanctuary. An invigorator. One male reviewer of my last book called it too feminine for any red-blooded Englishman. I wasn't offended by the criticism. His wife loved it.

I'm altogether comfortable with my feminine side. A garden requires a long-term commitment to care and nurture. You can get all macho about gardening, but I think it's a mistake. If your only relationship with a garden is to do with strength and posturing, you might as well abandon subtlety, suggestion and the idea that a garden can cater for more than one mood.

Nine: go local

Whenever you can't meet your own needs, support your local gardening enterprises. Small organic nurseries are a wellspring of local plant knowledge as well as being part of the glue that binds a community together. Local craftspeople can supply us with garden furniture, bird houses and feeders, fencing materials and other garden paraphernalia. Market gardens and box schemes can deliver much of our food.

My friend Sue Harper has her own cut flower business. It's called Sweet Loving Flowers. She wants to grow local cut flowers to reduce the need for those flown in from the four corners of the world. Sue's plants are hand grown and tended organically on a small, one-acre, south-facing field in Wales where, contrary to some of my occasional moans, the sun does shine. Sue was once the gardener for the famed River Café in London but moved back to Wales about five years ago to bring up her child. Her enterprise is tiny compared to some of the multinational companies that import a continuous flow of chemically produced, hot-house-grown, air-miles-laden, environmentally damaging plants from abroad. But she is only one of a handful of people meeting the growing demand for organic, local cut flowers.

Work with materials that are local to your area and learn how to fashion some of the things you need in your garden from natural, sustainable materials. Natural

Above A garden is a space for people as well as plants. Here the author relaxes with fellow gardeners in an eco-treehouse (see pages 53–56).

materials grown close to home are a fantastic and beautiful resource. As you will see later, this could include beautiful woodland materials such as willow, hazel and oak, or natural earthen products such as slate, local stone or clay. Very often they are also materials that the average gardener would feel happy to learn to work with. Some of the techniques for using them are very pleasing, almost therapeutic.

Half of garden design is about choosing plants. The other half is about materials and structures. The impact on the environment of buying a few plants is relatively small compared to the impact of some garden materials, furniture and accessories. The atmosphere and ecological footprint of a garden can be spoilt by poor material choice. Make sure you are not creating a paradise at home by destroying one somewhere else.

Above Use local materials and support local craftspeople, or even learn how to make your own garden furniture (see pages 42–46).

Ten: what we do in our gardens matters

It matters to somebody somewhere, even when we think it doesn't.

Many people have changed the direction of my life. Some of them I've never met. Top of this list is Chico Mendes. Chico Mendes worked in a small area of rainforest in a remote region of Brazil. His job was to extract a harvest of natural rubber from trees – a job he could do without harming the trees. Chico supplemented his income by collecting other things from the forest too – Brazil nuts, herbs and fruits. He believed in harvesting from the forest in a way that would keep the forest intact for ever. Being totally reliant on it he was horrified to hear that his area of rainforest was to be cut down. Faced with the loss of his own livelihood, he organised a peaceful campaign of protest and resistance. He was sitting on the steps of his home when two gunmen hired by loggers shot him dead.

What could be so important to take the life of a man like Chico Mendes? The sad reality is that the wood Chico died to protect was turned into charcoal, garden furniture and plywood fences. It appeared in chain stores around Britain and we bought it.

How extraordinary it must have been to garden a rainforest. To walk amongst giants every day. To be no bigger than an ant nor older than a child in comparison to the living things around you. How brave to go into your garden every morning wondering whether you will return to sit on the steps of your home each night. As gardeners we can imagine how it must have been for Chico Mendes as he heard the bulldozers move onwards through the forest. Wondering when his garden would be next.

I can picture the landscape after the bulldozers moved on. It doesn't take much imagination. We've all seen the photographs. Can there be anything more ugly than the jagged edges of felled tree stumps poking up from empty soils?

But however vivid these pictures are, they still don't tell the whole story. We might think that within a few years farmers are happily ploughing and harvesting crops on this new landscape but the truth is that once a rainforest has been removed from a piece of land nothing on that land is ever quite the same again.

Rainforest soil relies on rainforests. Once they are removed the soil loses its fertility. It is a story that 300 million slash-and-burn farmers know all over the tropical world. Each one cuts, farms and moves on, chasing ever-decreasing circles of fertility until they are forced off the land altogether, into city slums. This is competition at its most brutal. Competition amongst men for land, and with nature for fertility.

> Can there be anything more ugly than the jagged edges of felled tree stumps poking up from empty soil?

Making ethical decisions

You're going to need to be equipped to start living organically, so I thought it would be helpful to list the thought processes that go through my mind when I'm making an ethical decision. I don't want to give the impression that I'm a puritan and never buy anything brand new. It's just that I like to think carefully before I buy anything.

Before you buy... DIY

- Do I need it? This is a classic example of an obvious question often overlooked. How many times do you buy something on impulse and then realise that you could have done very well without it? This may seem a bit puritan to people who like shopping without boundaries, but the first step to ethical living is think before you engage credit card.
- Can I make it at home? In Chapter one I rattle on about a garden bench I made. It's not a particularly amazing bench but, because I made it, it's the best thing since unsliced bread. Making stuff yourself is the best ecological option. You can choose the materials yourself and put it together in the least energy wasteful way.
- If I can't make it myself, can one of my friends or swap buddies make it or offer me another solution? Check out www.freecycle.org for a national network of swap-crazed freeloaders.
- If I have to buy something, can I buy recycled, secondhand or reused?
- If I have to buy new, can I buy products that are sustainable, local, natural and carry an approved symbol? (Be it a Soil Association, Forest Stewardship Council or other ethical standard.)
- If I can't buy local or natural, can I buy sustainable from the UK or Europe and from an ethically minded national company?
- If I can't buy from Europe, can I buy fair trade, organic and sustainable from developing countries?
- If I can't buy within these criteria, should I bite the bullet and buy it or is there another solution I hadn't thought of?

This sounds like a laborious process but actually after a while you can make these decisions quite quickly. It's just another skill to learn.

Buying new products

If you're buying new stuff how do you know what you're getting is really green, organic or ethical? There's a whole host of different symbols and standard-setting organisations out there but which are the ones that ensure the highest standards? I've tried to pull together the best symbols and organisations here, give you an idea of what each of them stands for, and a contact point to make further enquiries.

Understanding ethical symbols

 Soil Association. The Soil Association symbol covers things such as food, compost, liquid fertilisers, seeds and plants. A full list of organic certifying bodies is available from www.defra.gov.uk/farm/organic/standards/index.htm. The Soil Association is the most widely recognised symbol, and comes from the grass roots organic movement: www.soilassociation.org.

 Organic Farmers and Growers. One of the other main organic symbols. Check www.organicfarmers.org.uk for full standards.

 Vegan Organic Network. This symbol guarantees that your food comes from a supplier that does not use animal products to grow food. Support Vegan Organic Network to combat climate change and for help in growing your own food the green, clean and cruelty-free way: www.veganorganic.net.

 Vegan Society. Guarantees products are free from animal products and have not been made using any processes that might have harmed animals: www.vegansociety.com.

 Vegetarian Society Approved. Signifies products have met the following criteria: free from animal flesh, contains only free-range eggs, GMO free, cruelty free and no cross contamination with non-vegetarian ingredients. www.vegsoc.org.

 Leaf Marque. Affordable food produced by farmers who are committed to improving the environment for the benefit of wildlife and the countryside: www.leafmarque.com.

 Marine Stewardship Council (MSC). Internationally recognised standard for sustainable and well-managed fisheries: www.msc.org.

 Forest Stewardship Council (FSC). Indicates products which contain wood that comes from a forest that is well managed according to strict environmental, social and economic standards: www.fsc-uk.org. See also page 48.

European Energy Label. Manufacturers of certain household electricity products must label these products with information on energy consumption and performance: www.defra.gov.uk/environment/consumerprod/mtp.

 European Ecolabel. Europe-wide award for non-food products that minimise impact on the environment: www.defra.gov.uk/environment/consumerprod/ecolabel.

 Rainforest Alliance. Goods from farms and forests that are managed in an environmentally and socially responsible way: www.rainforest-alliance.org.

 Energy Saving Recommended. This logo is your guarantee that the product will save energy, cost less to run and help the environment. Managed by the Energy Saving Trust: www.est.org.uk/recommended.

 UK Fuel Economy Label. Shows how much carbon dioxide a car emits: www.lowcvp.org.uk.

 VOC Labels. Indicate the relative content of harmful VOCs (Volatile Organic Compounds) in paints and associated products. VOCs cause air pollution and may be harmful to human health: www.coatings.org.uk.

 Mobius Loop. Indicates that part of a product can be recycled where facilities are available. The inclusion of a figure shows the percentage of recycled material that has been used to make a product. www.biffa.co.uk/getrecycling/symbols.php.

 **FAIRTRADE Mark.** Products that meet international Fairtrade standards. These include long-term contracts and a price that covers the cost of sustainable production and living. Some money also goes to community groups: www.fairtrade.org.uk.

Reading between the symbols

Organised standards are almost always the best way to ensure that products are ethically up to scratch. However, there are some exceptions. Many local suppliers in my area have not been through the certification process, but because I know them and what materials they use and how they grow and harvest their materials and plants, I know I am getting an environmentally sound product. Mail-order catalogues and websites do not always brand products with a logo but use words such as 100 per cent recycled or made with organic materials. If you're not sure, ask the supplier which standards they meet and decide on face value whether you want to buy the product – with or without the logo.

Wherever possible in this book I've tried to make suggestions for new products to save you the trouble of doing all the research, but products and companies change all the time so please use the information I have provided as a guide rather than an absolute recommendation. Also I am one writer working alone. If you have any doubts concerning a product or a company then you should refer to those organisations whose job it is to monitor standards and provide information (see above).

When you're looking for a supplier, use these questions to know if they really are what they say they are. Ask them where do their products come from? What is their policy on recycling? What are they doing to reduce CO_2 emissions? There are plenty of great ethical companies now who share your values. It takes time to find good suppliers but often the rewards are much greater than the effort. I get an enormous buzz from discovering a new company selling a new range of well-thought-out products.

Where to go for independent information and advice

CAT provides one of the best information services in the country. It has a huge database of contacts working in the environmental sector. CAT does not set standards or review company performances but will act on complaints made about companies, which can result in their removal from the database. Phone their information line on + 44 (0) 1654 705 989.

Ethical Consumer magazine is the single most important source of information about products, services and companies available to the average consumer. Each month it analyses a different set of products for their environmental and ethical performance. A must read.

Gardening Which? magazine does not necessarily focus on environmental and ethical considerations so much as quality and performance of products, but sustainability is also about how well a product performs and lasts. It does have special environmental features and as a general read for the average gardener it is extremely good.

The World Wide Fund for Nature (WWF) has extremely strict buying criteria for all of its products. Each supplier has to fill out a ream of forms before the organisation will stock its goods.

Greenpeace and Friends of the Earth both produce wide-ranging reports on ethical and environmental standards and whistle-blow the illegal activities of polluting companies worldwide.

Other magazines: *Organic Gardening*, *Permaculture*, *The Organic Way* – the magazine of Garden Organic (HDRA) – *The Ecologist*, *New Consumer*, *Free Range*, *Growing Green International from VON* and *Clean Slate* – CAT's membership mag – are all good sources of information.

Useful websites include www.ethical-junction.org, www.greenguide.co.uk and www.reuze.co.uk.

Buying tools – used or new?

Before you buy anything new go along to a local car boot sale, ask around your mates and check on www.freecycle.org. Don't buy anything until you've exhausted all these secondhand options. Apart from secateurs – which have to be clean and sharp to prevent the spread of plant diseases – and some specialist tools (of which more in a moment), all these tools are just as effective secondhand. Tools need to be rigorous and tough. Check that handles are strong and that the blade or prongs do not bend easily. Some cheap hand forks and trowels bend easily. Press them onto a surface to test them.

There are thousands of unwanted tools cluttering up sheds all over Britain and some companies are getting into the recycling spirit by reclaiming, reconditioning and selling them on. These 'vintage' tools are sometimes difficult to get hold of and have special features not normally available. I curse the day I missed an opportunity to buy a reconditioned Victorian daisy grubber from Wales-based group Tools for Self Reliance Cymru (www.tfsrcymru.org.uk). It was a lovely piece of work that would have made my weeding a lot easier. Buying secondhand tools saves energy and materials and avoids difficult ethical questions about where the tools came from.

When to buy new

In some situations it's worth buying new. People with back problems or disabilities that prevent them using run-of-the-mill secondhand tools can access good ergonomic tools at www.carryongardening.org.uk, the website of Thrive, an organisation specialising in horticultural therapy. One example is the Swoe cultivator – an extremely useful type of hoe that looks like a golf club. It's lightweight, but extremely strong and can clear weeds on the backwards and the forwards motion. Turned on its edge it can be used to dig holes for planting, to draw seed drills, and for ridging soil. It is not necessarily designed for people with disabilities but its flexibility and lightness make it a particularly handy tool. The excellently named Lazy Dog Tool Company produce handmade back-saving tools in Yorkshire. Their RIP (removal of individual plants) system keeps bending to a minimum. I also found something called a speed weeder (a small hand tool that enables you to hook weeds out under the root; especially useful for removing weeds from walls and the cracks between paving), which is made in the UK for the Gardeners' Royal Benevolent Society.

Many new tools are made in developing countries. Most of the time it's impossible to know in what conditions these tools have been manufactured. It is certainly true to say that health and safety regulations for workers are nowhere near as strong as ours; similarly environmental regulations will be less stringent. Some high-street retailers have made efforts to improve the rights of the workers who supply their tools. B&Q has a long-term goal of transforming the working conditions of suppliers and reducing the environmental impact of their work. If you want to know how good the claims are you need to check out *Ethical Consumer* magazine's website www.ethicalconsumer.org.uk.

Most power tools get used for a total of just fifteen minutes in their entire lifetime so cut down on waste by renting from hire shops, borrowing from friends or asking on a swap shop. Of the ten companies investigated by the magazine *Ethical Consumer*, Draper came out top, followed by The Stanley Works and Makita Corp. and then Black & Decker. The WEEE Directive (Waste Electrical and Electronic Equipment) requires member states of the European Union to set up collection systems for all old electrical equipment by the end of 2006.

Basic garden tool kit

One **fork** for digging out weeds, turning over soil, lifting plants, forking
   in compost and manure
One **spade** for digging holes, moving soil, making trenches
One **rake** for levelling soil ready for planting seeds, removing some
   lawn weeds, gathering grass clippings, etc
One **hoe** for removing weeds, marking seed trenches
One **hand trowel** for digging small holes and removing some weeds
One **hand fork** for removing easy-to-lift weeds
One pair of **secateurs** for light pruning
One small **pruning saw** for removing slightly thicker unwanted growth
One pair of **scissors** for cutting flowers, string, etc
One **knife** for removing difficult weeds from patios, walls, etc
One **sharpening tool** for keeping your cutting tools sharp

Chapter one

My space: planning your garden

My granddad detested disorganisation of any sort. He kept all his files in immaculate order and planned everything exceedingly well. If my granddad was writing this book he would expect you to prepare detailed plans of your garden on paper to which you could refer later. And you would need to work out exactly how much spare time you had, and whether or not it was feasible to do the things you wanted to. I am ashamed to say that I have not inherited his sense of order or preparation, I can't draw and I'm not too good at keeping records. What I can do is appreciate how the seasons change the garden, work out what type of soil I've got and what plants I can grow, shape the garden to suit my needs and see that the wildlife get their fair share. None of this is difficult. It just takes time, knowledge and a sense of calm understanding. I tend to keep all the information about my garden in my head and move it around from time to time to come up with the next stage of my slightly baggy long-term development plan. Your impression of a garden changes over time and you learn things that you couldn't possibly have imagined when you first encountered the space.

Take a gap year

Unless you've just bought a new-build house, you'll come into a garden as a small link in a great chain of people who have come before and who will enter after. New-build gardens come without any of the emotional and physical clutter of other people's plants, sheds, ornaments and rubbish to worry about. If you're starting work on an old garden, it's rarely advisable to tear the whole lot down and start again. It takes up more energy, materials, time and money and is not environmentally, financially and emotionally sustainable. Decide what you can live with and work with what you've got.

Whether your garden is new or old, it takes a good year to get to know it well enough to really start pulling a plan together. Plants are either sun-loving, shade-tolerant or semi-shade tolerant and the shade cast in your garden will vary from month to month over the whole year (see page 68). You'll need to learn how other weather conditions such as rain, wind and frost affect the garden (see pages 72–85), because they will all affect plant growth too. If you're planning to put in fencing, hedging or any structural elements, you'll need to site them carefully to make the most of these conditions (see page 38). You'll also need to know what kind of soil you have – clay, sandy, boggy, dry, stony, rich, poor, acid or alkaline – and what sort of plants will grow there (bog-loving, drought-tolerant, acid- or alkaline-loving, and so on). For the sake of clarity I've put all this important information in Chapter three.

Plant editing

After about two years of being in my current garden I've really started to appreciate all the wildflowers that come up. I haven't had to do anything to encourage them – just leave them be. In fact, in large parts of my garden I've developed a policy of editing what's there naturally rather than buying and planting seeds. This means digging up those weeds that will become invasive (see pages 190–207) and leaving those wildflowers I know I want. Foxgloves (*Digitalis*), cambrian poppies (*Meconopsis cambrica*) and red campion (*Silene dioica*) are all mainstays in my garden and they're all fantastic for pollinating insects. They are also resistant to attack from slugs and snails. Editing is a good way to learn about the differences between weeds and wildflowers if you're just starting to garden.

But editing has obvious limitations. You can't edit yourself a vegetable patch. Or an orchard. Or a perennial flower border full of your favourite plants. If you want to grow the plants you prefer, rather than those the soil throws up, you have to write your own story – not edit nature's. This means working out what sort of planting schemes you want, what shape beds to make and how much room to give to each different element within the garden. You'll also have to decide how to enclose your boundaries and where to put your paths. If your pencil skills are like mine – only fit for French caves – don't feel you have to draw everything. Keep it in your head. For once it may be better in than out.

Hopefully as you read this book, you'll get an idea of what sort of plants you might want to put in your garden. If you're like my mum you've probably already overstocked it in your imagination to Kew Garden proportions. Remember to leave room for all the other things you need: paths, seating areas, hot tubs. The last one is optional, obviously, but unless you're in possession of a Harry Potter broomstick you'll need the first two. A balance has to be struck between plants and infrastructure. And if you're starting with a clean sheet you need to plan both at the same time.

Pulling shapes: landscaping and other materials

Most of the hard landscaping materials in my garden were chosen by the previous owner. Luckily he landscaped the garden sensitively, creating terraces using walls made of slate, largely reclaimed from the part of the house he took down to make room for an extension. It must have been a huge job – one that I'm very glad I didn't have to do. I can live with my hard landscaping, and I don't intend to change it or add to it. If you're starting from scratch or want a change, however, you'll need some eco-options for paths, walls, fences, seating areas and any other random garden features like trellis, arbours, and so on. Perhaps, more than anything else in your garden, it is important to get your landscaping features right. If chosen badly they can make a big impact on your garden and the environment.

Soft landscaping vs. hard landscaping

It is possible to garden entirely with so-called soft landscapes. Soft landscapes are created using living materials and include lawns and grass paths, hedges made using trees, shrubs and other plants, as well as arbours and other living structures made out of trees such as willow. If it is managed sensitively, soft landscaping is mostly more environmentally benign than hard landscaping. Hedges need to be trimmed responsibly and regularly – preferably using power-free tools or power tools that use renewable energy – and can produce a number of useful by-products, such as fruit, poles for staking peas and beans, decorative material, and so on. Lawns and grass paths are lovely to walk on and fairly low maintenance, but be careful how you cut them. A study funded by the Swedish Environment Protection Agency found that using a four-horsepower lawn mower for an hour caused the same amount of pollution as driving a car 150 kilometres. In preference use an electric mower or, even better, a non-powered mower.

Hard landscaping is made from quarried materials or cut from timber and includes decking, walls, fencing and hard paths. Common materials include stone, cut timber, concrete, brick, plastic, metal and glass. Wood is the most environmentally benign material if it is cut from responsibly managed woodland (see information on FSC approval, pages 26–27) or, even better, if it is reclaimed waste wood. Avoid MDF (medium-density fibreboard). It is made using wood and a bonding agent called urea-formaldehyde, a dangerous material described by some as the 'asbestos of the 90s'. In preference use untreated wood.

Quarried stone usually comes in its raw unprocessed form. Quarrying is hugely destructive of local environments so look for reclaimed materials if you can. If you can't, use materials that are local and traditional to your area. Unprocessed materials are generally better for the environment because processing usually involves the use of more energy. A prime example is cement, a major component of concrete. Cement has to be burned at 1500°C (worldwide the cement industry creates 10 per cent of all CO_2 emissions).

The range of reprocessed materials available to the gardener has increased over the past few years: look out for paving materials made out of reclaimed brick, chipped slate, recycled glass and reclaimed aggregates. A lot of energy is needed to produce glass, and likewise plastic, but both materials are used extensively by the gardener to capture heat and speed up the growth rates of plants. Old windows can be recycled into cloches and although polytunnel plastic wears out after a few years it can then be turned into mini cloches or laid on the soil to heat it up in early spring. Plastic is used extensively to make water butts, watering cans, compost bins, raised beds and other common garden objects. Look for products that are 100 per cent recycled.

Fencing, hedges and walls

Possibly the first thing you need to do in a garden, if it hasn't been done already, is to fence, wall or hedge it off. A barrier between you and the rest of the world helps to keep out four-legged pests like rabbits, deer and sheep (although will rarely deter foxes and cats); gives shelter and privacy to a garden; and helps to screen out ugly noise and views. Fences and hedges also offer protection from wind, but a solid fence that stops the wind dead is less stable than one that slows the wind speed down. Fencing can cast shade on a garden so you need to strike a balance and plan your materials carefully.

Fencing options

If you're buying a standard cut-wood fence, the sort of thing found in most garden centres, look for the FSC symbol, as before. A company called Forest Garden supply a huge range of DIY shops and garden centres with a massive range of wood products for the garden, including fencing, gates, sheds, storage boxes, trellis, and so on, using wood cut from FSC-approved UK forests owned by the Forestry Commission. Hurdles are a nice alternative to wire fencing and the more conventional garden fencing in most DIY stores and garden centres. They are made from untreated coppiced wood and can be bought or made at home using the same skills as for rustic furniture-making. The best website I found on the subject was www.allotmentforestry.com. Not only does this have a whole set of wonderful free fact sheets explaining how to make gates, fences, tables, arches, bird tables, hurdles, plant supports and a laptop table, there is also a directory of craftspeople working with coppiced material in England. For more information on fencing, see page 79.

Hedges

NEVER PLANT LEYLAND CYPRESS! Sorry, had to get that out of my system. Leyland cypress (*Cupressus leylandii*) is a fast-growing conifer that needs to be trimmed to maintain a good hedge, and rarely is. You usually see hedges brown, dying and ugly because the owner panics as they grow and grow and grow... and cuts the top off. Or else you see them more than 6 metres high, from which height they shade everything in sight. See www.hedgeline.org for some truly awful hedges gone wrong and try to avoid doing the same in your garden. I've picked out some good hedging trees on page 81: check them out before buying.

Hedging takes a few years to establish and will not keep out pests until it is thick with growth (and even then rabbits may still get through). In the interim use a wire fence as a temporary shield. The height and type of wire fence required varies from pest to pest (see page 216), as does the lengths of the stakes used to support it. For the

Ethical choice: natural finishes

Gone are the days when everyone covered their fences with creosote or white paint as a matter of course. The average can of paint contains fungicides, heavy metals such as cadmium, and polycyclic aromatic hydrocarbons. Titanium dioxide, used in most shades but particularly in 'brilliant white', is a possible carcinogen and can cause respiratory problems and skin irritation. Paints also give off VOCs (volatile organic compounds) when drying. VOCs are known to induce eye, nose and throat irritation, headaches and dizziness; some are suspected or known to cause cancer in humans. There is now a range of environmentally sound alternatives for waxing, polishing, painting, decorating and otherwise preserving internal and external surfaces. CAT sells some of them, as does www.greenshop.co.uk and www.greenbuildingstore.co.uk. Brands include Auro, Green Paints, Stuart Furby's Lime Earth Paints, Ty Mawr Lime, Eco-strip, Holkham Linseed Paints, Osmo Uk, Earthborn, La Tienda, Treatex and Clearwell Caves.

Above Manufactured bricks are fired (heated at high temperatures) using large amounts of energy. These earth bricks were made by hand without firing, during one of CAT's empowering self-build courses.

stakes use local untreated chestnut, which lasts longer in the soil. Bash the stakes in at 2-metre intervals with a sledgehammer and draw the wire as tight as you can before fixing it in place using a hammer and 10-mm fencing staples. For more information on hedges, see pages 80–82.

Making a wall

Walls tend to be made out of earthen materials (i.e. those that come out of the ground), although you do get some very nice walls that mix earthen materials with wood – a technique known as cordwood masonry. If you want a stone wall, research which stone is local to your area and buy accordingly for a wall that fits in with your local environment. Alternatively, use reclaimed brick (www.salvo.co.uk or check with local builders' merchants), or make your own – see left. Making your own bricks gives you a great sense of pride. Organics is all about gaining confidence by doing it yourself. Avoid using concrete blocks. Many show gardens have experimented with walls made with recycled materials, including old bottles, tin cans, rubble, and so on. These are either built using a binding material such as mortar, or more simply stacked in rows using gabions. Gabions are steel mesh boxes primarily used in the road building and construction industries. Now you can get garden-sized gabions from www.stones3.co.uk. Fill the mesh up with natural stone, reclaimed building rubble or any material that will hold weight.

Cob is used extensively by eco-builders. It is made by mixing subsoil with straw and water, and then pounding or treading it down to form free-standing walls (see page 57). In a similar vein, rammed earth, mud bricks and stabilised earth blocks are all popular natural building materials for walls.

Seating areas and paths

Grass is the most obvious soft landscaping choice for a seating area. If you've got a large lawn and want to cut down on the mowing, think of leaving some of it to grow longer into meadow and keep only a small patch of regularly cut lawn for seating. Meadow lawns need only be cut two or three times a year, saving energy and creating a habitat for wildlife (see page 165). You can get different mixes of grass seed nowadays, catering for different uses and sites: www.organiccatalog.com is a good place to start looking. Wiggly Wigglers, www.wigglywigglers.co.uk, have also launched their own cut wildflower turf which you can lay like ordinary turf.

For something a little shorter than a meadow, plant an informal lawn with flowering bulbs. Plant spring bulbs and your lawn will be free of flowers and ready to walk on by the time it comes to summer socialising. Remember that lawns get very scuffed up if you have to do heavy work in the garden. My own lawn is more or less dead but I plan to reseed it with a shade-tolerant seed mix when work is complete.

Woodchip can be used as a non-living soft landscape material for seating areas and paths. It can be laid directly onto the soil, but to ensure seating areas and paths are kept weed free, it's best to use a permeable geo-textile membrane underneath. The membrane is laid in a single layer and the woodchip poured on top until it covers all the membrane to a depth of at least 5cm. Most garden centres sell woodchip – usually recycled from forest waste. Geo-textile membrane tends to be made from plastic: for a more natural alternative try Hemcore Biomat. This is made in Essex from hemp grown in the UK without the use of pesticides and herbicides.

Woodchip is a low-impact material and will need replacing as it rots. Hard landscaping materials such as timber decking and concrete paving slabs last longer. Both of these can be destructive to the environment: source FSC-approved timber decking or reclaimed materials from salvage yards. Try Ashwell's Recycled Timber Products, and Wideserve and BPI Recycled Products for recycled decking. A wide range of long-lasting 'chipped' hard landscaping materials – shells, glass, crushed brick – are available. Again these should be laid on top of a permeable membrane to prevent weed growth.

www.traceytimber.co.uk, sell woodchip made from reused pallets. Biomat is available from www.amenity.co.uk and www.ewburrownursery.co.uk. Try www.rooster.uk.com, www.drgrowgood. co.uk, www.specialistaggregates.co.uk – all sell shells, a by-product of the fishing industry. Recycled glass chippings are available from these sites: www.derbyshireaggregates.com, www.decogem.com and www.rbgc.co.uk. Also try www.stevemassam.co.uk for crushed brick from factory rejects, and www.salvo.co.uk and www.reuze.co.uk.

Other garden essentials

The word organic doesn't just refer to plants, it means all the materials you use to make garden essentials such as sheds and benches. Here are some ideas to get you started.

The Bench

Now that you've decided on the basic structure of your garden, the next thing you need is a bench. Some people may argue for shed, tools, seeds, but I reckon bench. Of course, under the bench heading I'd include hammock, chair swing, stool, recliner, deck chair, turf chair, chaise longue or anything upon which one may park one's bottom – or, even

better, lie down. Somewhere from which to survey the garden, dream dreams, make plans and entertain guests. I've shaped a whole area of my garden around a bench and postponed planting the beds around it until I know it works as a good place to sit. That's how important this bench thing is to me, and my benches are organic.

The natural materials to use in my garden are slate and wood. These are the two materials that lie beneath and around me in huge quantities. So it's quite in keeping with the garden to use waste slate and wood materials wherever I can. The previous owner left copious quantities of both when he left and I've been cursing him ever since I moved in. But when I got round to making my bench I said a little prayer for him instead.

You have to know that my garden is made up of a set of flat and sloping steep terraces, a large, slightly messy pond and a variety of slate walls, all facing north-east. The sun shines in the morning on all parts of the garden but only on one part from the afternoon on (the small plot I have given over to those

sunlight-hungry families of plants we call vegetables).
My bench sits snugly into the sloping earth overlooking
the pond. It gets the morning sunlight beautifully (apart
from about one half hour or so when the sun passes
behind an enormous conifer planted by my neighbour
as a 30cm-high sapling thirty years ago). When the day
is at its hottest, the bench is only dappled by sunlight
and becomes a fantastically cool place to retreat to when
working the garden is no longer a pleasure. Before I cleared
the area it was a mass of old building timber, chicken wire
and felled conifer hedge – a combination of the previous
owner's waste and my own garden trimmings. Clearing it
has been a monumental task and it would have been easier
to have put my bench somewhere else, but nowhere else
would do. From here I am close enough to my pond
to see my frogs blink and far away enough from my
neighbour's titanic decking (which haunts my garden
like a hovering buzzard) to avoid the hot fat that I feel
sure will rain down upon me if they ever have a barbecue
when I'm lying on my lawn.

Far left and above The author's steeply
sloping garden is divided into terraces linked
by paths and steps. A slate bench, dug into the
earth, is ideally situated for pond-watching.

Ethical choice: turf benches

My bench is quite a rudimentary affair, in that it just sits
on the earth. My eco-builder friends Jenny and Medhi
have created many similar benches for their festival
gardens, including a long turf bench shaped as a snake,
with individual seats carved along the snake's back. Using
a natural material like earth is convenient if you happen to
be digging a pond or a sunken area and need to do something
with the earth you've dug from the hole. You can even buy
cardboard cutouts to help you shape the earth like a grass
armchair (www.purves.co.uk). There's also a plan for a turf
sofa at www.readymademag.com, an excellent American
website with lots of DIY projects.

Making furniture with green wood

Most carpentry work is done using wood that has been seasoned, which means it has been left until the moisture has completely gone (which takes a couple of years). The wooden benches you get in your average high-street store are made from seasoned wood. They are also usually treated with a preservative, which may contain toxic materials

harmful to the environment. Green wood, as the name suggests, is wood that has been freshly cut and not left to dry out. The tools and the techniques for using green wood are quite different than for standard carpentry but are actually very good for the average gardener prepared to spend a bit of time learning the tricks of the trade. This is mainly because most of the materials you need can come from your own garden, as long as you've got a few trees or a hedgerow. Or ask your local park, woodland or local authority if they have any hedge trimmings or unwanted felled wood you could use.

The simplest form of green woodworking is stick furniture. This is literally furniture made from sticks harvested from hedgerows and coppiced woodlands. Stick furniture doesn't last for ever but then it doesn't matter if your mood changes and you want to replace it with something else. Just use the old chair for kindling. I've seen the same principle applied to an office made out of cardboard. The whole thing takes very little energy to make and is completely recyclable once the client has tired of it. Stick furniture is a lovely addition to any garden and you can book yourself on a day course for not much money (www.bodgers.org.uk, or locally to me Sylvantutch +44 (0) 1654 761614). For slightly more advanced homemade benches you could consider investing in a pole lathe (a foot-operated device for turning wood), a set of lathe tools and a book such as Ray Tabor's *Green Woodworking Pattern Book*. This contains more than 300 projects, ranging from stick furniture to tool making to gates, fences, hanging baskets, bird tables, compost bins, arbours and trellis. For most of the projects you just need access to a handful of basic hand tools (no power tools are used) and some coppiced wood from a hedgerow or local woodland. If you just fancy having a go at green woodworking, check out local green fairs, festivals or country shows. There's usually an opportunity to make something simple with a wood lathe. If you live in London get yourself down to the Woodland Wonders Fair at Kew Gardens held every May Bank Holiday, see www.rbgkew.org.uk/events.

If you're a professional woodsman like Luca (**left**) trips to the gym become fairly redundant. The rest of us could probably use a tone up, although muscles like his are optional. Luca is cleaving (splitting) a piece of hazel to make slats for the panel you see behind him. The chairs and stools opposite and on page 46 were made with some gentle sawing, turning and bending.

Ethical choice: living willow

If you need a throne for your kingdom, how about a living willow chair? Better for the environment because you don't have to use materials that have been shipped over great distances and processed using machinery powered by fossil fuels. Majestic and alive, like something out of a Brothers Grimm fairy tale, living willow chairs carry on growing, providing fresh growth every year for you to trim and use for other willow projects such as basket making. Be careful where you plant it, though. Willow roots are notoriously aggressive and willows drink a lot of water. They're fast growing and are good for helping to reduce the moisture content in wet soils. They will compete with vegetables so don't plant too close to your crops. You can also make living willow hedges and arbours. Jon Warnes's book *Living Willow Sculpture* is an excellent place to start, as is www.thewillowbank.com. The Willow Bank is run by Steve Pickup, one of the country's most experienced willow growers and weavers (see below). You can pick up a bundle of willow cuttings ready for planting, a set of instructions to make your own dome and an extra DVD if you need a little bit of visual stimulation.

CAT runs a weekend course called 'Working with Willow'. Also check out Steve Pickup's courses at Ragman's Lane Farm, www.ragmans.co.uk, and the following websites: www.englishwillowbaskets.co.uk, www.sylvanskills.co.uk, www.simplywillow.co.uk. Finally, Garden Organic (HDRA) produce a factsheet: www.organicgardening.org.uk/factsheets/gg37.php.

Buying garden furniture

Buying stuff can be fun too and there are so many nice pieces of beautifully made, sustainable and ethical furniture out there, it's a shame not to support the suppliers if you've got the spare cash. Individually made items tend to be more expensive than the sort of factory-made furniture you can buy in chain stores, but you can guarantee what you're getting is unique. Agricultural and smallholding shows, green fairs, festivals and other events are always good places to find locally made handcrafted wooden furniture. Websites such as www.allotmentforestry.com, www.coppice-products.co.uk and www.greenwoodcentre.org.uk offer courses and directories of people making and selling handmade wooden furniture.

In Wales the Welsh Timber Forum produce a buyer's guide to buying (www.welshtimberforum. co.uk). If you go down the mass-produced route always look for the Forest Stewardship Council (FSC) symbol (see page 48), but also check whether the finished product has been made in Britain. Sometimes wood is shipped from Scandinavia to China, turned into furniture and shipped back again. This all seems a bit crazy when British-made furniture grown from UK or European wood is available. A UK or European product also gives you certain guarantees about the way the workers are treated. (See also pages 26–29.)

Right An arbour made from woven hazel.

What is the FSC?

The FSC (Forest Stewardship Council) ensures that natural forests are conserved, that endangered species and their habitats are protected, and that forest workers and forest-dependent communities are respected. Unlike other certification schemes, the FSC was set up independent of industry and has broad support from conservation groups, indigenous communities and forest product buyers. It gives equal decision-making rights to economic, social and environmental interests in its governing structure and standard-setting process. It is the preferred standard for gardening organisations such as the RHS and conservation bodies like The World Wide Fund for Nature and the RSPB. At www.fsc-uk.org, their buyer's guide includes a league table of mainstream retailers who stock FSC furniture. Top (A) ratings (100 per cent of furniture FSC-approved) go to B&Q, Asda, Wyevale, Tesco and Marks & Spencer.

The rainforest in our gardens

Felled timber from rainforests is often mixed with other fibres and hidden in chipboard products or turned into garden fencing. Rainforests are biodiversity hotspots, which means they are wonderfully species rich, and their destruction can lead to the extinction of whole species. There are only 60,000 gorillas left in the world and 5,000 are lost every year as their forest habitats are cleared. At this rate they will be gone within twelve years. We can help by avoiding products that may contain wood from felled rainforests. Always look for the FSC label. The Greenpeace online Garden Furniture Guide is the most comprehensive guide to finding FSC-approved garden furniture products: www.greenpeace.org.uk/forests. Think about contributing to some of the charitable organisations that buy up areas of rainforest to save them from logging (try www.rainforest-alliance.org). Boycotting is more effective if it is backed up with positive action to preserve and protect.

It's impossible to list all UK manufacturers of ethical garden furniture but here are a few for starters: www.britisheco.com, www.handmadehammocks.co.uk, www.hammocks.co.uk (Fairtrade hammocks from Mexico), www.pendlewood.com. I also liked www.tinglondon.com who make stylish hammocks out of recycled seat belts. If you look at only one website check out www.reelfurniture.co.uk, an imaginative company making entirely handcrafted furniture from old cable reels. Visit www.rd.se and www.purves.co.uk for cardboard seats, www.readymademag.com for plans for a turf sofa, www.salvo.co.uk for salvage merchants, and www.reuze.co.uk, www.marmaxproducts.co.uk and www.theurbangarden.co.uk for information about recycled products; www.ethical-junction.org is a general link to sites for green and ethical products. Enough already!

Shed's dead

I've never been a builder. My knowledge of carpentry is small. My aptitude for construction minimal. At school I got a U at woodwork, despite the fact I skipped PE for two years to take extra lessons. And yet, for some inexplicable reason, I think I'm going to build my own shed. This isn't a temporary thought: this is a long-held belief, stretching back a decade. One of the reasons I chose the garden I have now is the potential for it to house a shed on stilts. A shed on stilts! As if the task of constructing a shed on flat land wasn't hard enough. Nevertheless at some point a shed will be built and I will do the building. Why? Because really I want to build a house, and building an eco-shed is the first step.

Why 'shed's dead'?

Apart from wanting to reference Bruce Willis's performance in *Pulp Fiction,* why have I called this section Shed's Dead? After all, a shed is a wonderful thing – probably the closest thing gardeners have to a cultural icon. It's a triumph of simplicity and efficiency, combining as it does several important gardening functions within its four thin walls. Being a simple, effective place to store tools is probably the least important job it does. Most non-gardeners wonder what the allure of the shed can be: it's such a drab, soulless-looking place from the outside. Step inside, however. and you're immediately in another world. A place where a deckchair, a bottle of wine or a flask of tea is always close by. Where a wind-up radio can be kept wound and primed for a Sunday afternoon of *Gardeners' Question Time* on Radio Four. Where the world and its wife can just go and play somewhere else, quite frankly.

So why would I wish the shed dead? Well, I think we can do better. The first clue came midway through the last paragraph. Why are sheds so drab and soulless? Look at any of the seemingly endless number of shed websites and you will see the same bland carbon-copy boxes coming up again and again. They don't give any clue to the personality of the owner. They don't blend in with a garden. They don't add anything apart from convenience to a space. No character. No inspiration. No

I don't just want a shed, I want a home office with a wood stove and a place to sling a hammock if I feel like sleeping over.

sense of imagination. A shed is a thing to be hidden by plants, to be shoved into the corners of a garden, to be rendered invisible if possible. Or in the worst gardens, just placed without any thought whatsoever so it sticks out like a tower block amongst tiny rows of terraced-house vegetables. A towering example of mass-produced modernity.

All this could be forgiven if sheds met high environmental criteria, but unless you buy an FSC-approved shed you don't really know what you're getting. Buying the average shed is a journey into the unknown. Imagine you've just created your beautiful eco-friendly garden. Everything's carefully laid out to be pleasing to the eye and the soul. And now you need some storage. Well, the average shed is just not doing it for me.

What I haven't said yet is that I don't just want a shed, I want a home office with a wood stove and a place to sling a hammock if I feel like sleeping over. My shed will have star-gazing windows and a balcony. A hot plate for making tea and a little mouse-proof store for provisions. I imagine my shed will be a little like old Ratty's house in *Wind in the Willows*, only with a loftier view. Occasionally I'll get a visit from Mole and we'll take a picnic down to the lawn. Nasturtium flowers will hang down from small wooden pots and I shall graze on the peppery leaves. From the balcony I will be able to survey the weed situation in the whole of my garden with a small spyglass, like a sailor looking out to sea for a sight of the enemy. It's a fantasy, but, if you haven't got a dream, how you gonna have a dream come true?

I started having my shed fantasy way back at Robert Plant's place when my friend Kevin Beale built one of Britain's first straw bale buildings: a garden shelter constructed with bales, reclaimed timber, secondhand pallets and lime render (an eco finishing material). It's the first time I'd ever watched a craftsman at work. Building was a logical step-by-step process. But it was also an art form. The shed was finished off with sculptured lizards climbing down the corners towards the soil. It gave me a privileged close-up view of the art of making something out of nothing. Shed Zeppelin was a fairly bulky number – never use straw bales in a tight squeeze – and it lacked the finesse other materials would have allowed, but it was made on next-to-no budget and worked. It's still there on Robert's farm, even though the rest of the garden has sadly passed up the stairway to heaven to that great allotment in the sky.

The company Forest Garden supplies DIY shops and garden centres with wood products for the garden, including sheds, using timber cut from FSC-approved UK forests owned by the Forestry Commission. Look out for their label and visit **www.forestgarden. co.uk/stockists.asp** for the nearest place to buy. Also try **www.grange- fencing.com** for timber sheds and summerhouses. B&Q and Focus both sell FSC-approved sheds. Try **www.greatlittlegarden.co.uk** for a range of European-grown FSC- approved timber products, as well as **www.simply-summerhouses.co.uk**. There are now a number of recycled plastic sheds on the market. Look at: **www.langhalegardens.co.uk, www. hudsonwright.net/plastic-storage- sheds.htm, www.heskethsplastics.com /recycled.htm**.

Ethical choice: materials to avoid

Avoid using materials like PVC, vinyl and other non-recycled plastics. They each take a lot of energy to produce and they create harmful chemicals. Cindy Harris and Pat Borer, authors of CAT's *The Whole House Book*, state that the avoidance of PVC is now 'virtually a hallmark of green, environmentally sensitive building'. They also note that MDF (medium-density fibreboard) has been dubbed the 'asbestos of the 90s'.

So what's the alternative? The ecological shed

The first alternative to the dead shed is not to have a shed at all. If you just want somewhere to store a few tools, perhaps a lovingly constructed homemade waterproof box will do. The second is to buy a bespoke shed made to your specification, and the third is to make your own.

To give you some ideas I've enlisted the help of architects and eco-designers Jenny and Mehdi (www.jennyandmehdi.org). Jenny and Mehdi spend a month most summers creating the garden for Greenpeace at the Glastonbury Festival. This is always a showcase for low-impact, beautiful spaces made using reclaimed and organic materials. I've had the pleasure of helping them construct one of their garden structures – a cordwood wall using natural clay and cut logs of English hardwood. On a burning hot Glastonbury day I had the coolest feet in the field, treading straw into wet clay to form the principal bonding material for the wall.

The process of working with natural materials is much more pleasurable, fun and creative than working with bricks and concrete blocks. Jenny and Mehdi are fantastically imaginative people, able to combine a love of organic spaces with the practical know-how to do the building work themselves. In their treehouse described on the following pages, we have tried to put together a package of design ideas for different-sized gardens and different budgets, but what the three of us feel is that you can take any of the elements that we describe and adapt them to your own situation.

At the heart of Jenny and Mehdi's philosophy is the idea that the word 'organic' should refer just as much to the structures of a garden as to the plants. My only regret with this section is that it cannot go deep enough. Structures and plants need to mesh in a garden to create total atmosphere. It would have been lovely to give you a step-by-step guide to how to make this happen, but there just wasn't the space. I hope though that there is enough here to inspire you to look deeper. And see what's possible with a little thought and understanding.

Shed cred – welcome to the treehouse

Shed Zeppelin replaced an old caravan. The caravan was ugly and badly insulated. There was no fire and in the winter we shivered around a gas cooker, grilling tomatoes or cheese on toast. Kevin's straw bale structure was a luxury apartment compared to this. It was big enough to function as store room, mess house, meeting place and, occasionally (more in the summer than winter), crash pad for tired gardeners with early morning duties to perform. It was a good multi-function space for the whole year.

Jenny and Mehdi's garden structure in Kay Zitron's garden in Aberdovey is quite a different affair. Not at all chunky, it shows off the elegance of wood in an open summer stage topped with a curved roof garden and complemented by an enchanting (noises off) room for grandchildren. Kay wanted a structure that would connect an existing patio to a courtyard garden below, that would give her panoramic views of the Irish sea, that would allow her husband to do his office work outside during the warmer months, and provide a place for her grandchildren to play. She also wanted something that would give her the feeling of being in a treehouse.

Although I don't imagine many people will have the space or time to take on a project like this, it shows off all the main features of ecological design extremely well. It provides an example of a small shed project (the children's room), which is feasible in any small garden, and a larger open structure that would provide shelter with a minimum of materials.

Let's take a quick tour. Entering the garden courtyard you are immediately struck by the drop from the house to the garden. Before the structure was built the only way to get to the garden was down a set of old concrete steps. These did not sit well with the rest of the garden.

The solution was to incorporate a new set of steps into the overall design, to take people from the house, through the stage area and down to the garden. The whole structure is made out of green oak, which means it has been used freshly cut. Green oak lasts for decades without artificial preservatives and is extremely strong. Other woods, such as hazel, become brittle within a few years and cannot be used for this sort of structure. Most manufactured and homemade sheds are made out of seasoned wood, timber that has been left to dry for at least a couple of years. Green oak has a high moisture content and dries *in situ*. This means it shrinks on the job so you have to allow for this process. The green oak used here was cut to order from Powys Castle and sawn

locally but there are numerous suppliers around the country. The structure is held together with green oak pegs too.

The stairs are shaped inwards at the top to create a sense of being drawn towards the rest of the structure. Standing at the bottom, it almost feels like you are climbing into a painting by Escher.

The stage is a triumph of space saving and space enhancement. It is supported on four posts of green oak placed on four concrete pads. Because the load is borne by these four stilts there was no need to lay trenches for concrete foundations. This saved on labour, energy and materials. The stilts also freed up the space underneath the structure (for shade-loving plants, and a cool place to sit on very hot days). The structure itself is a vertical space for plants, with climbers trailing up to the roof. In a sunny, south-facing garden this is a perfect place to grow sun-loving fruits and maximise your home harvest.

Climbing to the top of the stairs you can turn left or right. Take the right turn and you come to the stage, but let's take a little detour first. Stroll along the boardwalk under the clematis bower a moment and you'll come to a small handmade wooden door. Open it and you enter the children's playroom – a magical little space with a unique view of the garden through a square window. It's made using a green oak frame and topped and sided with oak shingles cut by English company Carpenter Oak. To ensure

Ethical choice: the benefits of green oak

Green oak is used in ecological building not only because of its strength but also because it is a home-grown resource. Oak woodlands are a natural feature of the British countryside and provide valuable habitats for wildlife. A single oak tree can host hundreds of different species of wildlife and the loss or decline of many species in Britain can be directly linked to the loss of oak woodland. Oak woodland can be managed sustainably so that any trees felled are replaced by new trees. Oak has been an undervalued resource in the modern age because of the availability of man-made resources for building. By using green oak you can help to provide an economic reason for keeping old woodlands alive, protecting them from the bulldozer. Of course, there is a balance to be struck with the use of woodland resources – demand for oak should not be so great that it encourages unsustainable practices. Green oak is not the only timber that can be used to make sheds and other garden structures. Larch is often used for garden construction, and this is grown widely in the UK. Other woods suitable for heavy construction include beech, pine and Douglas fir. These are conventionally grown in plantations, which are less valuable habitats for wildlife. Whichever wood you choose to use for your shed look for the FSC symbol and, whenever you can, buy from local woodlands or plantations.

Clockwise from top left Hazel branches are placed in between handrails made from oak; an oak peg secures a step; oak shingles (small squares of wood) keep it watertight; stairs lead up to the treehouse.

complete protection from the rain, a single layer of breathable waterproof membrane has been placed beneath the shingles.

Leave the room and go back along the boardwalk and you come to the stage. This is topped by an amazing parabolic curved roof, an inspiring twist of a roof that really makes you feel as if you're in a unique space. The stage is all green oak, apart from the balustrades, which are made out of locally cut hazel with the bark stripped off to make them last longer. The balustrades are fitted in a pegged frame. The pegs can be removed, the frame dropped and the hazels replaced every ten years before they begin to rot. The green oak will not rot. It does not need weather-proofing with a chemical treatment, lacquer or paint, which is not the case with the kind of softwoods normally used in manufactured sheds (another environmental saving).

The frame for the stage was made flat on the ground and raised with block and tackle, just like the famous barn-raising scene in the Harrison Ford movie *Witness*, except without the costumes. Jenny and Mehdi's friends came to help, pulling the frame up by hand and inching it into place. A frame-raising is a real cause for celebration, a staging post in the building process. It's a joy you just don't get with concrete blocks.

Planting the roof

Leave the stage through the far entrance, head towards the house, turn round 360 degrees and look back. This should be your first glimpse of the amazing roof garden that tops the whole structure. Rolling along the twisted roof like the sea, plants rise and fall on waves of soil bedded on top of a hidden waterproof membrane. On one side a cascading rosemary sits proud to the bow, drooping purple flowers over the grey oak boarding. This is a rural garden but a roof like this could grace any urban shed or house. Not only does a roof garden provide vital garden interest in otherwise drab city streets, it soaks up some of the rainfall and absorbs airborne particles, helping to prevent flooding and reduce pollution.

And there we have it. A multi-functional covered space that combines all the elements you would expect to find in a handcrafted organic shed. It's made from a renewable resource cut locally, constructed with a minimum of 'unnatural' materials (a few stainless steel screws and ringlets, concrete pads and waterproof membranes). The structure fits the space perfectly, drawing the two levels of the house and the courtyard together while creating new garden space on the roof and around the frame. And finally, the clients' brief has been met: great views to the sea, a home office with electricity and broadband, an adaptable social space and a secret little room for the grandchildren.

Ethical choice: straw bales and other natural building materials

Straw bales are an agricultural by-product, the left-over stalks from the grain harvest. Bound together into square bales they form a tight building block. These are assembled in a brick pattern and staked together with connecting hazel rods to make a wall. They are then rendered with a lime plaster to keep the straw protected from the weather and attack by rodents. Interest in straw bale building has grown as the search for more sustainable building materials has widened. Other natural materials of interest to the eco-builder are cob, rammed earth and stone. In low-rise buildings all are a viable alternative to concrete, which uses vast amounts of energy to produce and is generally less pleasant to work with. CAT's website has a wide range of publications on all these styles of building (see www.cat.org.uk) and its courses department runs several natural

building courses throughout the year. These include Timber Frame Self Build, Straw Bale Building, Cob Building, Building with Earth, and Natural Rendering – Clay Plaster. If you want to make your shed out of recycled pallets, check out www.summerville-novascotia.com/PalletWoodShed for a pictorial record and explanations of the building process. And it costs less than $100 (around £54). Also check out Kevin Beale's factsheet from CAT, 'How to Build With Straw Bales', and www.strawbalebuildingassociation.org.uk.

Other ecological considerations

Jenny and Mehdi's structure is very much designed for summer use. If you want an all-year-round space, you need to think of your shed more like a miniature version of your house. Eco-homes use a range of techniques to make the most of natural heating and power sources and you can mimic these for your micro-house. Passive solar heating, the process of bringing more heat from the sun into a building, is a must for reducing winter fuel bills. At a basic level you can achieve it by giving your shed space large, south-facing windows, accompanied by smaller windows to the north. If you want to make the most of passive solar features I'd recommend getting hold of a book like CAT's *The Whole House Book*. It's packed full of useful information about green building materials and design features, most of which can be put to good use in a small structure like a shed or summerhouse. If you're treating your shed as a stepping stone towards buying, making or renovating your own eco-home, it's an essential purchase. *The Whole House Book* recommends the newer type of heat-loss-reducing glazing known as low-e glazing. It will also tell you what levels of insulation you require, and what heating options are available.

Kevin Beale (who built the straw bale shed on Robert Plant's land) is now working on a home office in Snowdonia that includes a woodchip boiler. A woodchip boiler, although more expensive than a conventional solid fuel woodburner (for solid fuel systems check out www.solidfuel.co.uk and www.stovesonline.co.uk), is more environmentally efficient because the rate at which the fuel is burned can be controlled and so less fuel is used. Woodchip or wood pellet can be made from recycled wood waste and comes in bags. This makes fuel storage less of an issue. However, a woodchip boiler needs electricity to run a fan and a thermostat to control the burn rate, so you'll need a power source.

You could generate your own power at home using solar PV systems or wind or water turbines, but it's easier to switch to a green electricity supplier and buy renewable energy through the national grid. On a global scale it's much more efficient to buy from a green supplier through the national grid than to install micro-power systems in every home. Check out www.foe.co.uk for supplier comparisons.

There are some situations where it will pay to go with your own system. Renewable energy systems are useful when the cost of linking to an existing power supply is prohibitively expensive. If you're connecting your shed to the house electricity supply the work will need to be completed by a certified electrician. CAT has a whole range of renewable energy books and factsheets, many of which are available both as downloads and in paper form. They will tell you how to assess your power needs, choose the right system and get one installed. Visit www.cat.org.uk/catpubs.

Wind turbines are less efficient in built-up areas: they are best sited away from buildings, woodlands and other obstructions on flat open ground. I'll touch on water collection overleaf but collecting water run-off from a shed roof will save time and money.

Shed's atomic dustbin

You never plan to turn your shed into a miniature landfill site, but that's what happens if you don't de-clutter. Old bicycles, unwanted tools, half-full cans of oil, batteries, random bits of plastic and metal, plant pots, and so on – most of these things can be taken to your local recycling yard and disposed of safely. Phone your council to check facilities. There are also a wide number of individual recycling initiatives for specific materials and unwanted products: www.reuze.co.uk is the best place to start looking.

Since 2003 a number of pesticides have been withdrawn from sale. Any left-over products should have been disposed of by 31 March 2004. If you inadvertently keep or use any withdrawn chemicals you may be prosecuted. Products might include:

- Moss and weed killers for lawns and paths
- Treatments for removing algae from decking and patios
- Ant, cockroach, fly, wasp and aphid killers
- Slug pellets
- Mice and rat poisons
- Anti-mould and fungus paints
- Timber treatments

If they are more than three years old, all of these products could contain banned chemicals, such as:
- Dichlorprop
- Dikegulac
- Resmethrin
- 2, 3, 6-TBA
- Tar acids
- Triforine

If anything in your garden shed is labelled as containing one or more of these substances, dispose of it safely with your local waste disposal authority. It is illegal to dispose of garden chemicals down drains, sinks or lavatories.

Non-permanent structures

A shed need not be a permanent space. There are some very fine temporary structures that can serve the same purpose: yurts, domes, tipis and benders (a very cheap structure made from cut hazel rods and a tarpaulin cover) being just four examples. A bender is the easiest to make, but not necessarily that pretty if you're using an old tarp. You'll need some flexible pieces of hazel, $2\frac{1}{2}$ metres or longer. These are pushed 30cm into the ground, bent in towards each other and tied together to form a frame. More pieces of hazel are then

placed across the bent poles around the outside of the structure to support it – cross bracing. Waxed cotton tarps are quite ugly but readily available and cheap from army surplus stores. The look of them can be improved using paints. Alternatively, order a specially cut piece of fabric from a nomadic tent supplier – the sort of material that would cover a tipi or a yurt. DIY domes can be made from recycled broom handles or cut hazel, assembled in a geodesic shape. A factsheet explaining how to make one is available from CAT, either as a download or paper copy. Also available from CAT are factsheets explaining how to make tipis and yurts. One of my favourite shed books is *Shelters, Shacks and Shanties* by DC Beard. Written in 1914, it is a classic of backwoodsman self-sufficiency, full of ideas for easy temporary structures the like of which you would find in some long-forgotten US frontier town or forest in the Mid-West. It's perfect for some unusual back garden projects, particularly for children in need of a den.

Butts and bins

Every gardener needs a compost bin. The most obvious solution is to make your own and there are various simple designs out there, all utilising a variety of recycled materials including reclaimed timber, pallets, chicken wire and old tyres. You can see various prototypes at the CAT visitor centre and at Garden Organic (HDRA) in Yalding, Kent. Also check out www.gardenorganic.org.uk/factsheets/gg24.php. This webpage provides a simple DIY bin design and you can also order a paper copy of the factsheet.

CAT found compost bins performed best when they were open to the elements, so that air can circulate and water percolate. See page 96 for more information.

Above left Everybody yurts, sometimes. This traditional Mongolian tribal tent makes a great extra room for guests in the summer, for yourself if you want to get out the house or for the kids.

CAT sells numerous compost bins, www.cat.org.uk, as do Wiggly Wigglers, www.wigglywigglers.co.uk, and many others. Look out for those made from reclaimed or FSC-approved timber or recycled plastic: www.greatlittlegarden.co.uk, www.forest garden.co.uk and www.grange-fencing.com. The Tank Exchange, www.organiccatalog.com and Blackwalls Ltd all sell water tanks made out of recycled material, while www.plantstuff.com sell ex-distillery oak barrels. The following companies sell trellis, planters, cloches, wildlife homes, etc., made from recycled material: CAT, Planet Friendly Products (+44 (0)1453 822 100), www.marmaxproducts.co.uk, www.intruplas.com, www.arborvetum.co.uk, www.linkabord.co.uk, www.gardena.co.uk (porous piping for irrigation), www.eric thepanda.co.uk (plant labels and supports).

Water butts make sense for any gardener and, with climate change and water shortages, each year they seem to become more important. *Gardening Which?* magazine (July 2006) trialled more than seventeen designs and chose the following as best buys: Harcoster Child Safe, Harcoster Space Sava Water, Sankey Beehive, Economy and Slim Water Butts and the Suffolk Barrel Water Butt (see www.which.co.uk). Regrettably, *Gardening Which?* does not grade according to any environmental or ethical criteria. Ask the manufacturers themselves about recycled content before you buy. Most water butts can be fitted to a downpipe using a rainwater diverter, but if you want something more substantial you should consider a rainwater harvesting system. Commonly used in places where drought is a real issue, the more sophisticated systems allow you to store water underground for use as and when required. Contact www.greenshop.co.uk for details. Download the CAT factsheet on reusing grey water from www.cat.org.uk/catpubs and see page 73.

And finally... a garden loo

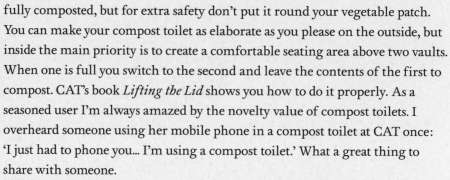

The compost dunny: for some people it's recycling gone too far; for others it's a must-have garden structure – especially if you're caught short in the garden! OK, it's probably not for every plot but it's a great way to cut down on water and make use of your own natural fertiliser. Composted toilet waste takes about a year to degrade fully but when it has you can put it on ornamental beds or around fruit trees. It's not dangerous when fully composted, but for extra safety don't put it round your vegetable patch. You can make your compost toilet as elaborate as you please on the outside, but inside the main priority is to create a comfortable seating area above two vaults. When one is full you switch to the second and leave the contents of the first to compost. CAT's book *Lifting the Lid* shows you how to do it properly. As a seasoned user I'm always amazed by the novelty value of compost toilets. I overheard someone using her mobile phone in a compost toilet at CAT once: 'I just had to phone you... I'm using a compost toilet.' What a great thing to share with someone.

Lots of people worry that compost toilets will smell, but they won't if managed properly. The worst you should get is an aroma, and although this may be unpleasant to the more sensitive nose, for most people it's not a problem. It's good to separate liquids and solids from one another and you can do this quite easily in a garden compost toilet by having a separate urinal facility.

The first time I used a compost toilet I was introduced to the gentle craft of 'peak knocking': levelling the Everest of excrement that rises threateningly towards you. For this you need to make a peak knocker, which is simply a piece of flat wood attached to a long pole. You access the chamber from an opening designed for the purpose, push in the knocker and knock off the peak. Apart from this, the only real job is to keep the toilet stocked up with wood shavings (a scoop is added after every visit to help the composting process), and to remove the finished product. Although you shouldn't have to remove the waste until it is safely turned into compost, you should still take the precaution of wearing some long gloves and protective clothing, and then washing well afterwards.

As a standard flush toilet uses 9.5 litres of water every flush there's a serious point to all this frivolity and it makes sense to get over any small fears we have about our own toilet waste. No one wants to go back to the bad old days of rank privies in the back garden, but a modern, well-thought-out compost toilet managed correctly by a careful owner offers a realistic alternative for people who want to give recycling that extra push.

Above and right Compost toilets can be grand or compact, as these two very different photographs show.

Chapter two

Garden micro-climate and soil care

In this chapter I'm going to identify the weak spots in a garden – those elements that slow or prevent plant growth – and show you how to put them right while still following organic principles. Starting with micro-climate control, we'll look at the five principal drivers of plant growth, and then at how to identify and enrich your soil. Later, in Chapter six, we look at weed management, pest and predator balance, and disease prevention.

Some plants are easier to grow than others but there are some general principles that help all plants succeed. I've called these principles Essential plant questions (EPQs); you'll find them in Chapter three, Choosing and Growing Your Plant Stock. Read them as you go along and they will help you understand how to pick the right plants for your garden when you are ready to start planting.

From time to time I refer to my own garden to help illustrate some of the points I've made. My garden is both atypical and typical. Atypical because it is a country garden and has slightly more unusual contours and nooks and crannies than the average garden. Typical because it has its fair share of weaknesses and problems that I have to rectify or work with as I go along. I think it's a good example to use because every garden space is quirky and different, and each needs an individual approach.

Observing and changing your micro-climate

Every garden has a micro-climate. Micro-climates are important because they determine the type of plants you can grow and the speed at which those plants will grow, flower and set seed.

Most plants prefer an 'open sunny aspect'. The garden capable of growing the widest variety of plants faces south to south-west, towards the sun. The sun rises in the east, moves over the southern part of the sky and sets at night in the west (unless you happen to live in the southern hemisphere, where this is reversed).

My garden faces in the exact opposite direction: north-east. On the south side the garden is shaded by a hill and a wood with some very large trees in it. Contact between soil and direct sunlight is low during the afternoons but higher in the mornings. During the winter months almost the whole garden is in semi-permanent shade. This means that none of the rainwater (of which there is a prestigious volume) evaporates, ever. The ground, and quite often the air too, is damp. Or frozen. This seriously restricts my choice of plants but it doesn't bother me unduly. There are still enough interesting shade- or semi-shade-loving plants to last me several lifetimes.

Above The author tending the sunniest part of his predominantly shady garden, the ideal spot for vegetable crops.

Further along my village, where the road bends outwards away from the hill, the houses are bathed in sunlight. If I lived in one of those houses I would garden in a completely different way. The contrasts between city gardens can be equally stark. Back-to-back houses are a classic example.

No garden micro-climate is sacred. They can all be altered by the gardener. When I first moved into my house there was a huge overgrown conifer hedge inappropriately planted to shade most of the sunniest part of the garden. I didn't notice it at first because it was winter but by spring it was obvious the hedge had to go. Since then I've also cut back copious amounts of overgrown and badly maintained hazel (*Corylus*) hedging, and one or two trees from the woodland behind. The overall effect is to lighten the garden as well as to warm it up and make it feel less damp and airless. The whole point being to make things more pleasant for me and the plants I want to grow there.

There are five climate drivers: sunlight, temperature, rainfall, wind and frost. Each one affects the growth rates of plants.

Sunlight

The kind of sunlight that interests plants most is middle-of-the-day direct sunlight that warms the soil and the air around a plant and causes water to evaporate. If you go to Lapland you can enjoy (or endure) weeks of 24-hour sunlight, but you still won't find any truly great gardens. Most of the sunlight skims over the gardens at far too low an

angle to be beneficial to the gardener. Plants cease to grow if the temperature drops below 6°C, so the position of the sun in relation to your garden is very important. As are the obstacles that get in its way. Direct sunlight is a blessing and a curse in the middle of summer when plants speed up their growth rates and fight to retain moisture, but in spring and autumn a little extra warmth from sunlight can make all the difference. If you trap heat plants will grow quicker.

The amount of direct sunlight that falls on a garden varies from month to month. The sun is higher in the sky during the summer and lower in winter. Start keeping a record of sunfall as soon as you move in and maintain it through a whole year. See how much of the garden is in shade and for how long. Plot out your entire garden on paper and mark on it where sunlight illuminates the ground and where it doesn't. Even small walls and hedges cause a certain amount of critical shading so you need to mark these on too. In the winter they can create little pockets of frost and in the summer starve plants of warmth. If you want to divide the garden up into 'rooms' you will have to take into consideration the effect any hedging or walling structures will have on the rest of the garden. Your initial shade and sun record will help you plan any future developments, enabling you to make a decision that's good for the whole year, not just the day you make it on.

Temperature

You can't really do anything about the direction in which your garden faces, but once you know where the sun falls you can start to enhance those spots that get all the sunlight and warmth. Plants need warmth to grow, just as they need sunlight, moisture and food. If you already have a nice south-facing spot, you can enhance growth by changing the angle of the soil, reducing the flow of cold air, and trapping heat. This is particularly important in spring when the air is still cold but you want to bring your vegetables on with a little extra heat.

Changing the angle of your soil

If you have a bed that faces the sun you can increase heat absorption by 30 per cent by shaping the soil at a 40-degree angle to the sun. This is particularly useful in early spring when the sun is low in the sky. Some vegetable growers bank up rows of soil and plant on the sunny side to take advantage of this.

Reducing the flow of cold air

Wind causes plants to become misshapen or damaged and blows away soil nutrients. It also stunts growth by reducing the air and soil temperature around a plant. Wind damage can be reduced by growing natural windbreaks or building walls and fences. These don't necessarily have to be big. Even low walls and terraces will trap more heat.

Trapping heat

Daytime temperatures at ground level are determined by the amount of sunlight falling on the soil, night-time temperatures by the heat that comes up from the earth. Find the warm sheltered spots and improve them. Walls trap heat. If soil is exposed to the sky it will lose heat. An area in the middle of an open space will lose more heat than soil next to a wall.

Above Covering plants with plastic sheeting or mesh will help trap heat and encourage growth early in the season, as well as protecting them from birds and other potential pests.

The west-facing part of the garden is the warmest but you can increase air temperatures in all parts by improving the ability of the soil to store heat – and by capturing that night-time heat around the plant when it rises up from the soil. Make sure you keep your soil in good condition (see page 91 for details). Good-quality soils retain more heat during the day to release at night. The simplest way to improve night-time temperatures around a plant is to cover it with glass or plastic. Heat released from the soil at night is captured under cover and the plant gets on with growing, when it might otherwise stop. Since plants don't grow below 6°C, this can be very important when spring temperatures drop rapidly at night. Heat-storage devices range from simple sheets of clear polythene pegged close to the ground, and low covers such as cloches and cold frames, right up to walk-in polytunnels and greenhouses.

The simplest way to improve night-time temperatures around a plant is to cover it with glass or plastic. Heat released from the soil at night is captured under cover and the plant gets on with growing, when it might otherwise stop.

Trapping heat on a large scale with a polytunnel (**above**) and small scale with a homemade cold frame (**right**).

Rainfall

There isn't much you can do about the amount of rain that falls on your garden. Your only options are to match the plants to the conditions and to manage the water when it arrives.

The first option is the easier. If you live in a wet region or your garden happens to be boggy, it is much easier to grow plants that love wet conditions. These range from lily-of-the-valley (*Convallaria majalis*), wild garlic (*Allium ursinum*) and narcissus, to iris, primulas and ferns. Vice versa, if you live in a dry region or have a dry garden it is easier to grow plants that prefer drier conditions. The oriental poppy (*Papaver orientale* 'Perry's White'), artemisia, sedum and euphorbia can all survive long periods of drought without watering (see page 117 for more examples).

This sort of approach is fine for decorative gardens but if you want to grow vegetables, the chances are you are going to have to water them at some stage. Definitely if you are using a polytunnel or greenhouse, and more likely than not if you are growing outside. The amount and frequency of watering varies from vegetable to vegetable and from garden to garden. If you are living with a hosepipe ban or other water restrictions, you need to think about how much water your plants need, how to store enough in the garden to satisfy these needs and how to get your plants watered without using a hosepipe.

One solution is to collect and store your own water, either in the garden or in the home. The simplest way to do this is to buy a water butt and collect any water that runs off your shed or house roof. Make sure the water is directed straight into the butt using a down pipe (pictured right). Wind tends to blow water away from the butt if it is just left to pour in without guidance, even if the drop is just a foot. You should also get a butt with a stand and a tap. The stand elevates the butt from the ground so you can shove your watering can directly underneath the tap. For more information on butts see page 61 and check out the websites listed there.

Ethical choice: reusing grey water

Water shortages aside, it's always better to reuse water when you can, because such a lot of energy has gone into processing it to make it fit to drink. Grey water is the name given to water that has already been used but can be used again for some lower order process that does not require clean drinking-quality water. It includes water saved from the bath, sink or washing machine. It does not include water that has been used in the toilet, which is known as black water, and should not be reused under any circumstances.

Using grey water is not as straightforward as it might seem: there are issues concerning the use of chemical cleaners and other toiletries. CAT has a tip sheet you can download from www.cat.org.uk/catpubs or buy as a paper copy from +44 (0)1654 705 959. It also produces *The Water Book*, a complete guide to managing your domestic water resource. The environmental impact of using grey water for reuse in the home can outweigh the benefits. CAT recommends reducing the amount of grey water you use in the first place, and avoiding pollutants such as salt, grease and detergents, which can be damaging if used for irrigation. Shampoos and soaps are fairly mild pollutants when diluted so water from the bath and shower is generally the easiest to use. If you want to reuse grey water from a washing machine use detergent that is low in sodium and phosphorus. Various non-detergent cleaning products are available but arouse much debate about their effectiveness. Some people swear by them, others say they don't work. These include Ecoballs, which are available from CAT. Water from the kitchen sink can be very dirty, and contains undesirables such as grease, oil and chemicals. Try to remove any grease from pans before you wash them. If you have a bowl full of very dirty water CAT recommends you don't use it in the garden.

There are various ways of getting the grey water to the garden. The simplest is to carry it out to the garden in a bowl. The contents can be poured around the base of fruit trees and shrubs and over flower beds. You should pour the contents slowly, directly into the ground and with care for your plants and wildlife. Soft soap solutions are used as a pesticide and it isn't a good idea to pour soapy water onto leaves, because it might damage some plants and you might kill beneficial garden creatures living around the plants. In many ways its easier to rig up your own drip-feed system that pipes the water direct from the house to the garden using standard irrigation pipes. These let a more gradual and controlled feed of water into the garden and you can direct the water to the base of the plants, closer to the roots where it is needed most.

Water and soil

Any good vegetable book will give you an indication of how much water a plant will need, but the amount of watering you have to do will also depend on the quality of your soil. Water rushes quickly through some soils and more slowly through others. There are ways of improving water retention in differen soils and I talk some more about these in the next section.

Gardens with soils exposed to direct sunlight will also lose water quickly, this time by evaporation. You can restrict the amount of water lost through evaporation by applying a thick layer of organic material to the surface of the soil. This is known as a mulch. Since mulches are primarily used as a weed suppressant, I talk more about them in the pages on weeds (see pages 203–4).

The presence of trees can also make a difference to the amount of water in the ground. A large oak in midsummer can send upwards of 1,800 litres of water a day into the atmosphere, leaving less for other plants to enjoy. Thirsty trees such as willows can be excellent for boggy gardens, but may steal too much water from other plants in dry gardens.

The importance of spacing and drainage

Plant spacing also becomes important in droughts. That's one of the reasons why most plants have specific instructions as to how much space should be allowed between them, and why a row of seedlings always needs to be thinned. Crowded plants can suck up water from the soil too quickly and leave the soil dry. Plants of the same species tend to compete more vigorously for water than plants from different species. This is one of the observations that helped Robert Hart develop his forest garden system, where crops of varying species are planted close together in what seem to be crowded conditions (see page 145).

Where soil is waterlogged, you could consider installing drainage channels to take the water away from the area. Showing you how to do this is beyond the scope of this book but, to give you an idea, it involves laying perforated corrugated plastic pipes underground. These collect the water and guide it towards a soakaway. This is a hole with sides lined with a geo-textile liner – the sort of material you would line a path with – and filled with gravel. Gravel drains more freely than soil and helps the water pass quickly to deeper soils where waterlogging is not an issue to the gardener. Obviously this is a lot of physical work and can be expensive, so, unless you have a severe problem, it isn't to be recommended. The RHS says that poor drainage can be confirmed by pouring water into a hole 30–60cm deep. If the water remains for

hours or even days, then the soil probably needs draining, if you want to grow dry-loving plants.

Flash flooding can happen anywhere, even in normally dry gardens, but wetter gardens are generally more likely to suffer waterlogging as a consequence. Outright plant death from flooding can happen within hours – or minutes if the waterlogging is severe. The water deprives plants of oxygen and they drown. If waterlogging is less severe but nevertheless serious, roots will not function properly. Since wet soils are often low in nutrients, as well as being cold, plant growth may be slow.

Environment Agency advice for coping with floods

The Environment Agency produces a guide for gardeners in areas prone to severe flooding. It is available in leaflet form online at www.environment-agency.gov.uk /floodline or call 0845 988 1188. This contains details of what to do in the event of a flood and the following advice on planning ahead:

- Familiarise yourself with the water table beneath your garden and know what the water levels are like at different times of the year. Follow the advice above to determine waterlogging.

- Check with local authorities whether excess water can be piped into drains.

- Consider laying land drains and soakaways and/or connections to public drains.

- Consider creating a bog garden or pond with supply ditches in naturally wet areas.

Ethical choice: thirsty plants?

Most common garden plants consume 140–160kg of water per 0.45kg of dry matter produced. On a sunny, warm, windy day a fast-growing pumpkin plant can consume almost its own weight in water every daylight hour. This is like you or me drinking 90 litres of water an hour. If you live in a dry region and don't want to water your plants, go for something much less thirsty (see page 117 for some examples).

The low-water garden

In a dry, sunny garden, take advantage of your conditions and grow drought-loving flowers. Don't think of dry as in dry and boring. Think of it as in dry and wacky, curious and ironic. With some of the drought-loving plants you do need a sense of humour to grow them. Take mesembryanthemums. Even if you can pronounce them, should you take them seriously? They are like something off the *The Magic Roundabout*. Drought survivors are loud and brash, and deserve to shout about it if they want to.

Low-water plants have a couple of ways of coping with drought. They take in water enthusiastically, and hold onto it fiercely. Various parts of the plant can be adopted to store water. Succulence (having parts that are thick and fleshy) is a key factor in desert plants. Some have succulent roots, some stems (like Wild West cacti) and some leaves. Most plants are happy to lose water through their leaves, just taking up more from their roots, but this isn't an option if you live in the desert. Our dry-loving plants have waxy or hairy leaves to prevent water loss.

When to water

It's easy to spot a plant that hasn't got enough water. It wilts. Once a plant begins to wilt, its growth rate has already begun to slow. If you don't water a plant that has wilted it may rush to flower before its time so that it produces seeds. If it is very short of water it will die. Watering is especially important for newly planted or transplanted plants, and those in shallow soils and containers. When growing garden plants indoors to give them a head start they should be hardened off before you plant them in their final position outside. Water should be gradually (not suddenly) withheld and the plants progressively exposed to the weather. If you don't do this and put plants straight out, they react as they would in a drought and growth slows.

Some plants have critical periods of growth, during which time water supplies are vital – for example, when fruits and tubers are swelling, or when a plant is setting seed. If you're growing veg you need to mark in the calendar when you've got to take special care of your crop. It's a difficult one because lots of people go on holiday when their plants need them most. You can get sophisticated drip-watering systems but it might be cheaper to pay a trusted friend or neighbour to help.

Wind

Gardeners are able to control wind much more effectively than some of the other climate drivers, which is a good job considering the damage wind can do to a plant. Wind can reduce growth by lowering temperatures, blowing soil away and causing frost to form, but it can also cause physical breakages and it can dry out leaves by removing moisture.

Gardeners can reduce all these symptoms of wind damage by erecting windbreaks. A sheltered plant is more comfortable and will grow far quicker. There is a balance to be struck, though. Very still conditions can support fungal diseases and solid barriers actually cause damaging wind turbulence by forcing the air up and over. An ideal wind barrier is one that lessens the pace of wind rather than preventing its movement altogether.

Spend some time walking around your garden to feel what's going on. You could buy expensive wind-monitoring equipment if you want to be very scientific about it, but it's just as good to walk round in different wind conditions and feel the force of the wind on your skin (no need to get naked, hands and faces will suffice). You'll soon discover where the flow of wind is strongest and weakest. You also need to know the regular direction of the wind – the prevailing wind: there's no point putting up your wind barrier the wrong side of your plants. You can get good clues from the plants for this one. Wind flagging is the term used to describe the way in which plants are pushed away from the prevailing wind. Although, having said this, the unusual wind can sometimes be the most damaging.

Shelter options

Wind should be calmed rather than blocked totally. High solid wooden panel fences are good for privacy but not necessarily brilliant for garden health. Totally still environments are more likely to create conditions that encourage the growth of fungal disorders in plants. Solid fences also create turbulence which can cause unnecessary damage to plants, and they are more likely to be pushed over in very windy weather. They are not good for exposed sites. It is possible to combine the privacy of the high fence while letting air flow through by buying a double-sided slatted fence. This is basically two fences attached to one another by a series of vertical timber posts. Each fence has spaces to let the air through but there are no visual gaps because the fence slats at the front cover the gaps at the back, and vice versa. The air is allowed to pass through the holes at a slower pace. As with all timber products look out for the FSC (Forest Stewardship Council) symbol (see pages 27 and 48).

The benefits of a hedge

Fences offer quick protection but wildlife gardeners will value the extra diversity provided by a hedge. Hedges are good for birds, insects and mammals, providing habitat, food and shelter. Some are better than others. Hedges made with evergreen conifers such as Leyland cypress (x *Cupressocyparis leylandii*) are much less valuable than hedges made with mixed woodland trees such as oak (*Quercus*), hawthorn (*Crataegus*) and hazel (*Corylus*). These deciduous trees shed their leaves in autumn and are bare throughout winter. If you want a hedge that keeps its leaves all winter and is not a conifer you could chose yew (*Taxus*),

Above *Rosa canina* produces hips for you and the birds to forage.

berberis, privet (*Ligustrum*), holly (*Ilex*), or beech (*Fagus*); although the latter is deciduous its leaves turn a russet colour in the autumn but do not fall off completely. Thick, formal hedges tend to act like a solid fence, blocking the wind completely. One other option is a willow fedge – both a living hedge and a fence. Willow (*Salix*) is a fast-growing plant that can be grown close together and shaped easily to form a decorative barrier (see overleaf).

Choosing a hedge

Before you choose your hedge trees make sure they suit your soil and climatic conditions. For example, beeches are more susceptible to damage during drought years and are said to be at risk in dry areas of Britain as a result of global warming. You could just plant a hedge using one species of tree but it's good to mix it up a little and make use of a wider variety. Mixed hedgerows are more interesting and will attract different species of insect, whilst providing flowers and berries at different times of the year. It's slightly more complex managing a mixed hedge but it's a skill worth learning.

> Mixed hedgerows will attract different species of insect, whilst providing flowers and berries at different times of the year.

Have a think about what additional purpose you would like your hedge to serve, apart from shelter. Planned carefully, hedges can also provide colour, food, nectar-filled flowers for pollinating insects, craft materials and support for non-tree species such as ivy (*Hedera*; a good wildlife plant), honeysuckle (*Lonicera*) and blackberry (*Rubus fruticosus*).

If you want to grow hedgerow foods, think about growing hazel, gooseberries (*Ribes uva-crispa*), elder (*Sambucus nigra*), *Rosa rugosa*, *Rosa canina* (dog rose), thornless blackberry and blackthorn (*Prunus spinosa*; for the sloe berries to make sloe gin). If you want year-round colour and interest pick dogwood (*Cornus*), red and yellow willow, holly and beech for winter; early-flowering blackthorn and hawthorn for the spring; elder and *Rosa rugosa* for the summer; and spindle tree (*Euonymus europaeus*), hazel, ivy, amelanchier and crab apples (*Malus sylvestris*) for autumn. Check out www.btcv.org.uk and www.cooltemperate.co.uk for hedge saplings.

We tend to think of larger trees for hedging, but smaller plants can create additional shelter at a lower level. Small herb hedges made with rosemary (*Rosmarinus*) and lavender (*Lavandula*) are quite common, fragrant and beautiful. They can be used to divide the garden up a little and create mini hot spots where plants benefit from the extra warmth created by the added protection from the wind.

Planning and planting a hedge

Depending on the species, hedges take three to five years to start looking like a hedge. Trees are planted as one-year-old whips (seedlings). These are available from hedge specialists and you shouldn't expect to pay much for them. When planted they need to be protected from pests like sheep and from any random tramplers, including children, partygoers, uninvited guests and, if you're anything like me, yourself. Protect with a wire fence.

Planning your hedge height in advance is a good idea, and also what level of neatness you are aiming to adopt. Formal hedges made from yew and privet can be clipped several times a year for absolute neatness. Deciduous hedging is usually pruned back to the required height and shape once a year in the winter when the trees are dormant (although I like to let mine go a little and cut back every other year). You can also layer a deciduous hedge. This is a traditional technique used by farmers to provide a secure hedge to keep livestock in. It requires a certain amount of skill, judgement and an ability to handle a cutting tool called a billhook.

Hedge maintenance

All hedges need some maintenance and a set of basic tools. I use a pruning saw, loppers and secateurs and like to take my time pruning. I like listening to the birds as I work and enjoying the feel of the wood in my hands. My hedge is quite informal. If you're managing a formal hedge you may prefer to use an electric hedge trimmer, though to me this is a less rewarding process. *Gardening Which?* magazine (August 2006) recommended the Bosch AHS 6000 Pro-T, Bosch AHS 48-16 and Gardena EHT 480 Vario as the best performers. Users of any cutter should wear goggles to protect the eyes.

Before you start cutting a hedge, whether using hand or power tools, check for birds. It is illegal to disturb an active bird's nest because disturbance can cause parents to abandon their nests and chicks. If you trim hedges during the mating season (usually between March and August) check for nesting birds first and delay trimming until you are sure the nest is no longer used. If you're too busy to maintain a hedge it may be better to stick to the fence option. Or plan to pay someone to do the maintenance for you.

If you want to see pictures of some truly horrific hedging go to **www.hedgeline.org**, the website of an organisation dedicated to helping victims of hedge bullying. These hedges from hell are usually Leylandii, but not always. Some of them are taller than houses and cast so much shade that their neighbours are unable to grow any sun-loving plants at all. In the ethical spirit of this book remember to be a good neighbour – keep your hedge under control! And if you are a victim of hedge bullying, find out about new antisocial behaviour legislation that gives you the right to make a complaint to your local authority about hedge bullies.

Right A willow 'fedge' growing in the CAT gardens.

Frost

In the middle of the winter it doesn't much matter how frosty your garden is because plants have more or less stopped growing. Some plants can survive temperatures of -196°C when dormant (the point at which liquid nitrogen freezes), but die at -3°C when growing. The danger for plants comes from March to June and from September to November. In other words, spring and autumn in the northern hemisphere. In these seasons plants are susceptible to damage by frost. There are two types of frost: ground frost and air frost. If the ground temperature falls to 0°C it will freeze. Small, non-frost hardy plants will die and those that have already shown signs of growth will be set back. If the temperature drops several degrees below freezing, the frost radiates a metre or more upwards from the soil. At this point it can collide with fruit blossoms on low bushes and trees. If blossom is killed by frost you won't get any fruit.

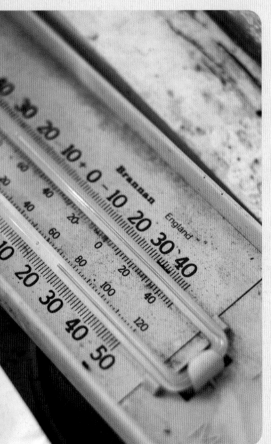

The duration of frost is another important factor. A frost of -3°C can devastate a crop if it is sustained over several hours, but causes no damage if it lasts for only fifteen minutes. As the winter sun moves lower in the sky, any garden shaded by a structure or natural object to the south or south-west will be more susceptible to day-long frost than a garden that opens out to a view.

Check the weather forecast if you are worried about the threat of frost. When it is predicted throw a protective cover over your most vulnerable plants. You can buy a range of protective fleeces online or through garden centres, but you can also use old sheets. It's amazing how effective a thin cover is against light frosts. Be careful not to damage any flower buds when you're covering or uncovering a plant.

Beware exploding plants

Plants can be damaged by freezing and melting. When air temperatures drop below zero the water crystals inside a plant freeze. If the drop is very serious the freezing crystals explode and kill the plant. On 31 October 1991 temperatures in Missouri suddenly dropped from 21°C to -26°C. Peach trees all over the state exploded. After a frost, when temperatures rise, ice crystals turn back into water. If these crystals melt too quickly a plant will struggle to reabsorb the water and become dehydrated. This can set back and even kill a plant. East-facing gardens, walls and beds feel the morning sun first and this is where most frost damage from thawing to plants occurs. Avoid planting vulnerable plants such as fruit there.

Frost pockets

Flat gardens are more frosty than sloping sites because there is nowhere for the cold air to go. They are however less likely to suffer from frost pockets. A frost pocket is a place where frost tends to gather. It occurs when a stream of cold air descending a hill hits a barrier such as a wall, a fence or a hedge. The cold air congregates around the barrier and causes the earth and air to freeze. Avoid planting all but the most hardy plants in a frost pocket. Herbaceous perennials that do not die back in winter should not be planted in these positions. It is possible to eradicate or lessen the effect of a frost pocket by preventing the downward flow of air or removing part of the barrier that causes it. If you have access to the land above a frost pocket (from whence the cold air descends), you could push the cold air away from its normal course by planting hedges further up the slope. Most of us don't have this luxury though and are better off working out some way of allowing the air to continue on its course or fitting the plant to the pocket.

Left Severe frost at the wrong time of year can affect flower growth in fruits, lowering eventual yields.

Understanding your soil

To a certain extent soil is what you make of it. Nothing is fixed. You can change the destiny of the soil quite easily. However, as far as basic geology goes there's nothing to do but accept what you're given. You can change the nutrient quality and structure of your soil, but you can't really alter its type, and this is determined by what's happening further down under your garden, in the layers of rock beneath.

Soil is actually made up of three layers: the bedrock (or parental soil), the subsoil and the topsoil. The topsoil is where most of the action happens, the soil that gardeners can influence with their composts and green manures. Topsoil is a combination of rock from the bedrock that has risen through the subsoil, and rotting or rotted organic matter accumulated both from activity in the soil itself and from the world above.

There are five basic types of topsoil – clay, silt, peat, chalk or sand – and the first thing you should do when you arrive in a new garden is work out what sort you've got. Pick some soil up and roll it between your finger and thumb. Clay is sticky and can be pressed into shapes. Sand is coarse and gritty and feels a bit umm… sandy. Silt feels silky. Chalk is dry and crumbly. Peat is blacker than all the rest and moist and has a lovely richness of texture.

> Personally, I'd have problems rolling a sample of my soil between my finger and thumb without getting a large piece of slate chipping under my fingernail. I have what you would call a stony soil.

Personally, I'd have problems rolling a sample of my soil between my finger and thumb without getting a large piece of slate chipping under my fingernail. I have what you would call a stony soil (pictured right). My parental soil is a rich seam of slate. As slate is a brittle material it chips off and rises easily to the surface. Stony soils are defined as containing a significant number of particles of rock with a diameter greater than 2mm. These 'fragments' can be classified as gravel, cobbles or boulders.

The two ends of the soil rainbow – if that's an appropriate metaphor – are (heavy) clay and (light) sand. Most garden soils fall somewhere in between, with varying amounts of clay and sand making up the greater proportion of the volume of the soil. The perfect garden soil for the majority of plants is called loam. This has a good balance of clay and sand and organic matter. Around 90 per cent of soil is rock (clay, sand, silt, slate, and so on) and minerals; the other 10 per cent is the organic fraction.

Acid, alkaline or neutral?

Soils are also said to be either acid, alkaline or neutral. It is possible to tell what kind of soil you've got by looking at the types of plants that are already growing there (unless you've ignored my earlier advice and bulldozed the garden already). Some plants will not grow in acid soils. Others not in alkaline. Rhododendrons, heather (*Erica* and *Calluna*), ferns, iris, camellias and azaleas are all acid-loving plants. Alkaline soils are good for buddleja, lilac (*Syringa*), pinks (*Dianthus*), euphorbia, tree mallow (*Lavatera arborea*) and evening primrose (*Oenothera biennis*). You may also be able to tell by looking at the kind of weeds you've got. Nettles (*Urtica dioica*), mosses, bracken (*Pteridium aquilinum*), dandelion (*Taraxacum officinale*) and ox-eye daisy (*Leucanthemum vulgare*) all like acid soils. Bladder campion (*Silene vulgaris*), white mustard (*Sinapsis alba*) and prickly sow thistle (*Sonchus asper*) all like alkaline or neutral soils.

> It is quite common to have several different levels of pH in one garden. I took four soil samples from my garden and found they ranged from alkaline, through neutral to very acid.

To be sure you can conduct a pH test. Kits are readily available and easy to use. The pH test gives soil a unit of acidity or pH, which stands for potential of hydrogen. A neutral soil has a pH of 7. An alkaline soil has a higher pH; an acid soil, a lower pH. The pH scale is logarithmic, which means each unit change represents a tenfold change in acidity or alkalinity. So a soil with a pH of 5 is ten times more acidic than that of a sample with a pH of 6. In comparison, milk is neutral, vinegar between 3 and 4 and battery acid between 1 and 2. On the alkaline side, baking soda has a pH of 9 and milk of magnesia 11.

The ideal soil pH is between 6.5 and 6.8. Most plants will thrive at this level. There are lots of acid-tolerant plants, including fennel, potatoes, rhubarb, blackberries and raspberries, and some which are relatively tolerant. These include beans, Brussels sprouts, carrots, cucumbers, garlic, peas, peppers, pumpkins, squash, sweetcorn, tomatoes, turnips, apples, gooseberries, grapes and strawberries. However, there are also plenty of plants that won't tolerate an acid soil: asparagus, beets, broccoli, cabbage, cauliflower, chard, leeks, lettuce, onions, parsnips, spinach. Acid soils also tend to be slightly impoverished. Plants can be slow to germinate, grow and mature, and are more likely to suffer outbreaks of disease and pestilence.

It is quite common to have several different levels of pH in one garden. I took four soil samples from my garden and found they ranged from alkaline, through neutral to very acid. The kit I bought came with an extensive and very useful chart of the acidity requirements of most common types of vegetables, fruit, herbs, flowers, ornamental trees and shrubs. Taking the test was very simple and each kit comes with enough material for ten tests.

Adjusting the soil's pH

Correcting acidity is relatively easy. You just add lime – regularly, in small quantities, rather than huge amounts in one go, which can scorch plants' roots. Heavy clay soils need more lime than light sandy ones. To increase the pH level of a sandy soil by one unit add 1kg of lime every 100sq m. A clay soil will need 4kg per 100sq m. Do this several weeks before sowing or planting and never directly after applying manure (it causes the formation of ammonia).

There are various different types of lime available: they include slaked lime, hydrated lime and ground limestone. Geoff Hamilton's favourite was ground limestone. It's more expensive but stays in the soil longer and contains magnesium (another useful nutrient). Avoid slaked or hydrated limes as these are caustic and harmful to soil organisms. You can use wood ashes in a garden to raise pH too but don't add more than 1kg per 9sq m in a year.

Clay soil

Clay is a heavy soil made up of minute particles less than 0.002mm in size. Water cannot easily pass between the particles on its way down. This means that a clay soil does not drain easily. When it is wet it becomes waterlogged, muddy and difficult to work. When it is dry it bakes and cracks, and water planes across the surface. It is important to work in plenty of organic matter to improve drainage and moisture distribution. On the plus side, because they do not drain easily, water and nutrients tend to stay near the roots of the plants where they are needed and not disappear out of reach into deeper soils.

Silty soil

Silt shares many of the characteristics of clay soil. It has small particles – between 0.002mm and 0.02mm. It packs down heavily and leaves the soil cold and badly drained but, like clay soils, its ability to keep water is useful when water is in short supply. It is also a fertile soil.

Sandy soil

Sandy soils are dry and lose water easily because they drain quickly, which can be a good thing in periods of excessive rainfall but can also lead to nutrient deficiencies where there are low levels of organic matter, as the nutrients get washed out. In dry conditions, sandy soils will benefit from top mulching and the addition of compost. Unlike clay, sandy soil particles are big – anywhere between 0.2mm and 2mm. Water passes between the particles easily.

Chalk soil

Chalk is another soil with big particles easily drained of water and nutrients. The topsoil is often shallow so you can't grow anything with very long roots. Chalk is very alkaline and the range of plants you can grow in a chalky soil is less varied than in some of the other soils.

Peat soil

In some ways, peat is the odd soil out. In all other cases the structure and fertility of the soil can be improved significantly by the addition of organic material. It will improve drainage in clays and silts, and water retention in sand and chalk. But peat is so rich in decomposed organic matter already it requires little extra treatment. However, it does waterlog easily and in very severe cases you may have to lay drainage pipes through the soil. Having said this, it's much easier and more sensible to grow plants that don't mind the damp conditions. Peat is an acid soil so you need to chose plants to suit.

Nutrient deficiencies

Once you've established a basic soil care routine you should keep it up and maintain the fertility in your soil year by year. If your soil is lacking some specific nutrient, plants are very good at giving you signs (see page 92). Even if you practise good general soil care you may find that some of your plants are short of one or two specific nutrients. If you can't rectify these problems by adding compost or by growing green manures, you should apply a specific liquid feed (see page 107) that is rich in the nutrient required.

How to spot nutrient deficiencies

Plants need a range of nutrients. Soils that are deficient in certain nutrients can lead to weaknesses in plants, making them more likely to suffer disease and attack by predators. The easiest way to spot soil deficiencies is by looking at the plants themselves.

- A shortage of nitrogen affects leaf and shoot growth and leads to pale foliage, poor growth and possibly a reddish or yellow discoloration.
- A shortage of phosphorus stunts overall growth, including the development of fruit and seeds.
- A shortage of potassium can lead to scorching on the tips of a plant and reduced flowering.
- A shortage of magnesium, iron and manganese will show up in the leaves, which turn yellow between the veins and around the edges.
- A shortage of calcium is seen on apples and tomatoes when the blossom end rots (the end of the fruit where the flower once was).

Poor soils

It's easy to be flippant about the value of poor soils, but actually poor and low soil gardens can be very effective and beautiful. It's perfectly legitimate to match plants to soil type and forget about trying to improve soil quality. In fact in some situations it's the most sensible and environmentally sensitive approach you could take. Writer and film-maker Derek Jarman created a beautiful, almost soil-less garden with pebbles, driftwood, scrap metal and a few hardy plants. The site could not have been more unpromising – a flat, bleak expanse of shingle near the nuclear power station at Dungeness, Kent. The book he wrote about it, his own record of how the garden evolved from its beginnings in 1985 to the day of his death in 1994, is an inspiring testament to the skill of matching the plant to the soil. (See pictures of the garden at http://www.flickr.com/photos/angusf/sets/656542.) One of the things I love about plants is their absolute determination to hold onto life in the cruellest of conditions. Sometimes we should just go with the flow. The results can be beautiful and enchanting

You can also send your soil off to a lab for testing. Elm Farm Research Centre is a leading organic research organisation and they offer a soil-testing service for all gardeners (www.efrc.com). The Royal Horticultural Society (www.rhs.org. uk/advice /soil_analysis.asp) also offer a soil-testing service. For commercial organisations try www.mrscrow.com, www.lancrop.com/indexlanc /indexlanc.htm and www.voelckerconsultants.co.uk.

Enriching your soil

There are two basic approaches to soil care. One is to do nothing. The other is to get stuck in and make things better for your plants and for the wildlife that lives in the soil. There's nothing wrong with taking the first option if you're quite happy to grow plants that like poor soil: meadow flowers, alpine rockery plants and the types of wildflowers that manage to appear from cracks in the pavement and walls. But if you want to grow demanding plants like vegetables and fruit, and the kinds of nutrient-loving flowers that fill the average garden border, you need to take the second option and learn how to enrich your soil with compost and green manures. It's more work for the gardener but work that will pay dividends in the long run with larger harvests, more bountiful blooms, stronger plants and less damage from pests. After climate, nothing determines the health of your plants like the quality of your soil. And this is one area you can control quite nicely, given the right knowledge and the willingness to put it into practice.

Composting

Soil is part rock (which is and has been, for a very long time, dead) and part decomposing material (which was once, and for a not very long time, living). Really good soil has much more formerly living material than eternally dead material because rock doesn't have much to offer plants in the way of nutrients. Compost is material that was formerly living, which has been placed by humans in a container to decompose so that it can be used for the purpose of enriching the soil, normally to grow food.

Compost doesn't happen magically; it is created by millions of living creatures eating and excreting, eating and excreting. What you eventually put back into the soil is mostly animal poo. Not the sort of poo that is dangerous or unpleasant to humans (such as that of dog, cat, rabbit, and so on), but deftly processed poo made by worms, woodlice and microscopic organisms. In its finished state it is perfectly safe, lovely and harmonious for nature, and full of nutrients that plants love. There are lots of different ways to make compost, and some of them are described here.

'Feed-and-forget' composting

The advantage of a wormery (see pages 102–103) is that it delivers high-quality compost very quickly. The disadvantage is that it can't handle large volumes of garden waste. CAT has developed its own type of composting system called 'feed-and-forget' or 'cool composting'. It's based on the needs of compost creatures, but includes all of them, not just the worms. For this you need a compost bin and a kitchen container. CAT called it feed-and-forget because in trials carried out with a group of homeowners in the Dyfi valley the best results came from doing nothing extra to your compost heap, such as turning it or adding a compost accelerator. The best thing you could do was just feed the compost in and forget about it. The system seems to work well in busy chaotic households where waste accumulates not as an organised mass but in dribs and drabs, and contrasts with the so-called 'hot composting' systems described below, which require the gardener to carefully place specific types of waste material in layers to generate heat. These compost heaps rely on different types of heat-loving composting bacteria to break down the compost, and regular compost creatures can't survive in the hot, hot heat.

> The random, disorganised style of feed-and-forget composting reflects the chaotic nature of soil decomposition in nature.

The random, disorganised style of feed-and-forget composting reflects the chaotic nature of soil decomposition in natural systems. When waste falls to the ground it is not in any way organised. Nature is messy. Many compost systems fail because they end up as neglected hot compost systems (hot compost heaps need turning regularly) or because they don't have the correct conditions for regular composters to work effectively. They become a soggy, slimy mess. This is not compost! Compost looks like a really rich soil. But in busy modern households there is an instant solution: cardboard packaging. Compost critters are more likely to occupy a compost heap that contains cardboard egg cartons, loo roll holders, cereal boxes (especially the small, variety pack boxes), fast-food packaging, and so on.

All compost creatures need a healthy balance of carbohydrates, proteins, fats, vitamins and minerals, suitable living conditions and plenty of air and water to survive. They don't like squashed and waterlogged conditions. The best way to prevent these conditions in a compost bin is to add cardboard and paper scraps. Cardboard on its own will not compost well. It is just a useful addition to the normal kitchen scraps and garden waste. All compost bins and heaps, as opposed to wormeries, need a good balance of nitrogen and carbohydrate to work properly. Cardboard provides a balance of carbohydrate-rich material to the more sloppy and nitrogenous (protein-rich) kitchen and garden waste.

Peter Harper of CAT created the feed-and-forget composting system and uses the analogy of a cheese sandwich as the best way to describe it. The cardboard is the bread (the carbohydrate) and the kitchen scraps are the cheese (the protein). It's a useful way to remember that you need both to make a fulfilling meal – or a healthy compost heap. When I've described the feed-and-forget composting system before, people have asked whether there is a danger in over-feeding with one or other material and want to know what the correct balance is. CAT's research with average householders mostly found that the system seemed to balance out. If you ate nothing but boxed pizzas you might have a problem, but if you have a healthy diet and have plenty of garden waste to put in the heap, it just seems to work.

Failing compost heaps will look either like slimy gloop or dry crackle. If your compost heap is too wet, add more cardboard. If it is too dry, add more garden and kitchen scraps. Experiment and you'll find a balance. Don't lay cardboard flat in a compost bin or tear it into little pieces. Instead scrunch it into rough balls, somewhere between the size of an egg and a small melon. Compost creatures love the air spaces these crumpled cardboard balls provide.

Collecting cardboard

The easiest way to collect cardboard is to get into a routine in the kitchen. Keep a dedicated container and it will soon fill up. Every time you go into your garden take the container of cardboard with you and empty it into the compost bin.

Large pieces of cardboard, newspapers or magazines should be recycled rather than composted. If you compost frozen food packets you may find they leave a thin film of plastic in the compost when the cardboard has disappeared. If you don't want the hassle of removing this, recycle the packets instead.

What sort of compost bin?

Most councils offer cheap or free home composters to get people recycling their kitchen scraps but the kind they offer do not necessarily give you the best results. They tend to be what I call the Dalek-type plastic composter (pictured below) – perhaps it's a secret invasion plan, Daleks disguised as compost bins...? CAT found the best design to be a square box with no lid. These sort of bins are more expensive to buy but you can make them fairly easily using pallets or straw bales.

The lidless square box bin allows air and water to circulate freely. It is also useful to allow air to enter the sides of the bin and quite often it will be a slatted construction with gaps between the slats. You don't need to build up heat in a feed-and-forget compost heap. Nor should you need to turn the compost. Let the soil community find their own way of working inside the bin and disturb them as little as possible.

I have two bins. One bin contains last year's finished compost. The other contains the current decomposing composting. Each bin is a basic square with four corner supports and slats in between. The slats can be lifted out of the corner supports at the front of the bin when it's time to empty the compost. Moving compost around is heavy work and being able to tackle it front on without having to bend into the compost bin saves back strain. The slats also allow you to see what's going on without too much disturbance. At the end of the year I transfer any uncomposted material at the top of the bin I've been using into the empty bin (by this time last year's finished compost has been dug into the vegetable patch before cultivation). I make sure I move plenty of compost creatures in there too to get things going.

My bins lie directly onto the soil to allow more composters to come up from below (although many slugs traverse the sides every night too). There is an argument for putting bins on hard surfaces – to make it harder for rats to enter the bin. Rats can carry disease. Of most concern to gardeners is Weil's disease, which is carried in rats' urine. It is not infectious when the urine is dry so is only a problem in compost bins when it is wet. No compost bin can be made 100 per cent rat-proof so I wear gloves when handling compost and wash my hands afterwards, just in case. If you have any worries take a look at **www.gardenorganic.org.uk/factsheets/gg1.php**.

Garden Organic (HDRA) provide a factsheet on how to make a simple square slatted compost bin. It is available in paper form and can be downloaded from **www.gardenorganic. org.uk/factsheets/gg24.php**. A brief guide to compost bin requirements is also available at **www.gardenorganic.org.uk/factsheets/gg14.php**.

Hot composting

If your garden is mostly lawn and borders, much of your compost will be made up of protein-rich grass clippings and weeds. It benefits the lawn to leave the grass clippings where they fall but neatness gets the better of us. Sometimes the addition of too much grass makes a heap go slimy, but if you're putting plenty of cardboard in the compost bin the addition of all this grass shouldn't be a problem. If it does become a problem it might be better to use a different system called hot composting. This approach uses alternate layers of flat cardboard and protein-rich materials stacked one upon the other. Because heat is trapped by the layers, the heap gets too airless for normal soil composters. Instead anaerobic fungi and bacteria (which can live without air) do the composting and heat the bed in the process. Eventually they heat themselves to death, so the compost heap has to be turned once a week to stop it overheating. Hot composting is time-consuming but fast: it's quicker than feed-and-forget composting. Some weeds should only be composted in a hot heap where the heat kills the weed seeds as well as plant diseases.

Composting meat

Another common question is about composting meat. Most councils advise householders not to compost meat or dairy products in the garden, because of the risk of attracting vermin and causing bad odours. But this leaves the problem of what to do with them if you don't want to send them to landfill.

A new method of composting from Japan called Bokashi is based on a product called Effective Micro-organisms – 'Ems' for short. Ems is a carefully controlled mixture of microscopic creatures such as bacteria, yeasts and fungi that work together to speed up composting, suppress pathogens, prevent putrefaction and eliminate bad odours. They come in the form of Bokashi, a dry bran-like material. You sprinkle the Ems on your kitchen waste, leave for a couple of weeks and then add it to your normal compost bin or incorporate it into the soil. According to Wiggly Wigglers the waste doesn't look as though it has decomposed. It just looks a bit pickled. However, when you add it to the soil or compost bin it breaks down quickly. Garden Organic (HDRA) is running its own trials on Bokashi: keep an eye on the website www.gardenorganic.org.uk.

The German Mound (see page 98) is one of several alternative composting methods that I don't really have space to do justice to in this book. If you start getting excited by composting, you'll need to do your own research. Try *Start with The Soil* by Grace Gershuny, the 'Cool Composting' factsheet from CAT, *All About Composting* by Pauline Pears (a Garden Organic/HDRA book) and **www.gardenorganic.org.uk /todo_now/faqs.php?id=93**

Dealing with woody waste

If you've got lots of woody waste (branches clipped from hedges and so forth) there are four ways of dealing with it:

• Establish a slow composting heap in a far-flung corner of the garden (if you have one) and let it rot back into the soil over several years.

• Shred it using a garden shredding machine and either lay the resulting material on the soil as a mulch, or put it in with your other composting waste.

• Take your woody waste to your council recycling unit to be turned back into compost.

• Put it in a German Mound. This uses a woody core as a base for layers of composted material topped off with topsoil and then used to grow shallow-rooting crops.

Composting leaves

In the US it is fairly common practice to go into the streets and kidnap leaves piled up for removal by the council. Leaves are very easy to compost. Just put a section of chicken wire around four posts and throw the leaves inside. The wire holds the leaves in place and you can see when they're ready. They rot down quickly and look like a very fine soil when fully composted. Just spade them straight onto the soil. Leaf mould, as the finished item is called, doesn't contain huge amounts of nutrients but it does add depth to top soil. If you don't want to compost leaves in a separate heap, or haven't the space, just pile them up around existing plants and let worms and other compost creatures do the rest. While they are still on the surface of the soil they act as a mulch (see page 203-204).

Right A typical high-fibre compost heap in action. It contains a mixture of card and vegetable matter.

Composting tips

Advice about what and what not to compost varies depending on who you talk to (see meat debate on page 97), but here are some general dos and don'ts.

What to compost

- Uncooked vegetable matter
- Smaller scrunched-up cardboard boxes like egg boxes, cereal packets, toilet roll holders, etc.
- Garden waste – excluding diseased plants, annual weeds which have already set seed and the roots of perennial weeds that might survive (and indeed benefit from being in) a compost bin
- Grass clippings
- Plants grown especially for the compost bin, such as comfrey and nettle leaves (see page 104)

What not to compost

- Meat and fish scraps
- Glass and tins
- Dog faeces
- Used cat litter
- Disposable nappies
- Coal and coke ash
- Plastics and synthetic fibres
- Large cardboard boxes, newspapers, etc. – although if you have a very big compost heap with lots of garden waste you may be able to accommodate such things

For more information see the How to Make Great Compost section on the Garden Organic (HDRA) website: www.gardenorganic.org.uk/organicgardening/.

Compost critters

Before we get down to the nitty gritty of soil improvement I want to spend some time with the little creatures that make it all possible: the decomposers. As I said earlier, gardening for wildlife helps us garden more successfully overall we just need to be a little more accommodating. Compost creatures have quite simple requirements: air, water, food. Whether they are doing their decomposing in the soil or in the compost bin it is always the same. But before we see what we can do to help them thrive, let's find out who they are.

       Broadly speaking, there are two types of composters: the ones you can see with your naked eyes and the ones you need a magnifying glass or microscope to see. The first group includes worms, ants, beetles, centipedes, millipedes, woodlice, slugs (yes, even they have their good points) – all creatures we can easily recognise. You will probably be less familiar with the second group: the micro-organisms. This group includes nematodes, protozoa, pseudoscorpions, actinomycetes, algae, Spirochaetes bacteria and springtails. Compost critters eat dead stuff for a living (i.e. rotting wood, fallen leaves and petals, other creatures, dung, and so on), and process it into a form that can be used by plants: compost critter dung. Some composters are also predators, but some are pure rotters.

Although the big boys are obviously more noticeable, it's the little fellas that do most of the composting. They account for 60–80 per cent of all soil life.

Meet the worms

Despite the microscopic decomposers' pre-eminence in the kingdom of composting, everyone's favourite composter is the worm. Worms have it all: they're visible for one thing, but still mysterious. They plough up and down soils looking for action, bringing up nutrients from the deep soils to the top soils and making useful water drainage channels as they go. They can get through half their own weight in rotting food every day and they drop the most amazing (yet precisely described) cast of excrement you'd ever want to have in your soil. Cast is one of those value-added words that really fit the object. A worm cast is a little golden nugget of nutrition. Plants love it!

Worm casts contain high levels of nitrogen (N), phosphorus (P) and potassium (K): the three key nutrients all plants need to grow strong and healthy. All composting activity generates increases in potassium, nitrogen and phosphorus. Worms just happen to do it better than most. In gardening terms the balance is known as the NPK ratio, named after the three chemical symbols (shown in brackets above). Plants take these three chemicals from the soil whenever they grow.

Tunnels of love

Worms are great tunnellers. They spend their lives moving through soil, dragging decomposing material into it and through it, casting off poo. Charles Darwin called them the 'intestines of the soil'. The tunnels they create allow air and water to flow freely through the soil. In hot weather worms retreat to deeper soils from which they bring back nutrients for the rest of the soil community.

This tunnelling activity is vital for a healthy soil community. Pockets of space filled with air (known as pores) account for 50 per cent of the volume of good soil. Soil without pores is said to be compacted. Life in very compacted soils is hardly possible because most soil creatures need air. Compacted soil will not handle floodwaters well either. The channels and air pockets that allow air to permeate through the soil also allow water to flow freely. When a plant label says 'needs good drainage', it is really saying it needs soil with air spaces and a thriving soil community. The quality of soil

structure determines the type and quality of plants we can grow. Just like the composters, all plant roots need access to air and water, as well as nutrients. The structure of the soil determines how much air and water the plant roots get.

If we think back to the story of *The Man Who Planted Trees* (see page 14), Elzéard Bouffier improves the structure of the soil by planting acorns. An oak tree takes a long time to grow but it does the job of breaking up the soil and facilitating a rebirth. It sheds its leaves to provide material for worms and other composters. It captures water and brings it into the soil. It provides shelter for other plants, and so on. Eventually the activity of the plants themselves creates good soil structure. The natural inclination of all soils is to return to forest. In a way the gardener is doing the work of the woodland by ensuring the fertility levels and structure of the soil are maintained.

Food for the worms

Worms are 80 per cent water and although they can survive for days submerged in water, they cannot survive a day isolated from it. Worms will leave dry soils for more hospitable places. Likewise any soil without food will be an unattractive proposition. Worms will live on freshly cut or rotting vegetation, meat, dropped leaves, the fallen petals of flowers and just about anything organic (although, interestingly, Darwin found that the worms he used in his experiments preferred carrot tops to cabbage and liked sage, thyme and mint least of all). We need to make sure our composters have access to plenty of food, water and air to allow them to carry on improving the structure of our soils. This can be done by adding rotting organic material to the soil to decompose or by sowing plants that will eventually be eaten by composters (green manures). Either way we have to keep on giving back to the soil what our plants take out.

Above A brandling or tiger worm at work in a wormery.

Keeping worms in a wormery

Worms love compost. Some species can live on nothing but moist kitchen scraps; keeping a wormery takes full advantage of the speed at which they will compost kitchen waste. A wormery is a specially designed home for worms. Normal earthworms (*Lumbricus terrestris*) don't like wormeries because they can't burrow into deeper soils when the wormery gets too hot. With nowhere to escape to they will die. Brandling worms (*Eisenia foetida*) are a much better species to keep in a wormery as they don't mind hotter temperatures. A brandling worm (also known as a tiger worm) can eat around half its own body weight in kitchen scraps a day: a wormery with a thousand worms can deliver a lot of worm casts. A colony of worms automatically regulates its numbers to suit the available resources; they are prolific breeders and you won't need to refill your wormery after you've started. You can find the occasional tiger worm in the garden but it's easier to buy them in *en masse*: 500g of worms is a good weight to start with.

If you don't want to make your own, there are some very efficient readymade wormeries available. Wiggly Wigglers supply the Can-o-Worms stacking wormery, the Waste Juggler and the Worm Factory, as well as various other composting systems, including the Bokashi (see page 97); you can phone them free on 0800 216990 or visit their website: www.wigglywigglers.co.uk.

Caring for your worms

You need to look after your worms when you house them in a wormery. They need to be fed regularly and kept moist. They're not overdemanding pets but they mustn't be forgotten about. Remember that they can't head off to other soils if the conditions aren't good for them. If neglected they will die. If the conditions are good – plenty of moist vegetable scraps – they can be left for up to a month. Make sure they're out of the sun though, a hot day will dehydrate the wormery very quickly.

You can put lots of different foods in a wormery. Vegetable peelings, cooked vegetable leftovers, apple peel, even things like coffee grounds and dog hair. Worms will eat meat scraps but most wormery specialists say its best to leave these out. And they definitely do not like citrus fruits. When you are starting out, add waste in small quantities until you get a feel for how much your worms can eat. Place the wormery as close as possible to the kitchen. Outside is probably best for air flow, but in a shed or garage is fine too. Worm activity is sensitive to temperature: they slow down when it's very cold.

Making your own wormery

This homemade method for making a wormery is based on a design created for the Garden Organic (HDRA) garden at Yalding. It's made with three fairly large polystyrene boxes – the type used for packing vegetables or fish. Ask around at your local veg market for any spares they may have. Quite often they're left out at the end of the day for waste collection so it shouldn't be a problem finding some. Each box usually comes with a lid but you only need one; discard the others or use them as seed trays.

Make a hole at the centre of the bottom box, 2.5cm wide. Place the box on two small columns made of some scrap material like old wood, bricks or concrete blocks. The hole in the bottom box allows excess moisture to run out. Place a small container underneath and then dilute the liquid that collects and use as a plant feed. It's powerful stuff – use ten parts water to one part worm juice.

Take the second box and make seven or eight holes in the bottom. These holes are for the worms to climb up and down between the boxes so they need to be at least worm-sized. Place this box on top of the first. Take the last box, make the same number of holes and place on top of the second. Put the lid on top.

To start, place kitchen scraps and small amounts of scrunched up (not flat) cardboard in the bottom box, along with 100 tiger worms. When that box is full move onto the next box and then the top box. The worms will move between layers in search of food. When the top box is full the bottom box should be full of worm casts by then. Take the worm casts out, add them to the soil surface, dig them into the soil before planting or use them as a potting compost.

Increasing fertility using plants

The use of plants as soil improvers is becoming increasingly common. They complement the use of compost and in some cases, where compost is in short supply, provide a valuable alternative. The Vegan Organic Network (VON) is pioneering their use as an alternative to animal and chemical fertiliser, and most organic gardeners use them in combination with other soil-care methods. See www.veganorganic.net and *Growing Green* by Jenny Hall and Iain Tolhurst.

There are two main ways of using plants to improve soil fertility. One is to grow nutrient-rich leafy plants, harvest the leaves and turn them into compost or liquid fertiliser. The other is to use them as a so-called green manure, ploughing them back into the soil directly after they have grown. I explore both these methods in turn.

Comfrey: the compost plant

Russian comfrey – *Symphytum* x *uplandicum*, a hybrid that is different to our native wild comfrey – is the closest thing we have to a compost plant. It has almost the same chemical composition as compost (ten parts carbon to every one part nitrogen). Moreover it has very high levels of NPK, just like a worm cast (see page 100). In fact, according to analysis of its NPK content, it outperforms farmyard manure and ordinary compost. It is also one of the easiest plants in the world to propagate and can deliver four or five harvests a year.

The comfrey plant has very deep roots, which it uses to accumulate minerals and nutrients from deep soils. Once absorbed through the comfrey's roots, nutrients and minerals are transferred to the leaves, which can be harvested. Then through various methods described below, the nutrients can be made available to other plants in the garden. This redistribution of soil wealth is known as dynamic accumulation.

How to grow comfrey
You can grow comfrey from seed but it is easier to grow from a piece of root cut from a plant. You can buy root cuttings from www.organiccatalog.com (0845 130 1304). Comfrey grows in the wild but wild comfrey spreads like a weed; it's better to get a commercially grown 'contained' variety like Bocking 14 (pictured right).

Plant root cuttings in March, April or May or, if you miss the spring, September. Young plants can be attacked by slugs so you may wish to start off your comfrey in a pot

and plant it out when the leaves are at least 15–30cm high. If your root cutting has shoots, plant the cutting so the shoots face up. If not, plant the cutting horizontally. When growing more than one plant leave gaps of 60cm between each plant.

Within six weeks you can cut the first growth down to a few centimetres above the ground. Repeat the harvest every six weeks. Cut leaves can be placed under potato crops to aid growth, left on the surface of the soil to be decomposed by compost creatures, or thrown in the compost heap. If you grow a lot of plants in pots you can create your own comfrey potting compost by mixing alternate 7.5–10cm layers of leaf mould and chopped comfrey leaves in a black plastic sack. Leave it for two to five months, but check that the mixture does not dry out or become waterlogged.

Making comfrey liquid feed

Most organic gardeners who use comfrey also turn it into a liquid feed. For this you need two buckets and a homemade stand. One bucket is placed beneath the stand, and one on top. A hole is drilled in the top bucket and the bucket filled with comfrey. A weight is then placed on top of the comfrey to press it down. As the comfrey decomposes, it produces a syrup, which slowly drips through the hole, down through a gap in the stand and into the bottom bucket (pictured left).

This all sounds a bit stinky, and in fact it is if you add water to the leaves. But if comfrey is just left to rot on its own it produces a fine odourless syrup. Keep the bucket away from the house and children and always put a lid on it. Without a lid the bucket can become a breeding ground for insects. It takes four or five weeks to produce a comfrey concentrate. Remove the bottom bucket from beneath the stand and add the contents to your watering can. You have to

There are other ways of creating your comfrey tea. You can put it in a rain butt and lift the liquid out with a ladle (see how Alan Titchmarsh does it at **www.crocus.co.uk /organics/organicsmakeyourown plantfood**), or make a device using a plastic downpipe and a bottle full of water (see **www.organicgarden.org.uk/growing /grow/comfpres.htm**). Garden Organic (HDRA), **www.gardenorganic.org.uk**, also produces a 16-page booklet in its Step-by-Step series called 'Comfrey for Gardeners', which is packed full of good advice on how to process your comfrey leaves.

dilute the mixture with water. Garden Organic (HDRA) recommends one part comfrey concentrate to every fifteen parts water. Use it on tomatoes or peppers three times a week, other greenhouse plants twice a week, and pot plants and outdoor hanging baskets once a week.

Other liquid feeds

There are various Soil Association-approved organic liquid feeds available to buy (see www.organiccatalog.com). These tend to be mixtures of plant materials combined with minerals and provide a very precise combination of nutrients. For example, one product I have seen advertised combines amino acids, seaweed and vinasse – a by-product of the sugar beet industry. Another, lucerne, vinasse, rock phosphate, molasses and sugars. Each provides a good NPK ratio.

Of course it is more sustainable to make your own at home or down the allotment. I've used nettles before as a liquid feed (pictured above), processed in the same way as comfrey, and lots of truly dedicated recyclers collect and reuse their own urine. There's even a book on the subject called *Liquid Gold*. Urine is full of nitrogen and when diluted can be added to compost to speed up decomposition, or direct to the garden (www.liquidgold-book.com).

Green manures

A green manure is a crop grown for the soil community. It is not harvested for food for us but instead cut and ploughed backed into the soil to be munched by composting creatures. When a green manure is alive and growing its root systems help to create a better soil structure. The crop also suppresses weed growth by acting as a mulch and reduces the loss of soil through wind erosion. The cut dead plants are vital food for soil composters. They are also an easy way of adding organic matter to a soil, increasing water retention in dry soils and keeping soil temperatures warm.

Nitrogen fixers

The fourth most important nutrient required for plant growth after oxygen, carbon and hydrogen is nitrogen. Although it accounts for only 1.5 per cent of that nutritional requirement, a shortage in the soil can lead to slow growth and an increase in the risk of attack by pests and diseases. This is especially noticeable in vegetable crops. Not all green manures are used specifically to increase levels of nitrogen in the soil but it is the attribute they are best known for.

The ability to increase levels of nitrogen in a soil is called nitrogen fixing. Only a small percentage of plants have it. Those that do are very useful to the gardener and are referred to as leguminous plants. They include peas, beans, pulses, peanuts, vetches, lupins, lucerne and clover. I'm always astonished at how the process of nitrogen fixing works. It relies on the relationship between the leguminous plants and microscopic bacteria called rhizobia. These live freely in the soil until they find themselves in close contact with the root of a legume. The root releases a substance in the soil that attracts the rhizobia, which then enter the roots and stimulate the formation of swellings, called nodules. Inside these nodules the bacteria morph into a different shape, become known as bacteroids and start fixing nitrogen from the air. In return for a share of sugars from the plant, the bacteroids pass on nitrogen in a usable form to the host plant, to adjacent plants and to the soil. If you dig up a legume and slice open one of the nodules it should be pink or red. This indicates a high level of bacterial activity, a healthy nitrogen-fixing plant.

Non-leguminous green manures do not support nitrogen-fixing bacteria, but they are generally fast-growing and still provide the other benefits of a green manure. They include buckwheat, small grains, grasses and brassicas.

Left Phacelia, a green manure plant. **Above** Runner beans (*Phaseolus coccineus*): tasty nitrogen fixers.

Planting, growing and harvesting green manures

Green manures are easy to grow from a small packet of seeds. They are most commonly grown in vegetable rotation systems where an area of soil has been left to recover after being occupied by a particularly nitrogen-demanding crop such as potatoes. They can also be used as a so-called under-crop: in other words, planted around an existing crop to keep the soil covered and build fertility.

The following crops are all suitable for green manures: alfalfa, buckwheat, fenugreek, field beans, lupins bitter blue, mustard, phacelia, red clover, ryegrass, sunflowers, tares.

Planting them is easy. Smooth over your soil with a rake. Sow according to instructions on the packet (each crop will be slightly different), though generally you broadcast sow onto the surface of the soil. Then rake the soil lightly over the seeds. Water if the soil is dry and sprinkle a layer of mulch on top to conserve moisture.

Each green manure has a different growing pattern and harvesting time. The trick is to know what your soil needs, understand the crop you want to grow alongside the green manure and chose the most appropriate green manure accordingly.

There isn't the space to go into each crop in depth here but any good supplier will provide full instructions for use on the seed packet. If you choose the wrong type or leave them to set seed, they can become a real weed problem. Cutting a green manure is not particularly difficult if they are cut young (just a few centimetres high). They can be spaded into a trench to the depth of a spade head or just chopped up and mixed thoroughly into the top few centimetres of soil with a hoe and a fork. If they are bigger they need to be cut down and left to dry for a couple of days before doing the same. The soil community do the rest, breaking them up, eating them and turning them into compost.

The UK-based organic seed company Beans and Herbs stocks many crops for green manures and has descriptions of how to grow them on **www.beansandherbs.co.uk/greenmanures**. For more technical information about growing green manures try **www.veganorganic.net /images/greenmanures.pdf** and the book *Growing Green* by Jenny Hall and Iain Tolhurst, which contains the most up-to-date research on the use of green manures. See also Garden Organic (HDRA)'s leaflet 'Green manures/cover crops', available as a printed copy or from **http://www.gardenorganic.org.uk/pdfs/international_programme/GreenMan.pdf**.

Soil care: a conclusion

The intricate details of soil care are a source of endless fascination and I'm quite satisfied I will never know all there is to know. Nevertheless, it's a far cry from my fourteen-year-old self. In those days soil was just a boring inert material to which I added chemicals to make everything grow. I now know different.

I've given a lot of time to soil care because it is the most important thing to get right from the start. To recap:

- Find out what sort of soil you have
- Think about what types of plants you would like to grow
- Match the plant to the soil type
- Look after your soil community
- Build up general soil fertility by creating compost
- Rectify specific deficiencies with liquid feeds and green manures
- Use a four-year crop rotation system for growing vegetables (see page 140)
- Carry on learning!

Chapter three

Choosing and growing your plant stock

There are thousands of different species of plants you could put in your garden, but how do you go about choosing the ones that are most likely to do well? I've already touched on the subject in the section on climate and soil. In this chapter we delve a little deeper. I've tended to stear clear of food – that's all in Chapter four – and concentrated on matching your plants to your garden conditions. At the same time, I've introduced some of those frequently asked questions all starter gardeners need answering when they're about to delve for the first time into the fantastic world of plants. Which plants are harmful? Is my plant shade loving? Will my plant be tolerant of frost? And then there's the greatest mystery of them all – sex. How do plants get it on? Because this book isn't meant to be an encyclopedia of gardening techniques but an introduction to ethical gardening we haven't described common methods of reproduction such as cutting, grafting and root division but concentrated on the starter gardener's common dilemma, whether to buy plants that are ready to go or seeds that are ready to grow.

A healthy plant is a happy plant

Always make sure you've got the right plant for the conditions in your garden. Don't buy cheap plants or seeds from dubious sources. They may carry disease or be bred to a poor quality. These days you can chose varieties (or cultivars to give them their correct horticultural term) of seeds and plants that are more resistant to certain pests and diseases. If you grow seeds one year that suffer attack and you can identify the source of the problem, choose a resistant variety the following year. You should also seek out plant varieties local to your area, as they are more likely to suit your growing conditions (see page 117).

Always follow the growing instructions. Plant with the correct space between each plant. Sometimes when you grow plants from seeds you have to sow them in one seed tray and separate them from one another into larger pots when they are small seedlings. Do this promptly: never let the seedlings grow straggly or allow them to wilt or, conversely, to get waterlogged. When you separate them, select the stronger seedlings and remove them carefully, holding them by the leaf between thumb and finger. Use a seed separation tool, such as a widger, with the other hand to loosen the roots from the soil and lift gently. Mishandled plants will damage easily at this early stage. Always transplant into the correct-sized pot (as per instructions) and remember to harden off slowly before planting (see pages 128–130).

Throughout the growing cycle of your plants look after them carefully. Remove unwanted growth (leaves, stems, branches) and any dead, diseased and damaged growth. Do not put diseased material on a compost heap. The disease may spread to other plants

Essential plant questions: what is meant by a short-day plant or a long-day plant?

This is rather like asking if a plant likes a lie-in. Some plants get going later in the season than others because they like to know that there aren't going to be any more really long nights. They need a lot of light to grow and save themselves for long days when they can produce more sugar. Although the globe has experienced huge climatic changes throughout its history, the one thing that hasn't really changed is the length of day and night. Because of this, plants have evolved to react to day and night in a very specific way. Short-day plants need less light to get them going, and in fact bolt and go to seed when the long days come. Long-day plants do the opposite. And then there are those that are day neutral and flower when they reach a certain maturity, regardless of the amount of light. These include tomatoes, cucumbers and grasses (pictured right).

You may think it would be an advantage to be a long-day plant soaking up all that sunlight – examples include spinach, evening primrose (*Oenothera biennis*) and pot marigold (*Calendula officinalis*; pictured below) – but it is no coincidence that most annual weeds are short-day plants. They steal a march on the long-day plants by flowering and setting seed first. Of course there are lots of nice short-day plants too, such as strawberries and florist's chrysanthemums, but it's a useful reminder that you have to do something about your weeds before the long days come around.

The Christmas poinsettia is a classic example of a tropical short-day plant forced to flower in our winter. Breeders control the plants' exposure to light so that they flower for Christmas, and it takes a lot of energy and carbon dioxide emissions to create these artificial conditions. It is rare to see the terms short-day and long-day on a plant label, but still useful to know why your plant needs to be planted at a certain time of year and behaves in a certain way when it passes a critical level of exposure to darkness. Some crops, such as rhubarb, can be 'forced' to grow quicker by depriving the plant of light. Other plants are affected by the presence of street lighting or garden lighting. High-intensity street and security lighting have even been known to disrupt plant development cycles by altering day–night cycles.

around the garden. Burn it instead or take it to a council composting scheme to be hot composted. If you have plants that need to be pruned, make sure you cut the stems correctly (see page 218).

Disease is more likely to occur in annual crops if they are planted in the same bed year after year. Especially if they are vegetables. A crop rotation system should be used to reduce the risk (see page 140). Some diseases are so pernicious when they strike that gardeners are advised to stop growing the affected plant for several years. Potato blight, tulip fire and onion white rot are three examples.

Mostly importantly, remember to weed. Weeds tend to grow earlier and faster than the plants we want to grow and they take much needed nutrients, water and (if you don't dig them out soon enough) light from 'our' plants. They also harbour pests and stifle air flow. (Air flow should be encouraged in gardens to reduce the risk of fungal problems.)

Essential plant questions: which plants are harmful?

When choosing your plants, be aware that plants from garden centres and catalogues should carry a warning label if they are dangerous. If there's no label and you're not sure, look it up or go online. There are two ways for plants to affect a human: via ingestion or skin contact. Inedible plants can range from the mildly annoying to the downright deadly. If you have children around avoid planting known poisonous berry-producing plants such as yew (*Taxus*) and wild arum (*Arum maculatum*). Skin contact plants to worry about are the stingers and the prickers. Monkshood (*Aconitum*), rue (*Ruta graveolens*) and euphorbia are all stingers. And berberis, blackthorn (*Prunus spinosa*), pyracantha, yucca and of course roses (except those varieties that are thornless, such as 'Goldfinch') can all have dangerous pricks. Plants like comfrey (*Symphytum*) can also cause mild skin irritation.

Match your plant stock to your garden conditions

Some plants are fussier than others, but all have their own special likes and dislikes. It pays to clue up on your plants' little hang-ups before you fork out your hard-earned cash for something that will just wilt and die in the wrong conditions. Here's a list of some different conditions to look out for and a handful of plants for each one.

Plants for poor soil

Beech *(Fagus sylvatica)*
Cambrian poppy *(Meconopsis cambrica)*
Pasqueflower *(Pulsatilla vulgaris)*
Sea buckthorn *(Hippophae rhamnoides)*

Plants for clay soil

Delphiniums,
Perennial sunfowers *(Helianthus multiflorus and other species)*
Cornfowers *(Centaurea cyanus)*
Asters
Common bugle *(Ajuga reptans)*
Daylily *(Hemerocallis)*

Plants for silty soil

Ivy *(Hedera)*
Roses
Witch hazel *(Hamamelis)*
Honeysuckle *(Lonicera)*
Primulas

Plants for sandy soil

Artemisia
Oregano *(Origanum)*
Globe thistle *(Echinops)*
Pampas grass *(Cortaderia selloana)*
Mullein *(Verbascum)*

Chalk-loving plants

Lilac *(Syringa)*
Buddlela
Yucca
Anemones
Primulas
Honeysuckle *(Lonicera)*
Clematis

Acid-loving plants for peat

Magnolia
Heather *(Erica and Calluna)*
Witch hazel *(Hamamelis)*

Planting ideas for drought tolerance

California lilac *(Ceanothus spp.)*
Foxtail lily *(Eremurus spp.)*
Livingstone daisy *(Mesembryanthemum bellidiformis syn. Dorotheanthus bellidiformis)*
Sea holly *(Eryngium maritimum)*

Essential plant questions: will my plant survive frost?

Plants are said to be hardy, half hardy or tender. Hardy plants can tolerate temperatures as low as -15°C and can survive cold snaps of -5°C for several weeks. Half-hardy plants cannot tolerate any temperatures below freezing but will withstand between 5°C and 0°C. Tender plants do not survive under 5°C. Some tender plants may have to be grown in pots and moved inside on colder nights or kept permanently in greenhouses or conservatories. Others (pumpkins, for example, pictured left) can be grown outside but harvested before the first frosts. There are different ways of protecting plants from frost and if there are any plants you are worried about you should consult their particular cultivation details.

Plants that will cope with occasional flooding

Alder *(Alnus glutinosa)*
Ash *(Fraxinus excelsior)*
Daylily *(Hemerocallis* spp.) **pictured right**
Dogwood *(Cornus* spp.)
Elder *(Sambucus nigra)*
Guelder rose *(Viburnum opulus)*
Hornbeam *(Carpinus betulus)*
Meadowsweet *(Filipendula purpurea)*
Hosta spp.
Purple loosestrife *(Lythrum salicaria)*
River birch *(Betula nigra)*
Rowan *(Sorbus aucuparia)*
Sedge *(Carex* spp.)
Siberian iris *(Iris sibirica)*
Silver birch *(Betula pendula)*
Willow *(Salix* spp.)

For a more comprehensive list go to www.environment-agency.gov.uk.

Planting ideas for ponds

Oxygenators include water milfoil
   (*Myriophyllum spicatum*)
Water starwort (*Callitriche stagnalis*)
Curled pondweed (*Potamogeton crispus*)
Rigid hornwort (*Ceratophyllum demersum*)

Floating plants include

Duckweed (*Lemna minor*)
Waterlilies (*Nymphaea spp.*)

Shallow water plants include

Arrowhead (*Sagittaria sagittifolia*)
Bogbean (*Menyanthes trifoliata*)
Sweet flag (*Acorus calamus*)

Certain imported pond plants are damaging to wildlife

Floating pennywort (*Hydrocotyle
   ranunculoides*)
Parrot's feather (*Myriophyllum
   aquaticum*)
Australian swamp stonecrop (*Crassula helmsii*)
Water fern (*Azolla filiculoides*)
Curly waterweed (*Lagarosiphon major*)

Plants that do the job

Some people realise pretty early on that they just want to have a wide range of plants in their garden: vegetables, fruits, wildlife-friendly plants etc... Others find themselves leaning towards more esoteric pursuits: collections of night-time flowers for example. Whichever route you head down you need to know whether your plants like shade, semi-shade or full sun (see opposite).

Easy annuals to get you started

Cornflower (*Centaurea cyanus*)

Cosmos

Dahlia – go for single blooms rather than monster pompons

Honeywort (*Cerinthe major*)

Love-in-a-mist (*Nigella damascena*)

Pot marigold (*Calendula officinalis*)

Snapdragon (*Antirrhinum majus*)

Sunflower (*Helianthus annus*)

Sweet pea (*Lathyrus odoratus*)

Evening- and night-scented plants

Dame's violet or sweet rocket (*Hesperis matronalis*)

Meadowsweet (*Filipendula ulmaria*)

Mullein (*Verbascum* spp.)

Night-scented primrose (*Primula sikkimensis*)

Night-scented stock (*Matthiola longipetala* subsp. *bicornis*)

Phlox

Pinks (*Dianthus* spp.)

Sweet William (*Dianthus barbatus*)

Tree poppy (*Romneya coulteri*)

Twin flower (*Linnaea borealis*)

Evening- and night-scented climbing plants

Clematis rehderiana

Coral honeysuckle (*Lonicera sempervirens*)

Japanese honeysuckle (*Lonicera japonica*)

Wisteria (*Wisteria floribunda* and *W. sinensis*)

Flowers that open in the evening or night

Angels' trumpets (*Datura stramonium*) – highly toxic if ingested

August lily or fragrant hosta (*Hosta plantaginea*)

Bottle gourd (*Lagenaria siceraria*)

Citrus daylily (*Hemerocallis citrina* and *H. thunbergii*)

Daylily varieties 'Eenie weenie', 'Gentle Shepherd', 'Joan Senior', 'Lullaby Baby'

Evening primrose (*Oenothera biennis*)

Gas plant (*Dictamnus alba*) – said to emit a gas that can be lit

Moon flower (*Ipomoea alba*)

Miracle of Peru (*Mirabilis jalapa*)

Night phlox (*Zaluzianskya capensis*)

Nottingham catchfly (*Silene nutans*)

Tobacco plant (*Nicotiana sylvestris*)

Essential plant questions: is my plant sun loving or shade tolerant?

Plants need sugar to grow. They create their own when exposed to light and burn it to stay alive when left in darkness. The more light there is the more sugar they create – and the more sugar they can burn to grow rather than just stay alive. In a rather small nutshell this is the process known as photosynthesis. If a plant needs a lot of light and doesn't get it, the amount of sugar it burns to stay alive (known as respiration) starts to exceed the amount it creates. Under these conditions a plant draws on its reserves and undergoes a process called low-light injury. If this goes on long enough its leaves will lose colour and drop off. It will become spindly and twisted as it tries to reach higher in the search for light. The pores on its leaves will open wide to admit carbon dioxide in an attempt to enhance photosynthesis.

Of course a plant can also have too much of a good thing. All plants have a light saturation point, beyond which photosynthesis becomes inefficient. The gardener has to appreciate how much light a plant needs to photosynthesise efficiently. The scientific term for this is called the light compensation point (LCP). This is the point where sugar creation exceeds sugar burning. The point at which the plant grows.

Most plants have high LCPs and like a lot of light. These include desert plants such as cacti, prairie plants such as corn (pictured above right), and most garden vegetables, fruit and flowers. Plants that love deep shade, such as calladiums, trilliums, coleus, hostas, philodendrons and many ferns (pictured below right) have low light compensation points. Most of us don't need to know a plant's exact LCP. We just need to know whether our plant will tolerate deep shade, partial shade or no shade at all. Choose plants appropriate to your garden. If your garden is more in shade than not, you need to buy shade-loving plants. If it is in total sun, the opposite. If you have a mixture you need to identify which plants will live with semi-shade and which will want full sun, and then plant accordingly. Some plants will live in full sun and partial shade, and some prefer partial shade. Crocosmia, cotoneaster, corkscrew hazel (*Corylus avellana* 'Contorta'), honesty (*Lunaria annua*) and lily-of-the-valley (*Convallaria majalis*) are a few popular partial-shade-tolerant plants.

Plants with early season flowers

Aubrieta

English bluebell (*Hyacinthoides non-scripta*;
   do not plant Spanish bluebells as they are
   invasive)

Flowering currant (*Ribes sanguineum*)

Grape hyacinth (*Muscari botryoides*)

Lungwort (*Pulmonaria* spp.)

Primrose (*Primula vulgaris*)

Sweet violet (*Viola odorata*)

Winter aconite (*Eranthis hyemalis*)

Wood anemone (*Anemone nemerosa*)

Yellow alyssum (*Aurinia saxatilis* syn.
   Alyssum saxatile)

Flowers for hoverflies and other beneficial insects

Alyssum (*Lobularia maritima*)

Blackthorn (*Prunus spinosa*)

California poppy (*Eschscholzia californica*)

Corn marigold (*Chrysanthemum segetum*)

Cornflower (*Centaurea cyanus*)

Coriander (*Coriandrum sativum*)

Dog rose (*Rosa canina*)

Fennel (*Foeniculum vulgare*)

Hawthorn (*Crataegus monogyna*)

Ivy (*Hedera helix*)

Yarrow (*Achillea millefolium*)

Flowers for adult butterflies: common annuals and biennials

African marigold (*Tagetes erecta*)

Ageratum (*Ageratum houstonianum*)

Alyssum (*Lobularia maritima*)

Candytuft (*Iberis amara*)

China aster (*Callistephus chinensis*)

Cornflower (*Centaurea cyanus*)

French marigold (*Tagetes patula*)

Heliotrope (*Heliotropium* spp.)

Honesty (*Lunaria annua*)

Pot marigold (*Calendula officinalis*)

Stocks (*Matthiola incana*)

Sweet William (*Dianthus barbatus*)

Verbena (*Verbena rigida*)

Wallflower (*Erysimum cheiri*)

Zinnia (*Zinnia elegans*)

Plants with late season flowers

Coneflower (*Echinacea purpurea*)

Black-eyed Susan (*Rudbeckia fulgida*)

French marigold (*Tagetes patula*)

Golden rod (*Solidago canadensis*)

Honeysuckle (*Lonicera* spp.)

Ice plant (*Sedum spectabile*)

Ivy (*Hedera helix*)

Michaelmas daisies (*Aster* spp.), **pictured right**

Perennial sunflower (*Helianthus* x *laetiflorus*
   and *H. salicifolius*)

Red valerian (*Centranthus ruber*)

Flowers for adult butterflies: perennials

Dahlias (single-flowered types)

Garden mint (*Mentha spicata*)

Globe thistles (*Echinops* spp.), **pictured left**

Golden rod (*Solidago canadensis*)

Jacob's ladder (*Polemonium caeruleum*)

Michaelmas daisies (*Aster* spp.)

Red valerian (*Centranthus ruber*)

Sweet rocket (*Hesperis matronalis*)

Plants with mid-season flowers

Buddleia (*Buddleia davidii*), **pictured far left**

Heather (*Erica* spp.)

Lady's bedstraw (*Galium verum*)

Lavender (*Lavandula* spp.)

Mallow (*Lavatera* spp.)

Purple toadflax (*Linaria purpurea*)

Wallflower (*Erysimum cheiri*)

Shrubs with flowers attractive to insects

Buddleja (especially *Buddleia* x *weyeriana* and *B.* x *weyeriana* 'Sungold')

Hawthorn (*Crataegus monogyna*)

Heather (*Calluna vulgaris*)

Hebe

Lavender (*Lavandula* spp.)

Thyme (*Thymus* spp.)

Willow (*Salix* spp.)

Lawn flowers for bees

Clover (*Trifolium* spp.)

Common thyme (*Thymus vulgaris*)

Daisy (*Bellis perennis*)

Dandelion (*Taraxacum officinale*)

Violets (*Viola* spp.)

Wildflowers

Comfrey (*Symphytum officinale*)

English bluebell (*Hyacinthoides non-scripta*)

Fox and cubs (*Hieracium aurantiacum*), **pictured above**

Foxglove (*Digitalis purpurea*)

Marjoram (*Origanum vulgare*)

Mulleins (*Verbascum thapsus* and *V. nigrum*)

Musk mallow (*Malva moschata*)

Ox-eye daisy (*Leucanthemum vulgare*)

Red campion (*Silene dioica*), **pictured left**

Teasel (*Dipsacus fullonum*)

Flowers for bumble bees

Anise hyssop (*Agastache foeniculum*)
Bergamot (*Monarda* spp.)
Bird's foot trefoil (*Lotus corniculatus*)
Clover, red and white (*Trifolium* spp.)
Foxglove (*Digitalis purpurea*)
Globe artichoke (*Cynara scolymus*)
Goldenrod (*Solidago canadensis*)
Horehound (*Marrubium vulgare*)
Honeysuckle (*Lonicera*, especially *L. periclymenum*)
Lobelia (*Lobelia cardinalis*)
Perennial cornflower (*Centaurea montana*)
Red valerian (*Centranthus ruber*)
Viper's bugloss (*Echium vulgare*)

Flowers for honey bees

Broad and field beans (*Vicia faba*)
Borage (*Borago officinalis*)
Blackberry, raspberry and hybrid berries (*Rubus* spp.)
Carrot (*Daucus carota* subsp. *sativus*) – vegetables
  left to flower can sometimes be quite beautiful
  and if you leave them to go to seed you're
  creating an extra crop for wildlife, but of course
  one less vegetable for you
Dog rose (*Rosa camina*)
Heather (*Erica* spp.)
Parsnip (*Pastinaca sativa*)
Russian sage (*Perovskia atriplicifolia*)
Rosemary (*Rosmarinus officinalis*)
Rosebay willow herb (*Epilobium angustifolium*)

Trees and shrubs for bees

Apple (*Malus domestica*)
Blackthorn (*Prunus spinosa*)
Broom (*Cytisus* spp.)
Californian lilac (*Ceanothus* spp.,
  spring flowering)
Cherry (*Prunus* spp.)
Cotoneaster
Currant (*Ribes* spp.)
Dogwood (*Cornus alba*)
Fuchsia
Gaultheria shallon
Gooseberry (*Ribes uva-crispa*)
Gorse (*Ulex* spp.)
Hazel (*Corylus avellana*)
Hebe

Hypericum
Loganberry (*Rubus* x
  loganobaccus)
Maple (*Acer* spp.)
Mountain ash (*Sorbus aucuparia*)
Pear (*Pyrus communis*),
  pictured left – and wasps
  love the fruit!
Plum (*Prunus domestica*)
Potentilla fruticosa
Raspberry (*Rubus idaeus*)
Rose (*Rosa* single-flowered
  species and varieties)
Virginia creeper (*Parthenocissus
  quinquefolia*)

DIY plants: the joy of seeds

It's perfectly feasible to fill your entire garden with bought plants, but it's boring, expensive and bad for the environment. Boring because you don't have any of the thrill of seeing seeds germinate and grow, expensive because you can grow a hundred plants from seed for the cost of buying one, and bad for the environment because one plant requires more energy to transport than a thousand seeds (although I should qualify this sweeping statement by saying that seed size varies enormously).

This is not to say that you shouldn't buy plants at all, just save the shopping trips for those that are better grown by a nursery. Working out exactly which plants are best grown at a nursery is quite a process, but with some plants it is obvious. Vegetables, herbs and most annual flowers are best grown from seed. Fruit trees and bushes are not. Something like a dwarf apple tree, which has its fruiting branches grafted (attached) to the root of another tree to limit its growth is one example of a plant that is commonly bought from a nursery rather than grown from seed. You can grow an apple from seed but the tree that you grow will not fruit as well.

Buying or swapping seeds

Environmentally speaking, buying seeds is a better bet than buying plants. Seeds take up much less room and therefore use less energy to transport than plants. However, most seeds for sale are not grown in the UK and are certainly not grown to meet organic standards. There are some notable exceptions though and the list of organic seed suppliers grows bigger every year. The ideal ethical seed packet would be made from recycled paper and contain seeds grown to organic standards in the UK. Some nurseries do specify seed as UK grown and this may be important if you wish to buy native wildflowers or other plants grown to suit local conditions. Otherwise stick to seeds grown to organic standards wherever you can.

Most seeds grown and sold to the UK gardening market are known as F1 varieties. F1 seeds are grown in controlled environments by crossing two different parent plants: combining the genetic material of two specific plant varieties. This process of genetic selection enables the seed grower to produce vegetables true to form.

There are, however, ethical issues with F1 seeds. Many gardeners like to save their own seeds to use year after year: when I was a child a proportion of my gran's peas and beans were always kept back and dried for seeds to grow next year's crop. You can't do this with F1 varieties. Only the seed company knows which parent varieties were used

Seed swaps and the Heritage Seed Library

In the introduction to this book I said that my area was full of people wanting to help each other to garden. But there are certain people who are, for want of a better word, hubs. Imogen is a hub – although this sounds like a terribly unglamorous title to be given. She makes sure all the gardeners are talking to each other. Imogen and her extremely active group of volunteers organise the Dyfi Valley Seed Swap Group. The group aims to organise at least four events every year to bring the gardeners of the Dyfi Valley together under one roof to swap seeds, plants, locally produced crafts, old tools, pots, stories, news, information, food, and in fact anything that we have produced ourselves. There is also a chance to hear speakers from national organisations and local groups. One such speaker was Sue Stickland, an associate of Garden Organic (HDRA)'s Heritage Seed Library (HSL). The Heritage Seed Library exists to maintain varieties of plants that are no longer available from commercial growers but are nevertheless excellent crops.

You can't sell seeds unless you've registered them on the National Seed List, a process which costs about £2,000 per variety. The National Seed List ensures that commercially sold crops are distinct from other varieties, uniform and stable from generation to generation, but because the cost of registering a seed is high, forgotten seeds drop off the register and vanish. Some of these varieties are perfect for gardeners to grow and the HSL exists to ensure their survival. You can't buy heritage seeds from the library but you can join as a member and receive seeds as a benefit of membership. Members get to choose up to six varieties from over 200 in the HSL and can also volunteer as Seed Guardians. It's fun to grow seeds that aren't commercially available and you're doing an important job of maintaining genetic biodiveristy.

Seeds are traditionally ordered well in advance of spring sowing. Get together with friends and share your order – most seed packets have too many seeds for one grower with a small plot. Have a seedy evening in the depths of winter, get carried away and order some crazy varieties you wouldn't have dreamt of buying on sober reflection. Well, we all make mistakes.

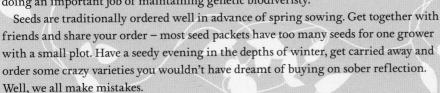

to create the Fɪ hybrid (the name given to a plant that has been crossed). If you save seed from an Fɪ hybrid, they are likely to be sterile or produce lower yields. This effectively keeps control of genetic material within the hands of the seed companies and prevents small growers from managing their own stock of seed. Seeds are cheap to buy so this is not really a financial concern for most people but it does restrict genetic diversity.

Gardeners who maintain their own stocks have quite often come across a seed that works well for the local climate and produces results that suit their tastes. In the event of a national emergency a supply of sustainable seeds (ones that can be grown year after year by ordinary gardeners) would be extremely valuable.

Saving seed takes time, and a certain amount of skill and knowledge. Seeds have to be carefully selected from the crop, checked for pests, dried and stored. Each species of seed is different to the next, so the methods used for saving each one are different too. Sue Stickland's book *Back Garden Seed Saving* is a recommended read.

> Many gardeners like to save their own seeds: a proportion of my gran's peas and beans were always kept back for next year's crop.

Growing seeds in pots

The basic ingredients for growing plants from seed are: seeds, potting compost (homemade or bought), pots, water trays, and a watering can with a rose head – a device that allows water to be showered over the seedlings rather than gushing out of the spout in a plant-swamping deluge. Watering cans are exactly the sort of low-quality plastic product that can be made out of recycled plastic. Also check out the section on secondhand tools on page 30.

When you buy a packet of seeds it usually has all the growing instructions on the packet, so I'm not going to repeat that information here. Just to say that many plants grown from seed have to be coaxed through several growing stages and sometimes different potting compost mixes before they are ready to be planted out in their final home. What starts out as a scattering of seeds in a one-seed tray can end up as hundreds of plants in separate pots. You can run out of time and space if you haven't thought through how much of both you actually need. Growing from seed in pots is undoubtedly more time consuming than planting direct into the ground.

Seeds are generally started off in single or module seed trays before being pricked out as seedlings into individual pots (separated, one plant from another, by tugging gently on the leaves; see page 114). If they are to be grown to maturity in a pot they are regularly 'potted on' into larger pots. If they are to grow to maturity in the soil, plants are generally hardened off first: acclimatised gradually to lower outdoor temperatures – for example, by standing pots outside during warmer days and bringing them in at night. Finally, they are planted in the garden when the outdoor temperature is right for that particular plant (usually defined on the packet as something like mid–May or late June).

You can grow some seeds in trays outside but mostly the reason you start them off indoors is to get the added advantage of a warmer protected environment. This helps the plants grow quickly and reduces the risk of attack from pests. I have a small, light room at the back of my house that passes for a conservatory. Anything I grow from seed in pots is grown here. It's south-facing so the sun warms it up nicely. Using the natural warmth of a sunny room is a great way of getting more value from existing energy sources. In the garden you can also increase this so-called passive solar gain by growing in cold frames, cloches, greenhouses and polytunnels (see pages 70).

If you don't have a naturally sunny room or you want to get a bit more heat around your plants, you can use a propagator – although as all they do is give your plants a few extra days' growth, it's questionable whether you really need one. To avoid wasting energy don't buy an electric propagator – unless you feel it is vital.

Ethical choice: what pot?

Millions of plant pots are thrown away every year, but it's hard to find a recycler who will take them. Most are the wrong sort of plastic. Pots can be quite expensive to buy new so it seems crazy not to find a way of reusing them. The best thing you can do with old plant pots that you don't want is to pass them on to people who want to reuse them. Hilltop Nursery in Dorset actively encourages shoppers to bring back their pots; allotment societies, local community gardens or individual gardeners in the community may all be able to use them. Searching on the net I did find one national organisation that wanted flower pots: www.oxfamireland.org, which has started selling plants in its shops.

If you need pots don't buy them. Ask around for people's surplus pots or make your own. Use the bottom of plastic milk or juice cartons. Old yogurt pots, takeaway plastic bowls and Styrofoam drink cups are all handy-sized containers. Likewise you can make pots out of old newspaper: www.poptel.org.uk/primalseeds/gpots.htm and www.ehow.com/how_1745_ create-seed-starting.html both show easy ways to make pots using an old tin can and a sheet of newspaper. Alternatively, you can buy a pot maker from CAT that uses a wooden 'mould' to shape pots out of paper (pictured above right). If you need larger containers, think about using old boots – anything in fact that you can drill a drainage hole or two in. When CAT took a recycled garden to *BBC Gardeners' World Live* in 2003 we used reclaimed children's toys, boots and even an old hosepipe coiled into a circle. Recycling is all a question of imagination.

Choosing an ethical compost

At some point during the writing of this book I came to the conclusion that there is only so much devil worth finding in the detail. There comes a point where the search for it prevents action.

To give you an example, I was looking around for a bag of potting compost (compost used for growing plants from seed) that ticked all the right ethical boxes: it had to be peat free (see below for reasons why); made from recycled materials; and UK-produced. I found one by TERRA Ecosystems: compost is made from biosolid waste from Thames Water's sewage treatment facilities. Perfect. Until I found out that TERRA Ecosystems is owned by RWE, a company that operates a number of nuclear power plants and coal-mining operations and donated money to the US Congress to support the hugely damaging 2002 US Energy Bill. Thanks *Ethical Consumer* magazine for pricking that bubble! And then Bob Sherman of Garden Organic (HDRA) patiently reminded me that organic standards do not permit the use of sewage sludge.

What am I to do? Is it better to recycle the toilet waste of the people of London and break organic standards, or boycott a company supporting a regime denying climate change? On the whole I think it is better to stick to the organic standards laid down by the Soil Association, but as I'd already made the cardinal sin of buying a bag without first checking that it was symbol approved I used it anyway. The first lesson of making ethical decisions is check the label. See pages 27–28 for details of all major labelling schemes.

The problem with peat

Peat is a perfect growing medium for most plants. It is full of nutrients and has a rich, fibrous texture that keeps water in the soil where it can be supped by plants. The problem with peat is that it is extracted from natural wetland areas, which are often vulnerable habitats, sustaining rare plant and animal life. The World Wide Fund for Nature (WWF) says that 'using peat as a growing medium is no more justifiable than digging up rare plants from the wild in order to adorn gardens; both threaten rare species'. Gardeners using peat are thus effectively robbing Peter to pay Paul. Because of this, peat composts are not approved under Soil Association standards. Peat bogs are non-renewable (the approximate growth rate is only 1mm per year) and they also act as massive carbon stores that play a part in combating global warming. In the UK 94 per cent of lowland peat bog has already been lost and we now rely on supplies from Eire, Estonia, Latvia and Lithuania. Always look for compost labelled peat-free.

Peat bogs are non-renewable (the approximate growth rate is only 1mm per year) and they also act as massive carbon stores that play a part in combating global warming.

Ethical Consumer did provide me with an alternative compost that is Soil Association approved and free of quarried peat. In its 2003 report on ethical gardening there were two companies that got full marks on all their ethical criteria (a mind-numbing list that includes environmental reporting – i.e. whether a company has a policy of telling us what environmental damage they cause and what they are doing to reduce that damage – links to nuclear power, animal testing, oppressive regimes, armaments manufacture, irresponsible marketing, political activity and genetic engineering). These were Fertile Fibre, a company that makes compost out of coir (the outer casing of the coconut) and Nature's Own, made by West Riding Organics. Nature's Own sounds like the sort of compost the fairies would make. It is made from peat, but only peat that has been filtered from streams before the water enters drinking water reservoirs. Because it is using only peat rescued from the water it is not classified as a quarried peat product. Of the other composts *Ethical Consumer* reviewed, Wessex and Gem Gardening were next best, followed by J Arthur Bowers, B&Q and then TERRA Ecosystems and Levington – all of which produce peat-free composts.

Peat on trial

The next important consideration is: does the product do the job? Gardeners use a variety of different types of bagged composts with very specific purposes. The most commonly bought is probably the multi-purpose potting compost used for growing seeds. In 2004 *Gardening Which?* magazine trialled a selection of peat- and non-peat-based potting composts and found that all the peat-based composts out-performed all the non-peat-based versions when used to grow plants from seeds. Germination rates were extremely poor in some of the non-peat-based composts. However they did not trial Fertile Fibre, TERRA Ecosystems or Nature's Own – only big brand composts from DIY chains. Of all the non-peat-based composts J Arthur Bowers New Horizon Multi-Purpose compost was the best. The RHS did trial two of these brands and published the results in *The Garden* in 2002. They found that none of the composts performed 'badly' but Fertile Fibre was better than TERRA Ecosystems, which performed least well of all the composts trialled (see test photographs at www.rhs.org.uk). Again J Arthur Bowers New Horizon did well.

A brief search around the internet reveals that many commercial growers who refuse to use peat go for a potting mix they have created themselves: www.samshrub. co.uk/compost.htm is an excellent website to visit for more information about how this is done. The nursery buys in green waste recycled from local councils and mixes it with coir, grit and an organic fertiliser mix. Contact your local council waste and recycling officer to see if you can buy a few bags of locally made compost. Roger MacLennan at CAT makes his own potting mix too: a combination of homemade compost, sand and top soil. Check out www.gardenorganic.org.uk/organicgardening/ cmp_recp.php where you'll find a number of recipes for making potting compost. Most domestic gardeners need relatively small amounts of potting compost so making your own is definitely an option. Asking around various gardeners I know, out of all the bagged composts available, most prefer to use Fertile Fibre. But then Fertile Fibre is made from an imported tropical waste product. It seems the search is still on for an effective UK-sourced compost product that ticks all the ethical criteria. Until then you could use the questions below as a guide to help you make a decision.

Ethical choice: buying compost

• Do I need compost? Many plants can be grown from seed direct in the ground without using compost. Would it be better to grow these plants?

• If I do need compost, what sort do I need? Potting compost for growing plants from seed in trays and pots? Or compost for improving soil in the garden (soil improver)?

• Can I make it myself? Compost making at home is easy, fun and good for the environment. Can I make enough to meet my needs? (See page 93.)

• Can I get compost from a friend, local business or local authority? Garden Organic (HDRA) publishes guidelines on which composts are considered to be organic. The list ranges from 'Best Practice', through 'Acceptable', 'Qualified Acceptance' and 'Not Recommended'. 'Best Practice' includes composted plant and animal wastes from the house and garden, and leaf fall collected in autumn. 'Acceptable' includes materials such as composted or well-rotted, strawy, farmyard manure, commercial manures and composts with an organic symbol, mushroom compost from an organic supplier, and so on (for full list see www.gardenorganic.org.uk).

• If I am buying compost in bags from a local or national supplier, is it peat free and recycled and if possible organic?

• If I am buying compost in bags from a local or national supplier are there any other ethical considerations that bother me?

Buying plants

The easiest place to buy plants is in a supermarket – just slip some into your trolley with your cornflakes. This is probably the worst thing you could do, if only because supermarket-bought plants are probably impulse buys – which means you probably didn't want or need them before you saw them. The other problem with impulse buys is that you don't really know whether the plants suit your soil and climate until you get back home. If you're planning to buy plants, first research what will work in your garden (see page 117) – hold back and think before you buy something that might die within a few weeks of planting out.

At the very least, check the label to see if it's Soil Association-approved and grown in peat-free compost. The Wildlife Trust has made a comparison between each of

the major supermarkets, outlining the policy each one has towards selling peat-free composts and plants grown in peat-free compost. The information is available in an excellent leaflet 'Where to Buy Peat-Free', downloadable as a PDF from www.wildlifetrusts.org. The government has set a target to eliminate the use of peat composts by 2010 so the supermarkets are trying to work towards this target. Until then consumers can identify which chains are making the most effort. According to the Wildlife Trusts, B&Q, Wickes, Focus, Tesco, Homebase and Asda all stock plants grown in compost made from peat but all of them except Focus and Wickes also stock plants grown in non-peat-based compost.

Check where plants are grown too. UK grown are obviously better – one of the reasons it's preferable to buy from a local nursery. Avoid plants grown out of season in glasshouses for a quick profit from festive celebrations, such as poinsettias at Christmas. They require a huge amount of energy to produce, compared to plants grown in season in unheated glasshouses or outside, and are very unlikely to be organic.

Nursery vs. garden centre

It's worth making the distinction here between garden centres and nurseries because some general garden centres are really gardening supermarkets. Nurseries tend to be smaller enterprises where the grower is also the seller, and usually on hand to offer advice about which plants will suit which conditions. I've already made the case for supporting local nurseries, but there are many national suppliers of plants I would also consider buying from, especially if I was looking for something more unusual. I have listed some nurseries in the directory on page 248. Some of them are very small enterprises and some much larger, but each one has a long history of supplying plants to environmentally minded gardeners. The Soil Association has a list of approved suppliers at www.soilassociation.org/web/sa/saweb.nsf/librarytitles/1956e.html as does Garden Organic (HDRA) at www.gardenorganic.org.uk/factsheets/gg22.php and *Permaculture* magazine at www.permaculture.co.uk/info/Useful_Organisations.html.

If you're looking for a particular plant the easiest way to find it is using the *RHS Plant Finder* guide. Updated every year and published annually, it lists a huge range of nurseries across Britain and the plants they sell (you can also access it from www.rhs.org.uk). If you want to make sure a plant has been grown peat free, www.peatering out.com offer an online plant finder service. Or ask your local nursery if they use peat-free compost. If not you could encourage them to do so, by putting them in touch with nurseries that have made the switch, such as Sampford Shrubs (www.samshrub.co.uk).

Chapter four

Gardening for food

Why grow food? What's so great about working your muscles and getting your hands dirty just for something that you can buy cheaply in the supermarket and already washed? Well, it's because you know where it's from. You know what has been put onto the soil because you put it there. You know how the pests have been outwitted because you outwitted them. You know what wildlife has lived among the crops because you listened to the birds chirping and the bees buzzing. You know how far it has been transported to your kitchen because you carried it there with your own fair hands. Food doesn't get any healthier than when it's plucked straight from the soil. So whether your plot's deep in shade, laid over with concrete, smaller than a gnat's tic, or the size of a football pitch, there's always something you can grow to eat. And what's the point of growing food? Just think fresh and local, and remember the food miles.

The ornamental kitchen garden

A kitchen garden will help you lessen your environmental impact: organic food with almost zero food miles. To grow organically, a diverse patch with good ecological balance is essential, and this makes it a wildlife habitat as well as a food provider.

Beautiful is best

Vegetables are beautiful. The ferny foliage of a carrot and the flowers of a runner bean are just as pretty as any ornamental garden plant. But grown in rows with bare soil in between – well, your average flower would struggle to look attractive. So why not plant your vegetables to show off their beauty? Plan the appearance of your patch as carefully as you would a flower border. Of course, there are some dos and don'ts. Brassicas must be grown together so that they fit into your rotation scheme (see page 140), but think about the colours and heights of your veg and how they will look together. Straight lines make hoeing easier, but a jumble of veg can help too, since it disorientates pests who find straight lines all too easy. We like to say we don't judge by appearances, but the likelihood is that your kitchen garden will get more attention the more attractive it is. Shiny ruby chard leaves and glowing yellow tomatoes will make you want to stop and look. The more you stop and look, the more you notice. There's a saying that the most

Right Chard 'Bright Lights'.

fertile land is that closest to the kitchen window. A kitchen garden should be right beside the kitchen or, if not, somewhere you go every day. You will be on hand when the plants need you, to put in a supportive stake if it's windy, to thin the rows of seedlings if they're getting crowded. An ornamental kitchen garden is a thing to cherish and dote on.

Not everyone is lucky enough to have a garden right next to the kitchen. You may have an allotment a few miles from home, but it can still be a beautiful, comfortable place to visit. Make room for a seat. Better still a shed. Tea-making facilities are a must. And flowers are essential: for attracting the pollinators and the good bugs, for confusing the predators and just for looking pretty among the brassicas (see pages 120–125). You might only be able to get to your patch once a week. Some crops, such as soft fruit, potatoes and pumpkins, are more suited to this sort of long-distance growing. Others, such as peas and radishes, need more regular attention.

Planning your plot

Planning a garden is fun, and it's easy to get carried away with big schemes, but go carefully or you might get overwhelmed! A kitchen garden is best as a small, intensive plot. It needs to be appreciated, observed and given time on a regular basis. A well-tended small or even tiny patch is much more rewarding than an out-of-control sprawl with some potato tops poking above the weeds. Your garden should call you, not torment you.

Most of your kitchen plants really do like the classic sought-after conditions, so try to give your kitchen garden a sunny position with well-drained soil. Flowers and other stuff can survive elsewhere. To start a vegetable patch you need to make your soil weed free and fertile (see page 93).

It is like having a living larder, but instead of having to fill it from the shops you replenish it with your time and love.

Crop rotation

Vegetables are very demanding plants. If you grow them in the same place year after year, the soil around them tends to suffer from a build-up of pests and diseases. Rotating crops so that they only occupy the same patch of soil once every four years avoids this and allows you to treat the soil in different ways to meet the specific needs of the vegetables you are growing.

Vegetables are divided into tribes of species that need similar conditions to grow. The big four tribes are *Solanaceae* and *Cucurbitaceae* (potatoes, courgettes, pumpkins, tomatoes); legumes (peas, beans); brassicas (cabbages, Brussels sprouts, broccoli); and root crops (carrots, beetroot, parsnips). Some other families of plants are included in the four-year rotation as minor players. They tend to partner up with a major tribe and move with them every year. In the system suggested by Garden Organic (HDRA), lettuces are grown alongside brassicas, onions planted with legumes, and sweetcorn and celery with root crops.

Creating your own style

As you create your garden, your own style will be imprinted on it. You can have neat, formal beds edged with herbs, or swirls of annuals and wacky tripods of peas. A well-designed kitchen garden might consist of an area of permanent plantings – such as fruit trees and bushes, and perennial herbs – and an area of annual vegetable beds. Permanent plantings provide shelter and give a pleasing structure to the garden. Fruit can be grown as free-standing trees or bushes, or trained against walls or fences.

Edged beds for annual vegetables allow easy organisation of crop rotation, soil additions, use of green manures, easy working of the land and preservation of soil structure. Beds with raised edges, which can be made from many materials including recycled plastic or wood, are good to work. The beds need to be designed so that all parts can be reached without treading on the soil, so a gardener with a short reach will have narrower beds. Bearing these things in mind, the shape is down to your creativity.

A kitchen garden may contain a greenhouse. This is useful for bringing on young plants, for growing salads in winter and heat lovers, like peppers, in summer. Don't feel you have to have one. You can raise plants on windowsills, and tomatoes do perfectly well outdoors in most areas. For indulgence, though, a greenhouse with a grapevine and a seat is a fine thing.

Ornamental kitchen garden must grows

Grow potatoes (*Solanum tuberosum*). There's something magical about brushing away the crumbly earth to reveal the white or red tubers. Simply boil and serve with olive oil and herbs – what a comparison between home grown and supermarket bought.

Grow a really nice-tasting squash (*Cucurbita* spp.). Squashes look fantastic and it's easy to grow them, admire them, pick them and leave them on the windowsill until they rot. Some taste much better than others, so select one for its taste. Uchiki Kuri (pronounced 'you cheeky coorie'!), or red onion squash, could be argued to be the tastiest: its strong, nutty flavour beats the scooped-out middle of your lantern pumpkin.

Grow soya beans (*Glycine max* syn. *Phaseolus max*). It's fun to grow things that other people think you can't. To casually mention your soya bean harvest can bring a pleasing smugness and also the hope that one day we won't have to import them from the other side of the planet. The variety Ustie can produce a reasonable crop in our climate. The seeds are best germinated on a wet paper towel and planted out when sprouting, but other than that it's not difficult to grow.

Grow a heritage crop. By growing something from the Heritage Seed Library catalogue you are protecting vegetable varieties that might otherwise become extinct. Your own endangered vegetables! Contact the Heritage Seed Library at Ryton Organic Gardens, Coventry, CV8 3LG, www.garden organic.org.uk/hsl, +44 (0)24 7630 3517. Or save your own: the tomatoes pictured above right are a variety called 'Aranger', sown from seeds saved from tomatoes bought on a heritage stall in France.

Grow flowers. For three reasons: because you can eat some of them, because they look nice and because the good insects will come to them and help control the bugs.

Grow the string plant (*Phormium tenax*). Also known as New Zealand flax, it's a big strappy thing, which comes in different colours and sizes up to 2m tall. You might recognise it from various bad TV gardening makeover programmes, where it provides 'instant structure'. What it is really for, though, is a handy source of string for tying in plants or lashing together canes (pictured right). Just rip the leaves into ribbons and use like garden twine.

The container kitchen garden

So you've got no soil? But you're still reading this book, and you're right not to let that hold you back. Container gardens can be very impressive. And there are advantages. Tender plants can be moved in and out of the house. The whole garden can be taken with you when you move. Acid-loving plants can be grown in ericaceous compost, lime lovers in lime-rich compost (see page 89). Even though you will not be literally connected to the land, you can still have a fully functioning garden ecosystem. Use a wormery (see page 102) and you can compost kitchen scraps and weeds, and for larger yards a compost heap will still work when sat on concrete.

Gardening in pots

Pot gardens can be very formal or very wacky. It's surprising what you can put a plant in when you start thinking that way. Take a trip to a car boot or jumble sale and buy anything you can fill with compost – old boots, babies' baths, footballs, pans, kettles, cycle helmets, handbags. You just have to drill holes in the bottom and hey presto – designer pots! They'll look fantastic and save you a fortune.

     Plants in pots are more demanding than those in the ground, due to their limited root run. If your potting compost does not contain loam, it's a good idea to mix some soil in with it. The clay particles in soil will hold onto nutrients and prevent them leaching out when you water. Pots dry out quickly and in hot weather can need watering twice a day. This makes water collection even more important. Set up as large a water butt as possible (see page 61). Maintaining fertility is also important. Potted plants need regular topdressing – replacing the top few centimetres of compost – and re-potting as they grow, and may also benefit from liquid feeds. The contents of a wormery (see pages 102–103) can be mulched onto the tops of your pots

Above A Cape gooseberry plant (*Physalis peruviana* syn. *P. edulis*) growing in an old motorcycle helmet. The sweet fruits are encased in their own 'paper bags'.

and the worm juice used to feed the more greedy plants, though dilution in water is essential as it is strong stuff.

Many edibles can be easily grown in pots, but herbs are especially well suited. The Mediterranean herbs such as rosemary and thyme do well and can cope with drying out a little. Mints are good to grow in pots as it stops their creeping roots taking over huge patches of the garden. If your pot garden is to supplement a real soil-based garden, perhaps an allotment, then herbs are what you should grow. Keep them by the kitchen door.

Fruit trees and most types of vegetable are also entirely possible. The only things that may present a problem are plants that need to keep their roots cool – blackcurrants, raspberries, and maybe some of the veg that bolt (go to seed) when stressed, such as spinach or leeks. Don't forget to grow some insect attractants to keep the system healthy. Fennel (*Foeniculum vulgare*) is a good one, and will add some height; chives (*Allium schoenoprasum*) are always a must, as are the annual flowers such as borage (*Borago officinalis*) and the poached egg plant (*Limnanthes douglassii*).

Container kitchen garden must grows

Grow a fig tree (*Ficus carica*). Figs like having their roots restricted. When planting them in the open ground it is recommended to line the hole with paving slabs so the roots can't run. It's obviously much easier to fill a pot with compost than to go burying paving slabs. Your pot can sit permanently in the same place and let the fig trail up against a sunny wall, or it can be pruned into a free-standing bush, which can be moved into a sunny room in early spring to get a good start and avoid frosts.

Grow strawberries (*Fragaria* spp.). A strawberry tower! Have it on the patio where you sit with your champagne. Grown at a height they are safer from slugs. Contained they are easier to net from birds. Close to hand they are easier to eat.

Grow blueberries (*Vaccinium corymbosum*). Unless you have naturally very acid soil it's hard to grow blueberries in the open. They are plants of heathland and suffer in neutral or alkaline conditions. But with a pot you are in control. You can grow blueberries wherever you live, by use of ericaceous compost. Cultivated varieties of the highbush blueberry are attractive and productive. In hard water areas always use rainwater for watering as tap water will contain lime.

Grow salads. Grow yourself some greens. By the kitchen door, a couple of old buckets with a rocket, mizuna or a cut-and-come again salad mix keeps meals healthy and fresh.

The edible forest garden

An edible forest garden is the greenest, purest, most balanced garden you can have. It is the Zen monk of gardens. Resembling a small natural forest, it is a collection of plants and trees grown together to share resources, shelter and shade each other, fertilise each other and generally be friends. It is a no-dig system. Weed control is carried out by ground cover plants and mulches (see pages 200–204), pests are slow to find the plants because they are not grown as monocultures. If you want an Eden to wander in, picking the odd leaf or fruit (odd often being the operative word), without year after year of hard digging, hoeing or weeding, then you will love a forest garden. A word of warning though – a forest garden is not something for nothing. For the design to work it takes careful planning; for the plants to thrive they need careful observation. The establishment phase can be very hard work. If you constantly wonder at the marvels of nature, want to learn more, to taste unusual edible plants and have time little and often to spend on your garden, a forest garden is for you.

'Forest' sounds rather grand. Actually you don't need a lot of space. A forest garden can be made in a couple of square metres. A small back garden – say 6m by 12m – is plenty. Any more and you'll find that a lot of the ground cover plants are just that – ground cover; there's only so much lemon balm you can eat. If you want to grow more trees in a much larger area then you are probably better off growing them in grass, or with a mulch. A forest garden can work well on 'difficult' sites. Being a no-dig garden, slopes do not present a problem, though you may want to create some flat paths across it. Poor soil, too, can be coped with, if plants are well chosen initially – more demanding ones can be added as fertility is built up over years.

So what actually is a forest garden?

A forest garden is a collection of mainly perennial edible plants of different heights and habit growing together. The main players are usually fruit and nut trees – apples (*Malus sylvestris* var. *domestica*), pears (*Pyrus communis* var. *sativa*), sweet chestnut (*Castanea sativa*) – which make up a canopy layer as in a deciduous woodland. This layer can be missed out in smaller gardens. Below this grow smaller trees and shrubs, such as hazel (*Corylus avellana*), elder (*Sambucus nigra*), dwarf fruit trees and some unusual edible berry plants such as Juneberries (*Amelanchier alnifolia*). Fruit bushes like blackcurrant (*Ribes nigrum*) and gooseberry (*Ribes uva-crispa*) grow beneath these. The ground layer is made up of creeping and vigorous plants such as wild strawberry (*Fragaria vesca*),

If you want an Eden to wander in, picking leaves and fruit, without year after year of hard digging or weeding, then you will love a forest garden.

Right Japanese plum yew (*Cephalotaxus harringtonia* var. *drupacea*), an unusual small tree or bushy shrub that produces lots of edible fruits even in dense shade, making it the perfect understorey plant for a forest garden.

mint (*Mentha*) and wild garlic (*Allium ursinum*) in the shadiest places. There can also be a vertical layer made up of climbers such as nasturtiums (*Tropaeolum majus*).

The idea is that the plants are going to help each other (and you) as much as possible. The ground covers will control the weeds. The trees will shade the shade lovers. The nitrogen fixers will improve the soil. Nitrogen fixers (see page 109) come in all shapes and sizes: trees such as the Siberian pea tree (*Caragana arborescens*), which has edible seeds like a lentil and likes alkaline soil; shrubs such as *Elaeagnus* x *ebbingei*, a shade-tolerant evergreen with edible berries; and low-growing plants like white clover (*Trifolium repens*), which can be grown among young plants to suppress weeds until the ground covers are established. Sceptics will say all these plants growing so close together will compete: true to some extent – you will probably get less from your blackcurrant bush in this system compared to one with no competition in a fruit cage. But above those blackcurrants you are also growing apples, below you are growing wild garlic. For the work you put in and the unit area, production can be greater.

Get the design right first

Design is the most important thing for a forest garden. If you're planning a large forest garden it should not be rushed! It is well worth going on a course. There's an incredible variety of stuff you can grow, and it really can be hard to choose. If you can, visit an established garden where you can taste a few of the more unusual food plants. You might hate them. But you might not. The Agroforestry Research Trust runs garden tours and courses, see www.agroforestry.co.uk. The plants need to be spaced just right for them to interact correctly and it is all too common a mistake to plant what seem like sweet little saplings far too close together. Making the site free of perennial weeds before you begin is of the utmost importance (see pages 194–199). It's more like planting a herbaceous border than a veg patch in that you will never be digging it again. If there is one bit of couch grass under the roots of a newly planted shrub, there will always be a patch of couch grass there, clinging on among those roots. You will never get it out!

A forest garden is not just for plants. It is a fun garden and, as such, benefits from incorporation of playthings such as treehouses and dens, and interesting bits like ponds, barbecues and seats. It's the kind of garden that you can really live in.

Edible forest garden must grows

Grow an apple tree (*Malus sylvestris* var. *domestica*). A forest garden can't be without an apple tree, but don't make your choice lightly. It needs to be agonised over. Cooker or eater? Traditional or local variety? Is it resistant to locally prevalent diseases? Is it compatible for pollination with an existing tree? Is it frost tolerant? Are the flowers pretty? With more than 2,300 varieties to choose from, you should be able to satisfy your every whim.

Grow climbing nasturtiums (*Tropaeolum majus*). Because they're fun. They're rampant, flower prolifically and you can eat the peppery leaves and flowers.

Grow wild garlic (*Allium ursinum*). Permaculture books and seed catalogues list a great many edible perennial salads. Many of them taste disgusting. Wild garlic is one you can't fault (unless you are a vampire). It loves shade, so is a perfect forest garden plant, and has beautiful white flowers in spring. The leaves have a mild garlic taste, and a pleasant texture. They can be eaten as a salad or, better still, dipped in batter and fried.

Grow a tayberry (*Rubus* Tayberry Group). A cross between a blackberry and a raspberry, it is a monster of a plant, and it is a thing that drapes. Grow it over an arch above a seat, where the prolific, long berries are within easy reach. Thrives in half shade. A real Eden plant.

Magic mushrooms
(no, not that kind)

Mushrooms are mysterious. They come up seemingly from nowhere, and they're not even plants. They grow from spores, not seeds. If you like weird things, grow mushrooms. If you prefer woodwork to digging then growing mushrooms on logs is for you.

Unlike plants, mushrooms do not get their energy from the sun but digest other once-living materials such as wood. They do this by use of living threads called hyphae, which make up what's called a mycelium network. The parts that we see and eat are the fruiting bodies that produce spores to reproduce. They emerge from the mycelium when the conditions are right. As mushrooms don't need energy from sunlight and quite like the damp, they will do well in a shady corner. They fit well into a forest garden, shady backyard or, if using the traditional method, in the loft.

Mushrooms are grown from spawn, which you buy growing on a substrate such as corn, or impregnated into wood. There are various ways of growing them. The ordinary white button mushrooms can be grown from organic kits, which is a good method to produce a fast crop growing on a tray of compost or straw. For longer-term growing and fancier species, mushrooms can be cultivated in the garden on logs.

Food from rotting wood

Growing mushrooms on wood is a very stylish option. Oyster mushrooms, shiitake and hericium mushrooms can all be grown in this way. You can buy logs already impregnated with the spawn, so all you have to do is bury them one third into the ground and let them fruit. Or you can impregnate the wood yourself. You will need logs 50cm long and 5–15cm in diameter of an appropriate hardwood such as oak, beech or birch. If you don't have a handy source of wood then contact a local woodland manager. The wood needs to be cut the winter before it is impregnated: check instructions carefully and plan in advance. You can keep the spawn refrigerated until needed and then it is just a matter of drilling the correct-size holes, inserting either the wooden dowels or the white spawn, and sealing with wax. Your logs will fruit the following autumn and for the next three or four years.

Mushroom spawn, kits and logs are available from The Organic Gardening Catalogue, **www.organiccatalog.com**, tel. +44 (0) 845 130 1304. To find a local woodland manager see **www.ecolots.co.uk**.

The fruit-lover's garden

If you like to plan well, put love and care into preparation, tend with passion, observe, think, do the right thing, and enjoy your successes, then grow fruit. It will be fantastic. If you're not that kind of person, then grow fruit anyway – you won't regret it. Growing your own gives you a huge amount of choice. Take apples (*Malus sylvestris* var. *domestica*): in the national apple collection at Brogdale Horticultural Trust in Kent, there are more than 2,300 varieties. In the average supermarket it is possible to buy about ten. And they're not chosen because they're the tastiest. They're chosen because they're the most resistant to bruising and have the right percentage of red and green on them. That's right, a red

Above Raspberries (*Rubus idaeus*) come in yellow, black and purple varieties, as well as the traditional red.

Jonagold apple will be measured for hardness using a thing called a 'penatrometer', and must be 40 per cent red and 60 per cent green. A Miller's Seedling, a very tasty, early apple, is too soft to survive the handling on the way to the shelves. Several well-chosen varieties can provide apples from the tree in August and from storage until June the following year.

When choosing your plants it is important to think about how the blossom will be fertilised, so that you actually get fruit. Some fruit is self-fertile, like blackcurrants (*Ribes nigrum*). This means that you can have just one blackcurrant bush and get a crop of blackcurrants – it will fertilise itself. Some fruit is not self-fertile and needs two or more plants of the same fruit type, but different varieties, which flower at the same time to ensure fertilisation. Some varieties of apple are self-fertile and some are not. This is yet another thing to think about when choosing fruit! Fruit catalogues should have information on this, or if you are buying from a local nursery ask them to advise you.

Fruit requires your attention in bursts. Most of the time it will look after itself, but at times of pruning and harvesting it needs a bit of enthusiasm. You can choose your varieties so that harvests are spread out over time, but you are still likely to get some gluts at certain times. So if you grow fruit it does help if you enjoy making your own home-made jam and wine, or freezing things. And such jobs can give great satisfaction, a sense of achievement in an activity that really makes you take note of the seasons.

In the national apple collection at Brogdale Horticultural Trust in Kent, there are more than 2,300 varieties. In the average supermarket it is possible to buy about ten.

How much space?

If you have very little space, but a reasonable amount of time, and are a bit of a control freak, then trained fruit is for you. Apples, pears (*Pyrus communis* var. *sativa*), redcurrants (*Ribes rubrum*), gooseberries (*Ribes uva-crispa*) and Tayberry (*Rubus* Tayberry Group) can all be trained against walls or into crazy shapes, such as step-over cordons where the fruit grows on horizontal 'branches' just above ground level. This can make really good use of the available space and micro-climates. For example, if you have a small garden enclosed by walls, you can get a good crop of pears, or even peaches (*Prunus persica*), by growing them against the south-facing wall, yet still make use of less sunny aspects by growing gooseberries or tayberries, which can put up with a bit more shade, on the other walls. Learning to train fruit takes practice, but it's a fun process to learn and very rewarding.

If you have more space than time, then free-standing trees are your best bet, particularly if you like a more natural look – a small orchard with spring bulbs underneath, or a single tree as a feature in the garden (pictured right). If you've selected the right tree on the right rootstock, it should require less pruning than a trained fruit tree. Tree fruit is usually grown on rootstocks. This means that the root and the crown of the tree are from two different types of plant and have been joined by a process called grafting. The rootstock affects the eventual size of the tree, so you will need to choose the right one for the size of tree you want. It is a good idea to ask the nursery for advice on this.

Soft fruit can be grown in a similarly informal style but it is not suited to growing in grass. However, it looks great with annual flowers such as the poached egg plant (*Limnanthes douglasii*) growing underneath. This will attract the hoverflies, the larvae of which eat those nasty blister aphids, a common pest of blackcurrants and redcurrants.

Fruit planting, pruning and protecting

It is important to plant fruit into soil that is free of perennial weeds. Mulching around the roots with cardboard or newspaper under a layer of straw or grass clippings will prevent them invading and preserve moisture. A mulch of compost in early spring will add fertility. You need not do this every year though: if your fruit is already growing green and lush, then too much fertility can make it sappy and prone to pests.

A lot of people seem to think that we must prune fruit trees, just because it's the done thing, but what we are really doing is encouraging the tree to grow in a certain way – to put on more vegetative growth or more flowering and fruiting wood. Pruning in summer encourages fruit buds and reduces leaf growth. Pruning in winter does the opposite. Different fruits need to be pruned differently according to whether they fruit on new or old growth, as well as many other factors. It is a skill to be learnt over time, with practice and the aid of a good book, such as the *RHS Pruning and Training*. However, a well-chosen tree, suited to its environment and growing healthily, can require less pruning.

Since fruit is so attractive it's not surprising that other things are going to want to eat it. You can be generous and let the birds have some, but they might not be generous in leaving you any. So there are various things you can do. Net the fruit to keep birds out, or use sparkly, jangly things to discourage them.

Other pests are of the small sucking or chewing kind that hide under leaves. Here the birds can help out by eating them, so it's good for birds to have access to fruit bushes and trees during spring and early summer before the fruit is ripe enough to be taken. Create a healthily balanced ecosystem with lots of good insects and half the battle is already won.

Fruit-lover's must grows

Grow a local apple (*Malus* spp.). An apple that has been traditionally grown in your area will be well suited to local conditions. You can order any variety from Brogdale (see directory) and they will graft it for you.

Grow autumn raspberries (*Rubus idaeus*) – easy-peasy. Prune them in winter by cutting the whole lot down to the base, just where the stems poke above the soil. Autumn Bliss is a productive variety, Fallgold has beautiful yellow fruits. Give them a cool, slightly acid soil if you can. They don't need much staking and produce fruit when other berries aren't around. Beats the summer varieties in every way.

Grow grapes (*Vitis* spp.). They can be grown in a greenhouse or outside, do not require fertile soil but do need a sunny spot. Pruning can be done in all sorts of styles. Trained over an archway, or as a shady climber over a seating area, the dangling fruits look fantastic, and the foliage colours up a rich red in the autumn. Varieties come suited to outdoor or indoor growing and for wine-making or dessert, so make sure the one you choose is appropriate.

Grow peaches (*Prunus persica,* pictured right). Yes you really can. There are a few things you need to get right, but it's worth it. They are best trained against the shelter of a wall, for two reasons – the need for a warm micro-climate, and the need to protect against peach leaf curl. It is easy to protect against this fungal disease by putting a clear plastic cover over the trees in late winter and spring. This keeps the foliage dry and so less susceptible to infection.

The salad-lover's garden

Salads are fast growing, rewarding and good for you. Raw green leaves picked straight from the plant are full of plant blood – chlorophyll, which in some ways is remarkably similar to our own, as both contain iron. Vitamin levels in fresh leaves deteriorate the minute they are picked so growing them yourself allows you to get them inside you straight away. Leaves produced for supermarkets are also very demanding on greenhouse gas emissions. They will almost certainly have been transported by road, possibly even flown in, probably in refrigerated containers and nearly always in plastic bags.

If you're a touch impatient, if you want to see that your plants have grown every day, then salads are for you. They're a great first crop for the novice: a bit of observation will teach you a lot about plants and how to treat them. If you're into being healthy you'll appreciate them even more; if you're not, it'll help you on the way.

Almost all vegetables can be used as salad when eaten raw – tomatoes, pepper, beetroot, onions, etc. – but we're going to concentrate on the leafy ones here. The stuff you buy in the shops tends to be pretty boring. Granted, salad doesn't just mean lettuce and cucumber any more, but believe it or not, rocket isn't the only alternative to lettuce. There are leafy salads to suit every palette, from mild to peppery to sharp to hot.

If you're a touch impatient, if you want to see that your plants have grown every day, then salads are for you.

Year-round salads

The most obvious way to grow salads is in beds as annuals. These can be included in your kitchen garden or in any handy free space. They can be grown outside all year round with the help of cloches and fleece (see page 84), but some space in a greenhouse will increase yields in winter. In the warmer months you can be picking your first leaves three weeks from sowing. Successional sowing – where you sow a row or two of your crop every few weeks – ensures a good supply all year round. There's a huge variety of lettuce (*Lactuca sativa*) on offer and a mix of red and green leaves look stunning in a salad patch (and on a plate). Some varieties are suited to winter growing.

Tasty annuals include peppery mizuna (*Brassica rapa* var. *nipposinica*), mustard greens (*Brassica juncea*), Chinese cabbage (*Brassica rapa* var. *pekinensis*) and, of course, rocket (*Eruca vesicaria*). Corn salad (*Valerianella locusta*) and miner's lettuce (*Claytonia perfoliata*) are alternative mild leaves that are good for winter cropping. Seeds sold as salad mixes are particularly good for 'cut and come again', where the plant is cut down to a few centimetres and allowed to regrow.

Some salads can be grown all year. Others need warmth and some need to be kept cool, as heat will make them bolt. They come from a wide variety of plant families. Some, such as mizuna and rocket, are brassicas – members of the cabbage family. This means two things. One is that they should be grown with the cabbages if included in a crop rotation scheme (see page 140). Another is that they are prone to flea beetle. This little pest makes very small holes in the leaves, which are not necessarily a problem unless it is particularly hungry and the holes start taking up most of the leaf. This is where your liquid fertilisers can be useful (see page 104). A dose of nettle juice can do the trick in making the plant grow faster than the holes. The other main pest of salads is of course slugs, so keep your beds clean, and if necessary select your favourite defences or attacks (see page 213).

Salads in pots and jars

The above advice all applies to growing in pots too. Salads are easy to grow this way right by the kitchen door. And if that's too far to go, maybe you should get into sprouting – growing seeds until they sprout but eating them before they get any bigger. This is a good way to supplement leafy salads in winter. A range of seeds for sprouting can be bought from catalogues or health food shops. They are loads of fun to grow and very nutritious. You need a jar with a bit of muslin over the top, or you can use a specially bought sprouting tray. All you need to do is rinse them twice a day – it won't take long for a spoonful of seeds to become a plateful of sprouts.

Perennials and edible flowers

There is a whole different way of growing leaves and that is as perennials. These require less maintenance and can be included in a perennial vegetable patch or forest garden. They tend to taste stronger, so if you like a salad with a kick, then these are for you. Wild garlic (*Allium ursinum*), buckler-leaved sorrel (*Rumex scutatus*) and pink purslane (*Claytonia sibirica*) are good ones to start with. Green is good, but you can have too much of a good thing. Maybe we need to add a little colour? How about flowers? Did you know you can eat daylilies (*Hemerocallis*) and dianthus? Flowers picked from the herbaceous border make a great addition to salads, but it can also be nice to have a special patch. The annuals borage, calendula and nasturtium (pictured right) are dead easy to grow and will complement your green leaves nicely. (Not all flowers are edible, check before you eat!)

Salad-lover's must grows

Grow yellow asphodel (*Asphodeline lutea*). Little known as an edible flower, but the sweetest and nicest there is. The plant is perennial, sending up spears of sweet star-shaped flowers in May. Don't get it mixed up with the bog asphodel, which is a smaller wildflower. You're unlikely to find it sold as an edible so check carefully by the Latin name.

Grow miner's lettuce (*Claytonia perfoliata*). A magical-looking plant in which the white flowers arise from the middle of a leaf. Another winter salad, but mild tasting, high in vitamin C, with almost succulent leaves. Perfect complement to mizuna.

Grow mizuna (*Brassica rapa* var. *nipposinica*). A peppery leaf, light green with a pretty shape. It can be grown under cover in winter and outside in spring and autumn. It doesn't like the heat, but does not bolt as easily as rocket. This one's a brassica, so include it in your crop rotations and watch for flea beetle.

Grow radishes (*Raphanus landra*). Obvious, but always fun to grow. There are lots of different types available, from little sparklers to big moolis, which grow about 20cm long.

The herb-lover's garden

If herbs were people they would be the Nobel prize winners. Sensual, aromatic, visually attractive, they are strong, yet giving. They'll perform in conditions of constant harassment or complete neglect and still be sweetness and light.

A herb garden is not going to make large demands on your time, but you're going to want to spend time there anyway. You'll want to sit among the smellies, have barbecues with some casually picked mint and rosemary thrown in.

The term herb is a bit ambiguous and seems to mean different things to different people. Herbs can be medicinal, or cosmetic, can be used to dye fabric or make pot pourri. But we're going to concentrate on the culinary ones here.

Your herb garden can be in whatever style you want. For the control freak there are knot gardens of tightly clipped aromatic shrubs. The wild enthusiast can have a loose, informal style with self-seeders and natural shapes. Herbs can take up as much or as little of your time as you like. Annuals such as basil, dill and coriander need sowing and tending each year, but most of the perennials such as chives, sage and fennel will pretty much look after themselves.

Herbs are touchy-feely plants: you'll want every excuse to be close to them. Plant them in raised beds backing onto seats, seed them into cracks in paving slabs, steps and the tops of walls.

> Herbs are touchy-feely plants: you'll want every excuse to be close to them. Plant them in raised beds backing onto seats, seed them into cracks in paving slabs, steps and the tops of walls.

Herb types

Herbs with tough, silvery leaves come from hot, dry places, such as the Mediterranean, where they keep hold of their water by reflecting sunlight and protecting their leaves with a layer of hairs. They will appreciate these conditions to help them feel at home and will thrive in a gravel garden with good drainage, a raised bed or south-facing slope. They'll respond to good soil fertility, but can cope with less.

The other group of perennial herbs can thrive in the other extreme – shady, damp ground – but don't necessarily need it. These are the more lush ones, mints and lemon balms, lovage and chives. So if your patch is in half sun, this is a fine use for the

shady corner, which can contain a welcoming seat for hiding from a hot day with a mug of fresh mint tea.

Herbs also do well in pots. This makes it easy to keep them by the kitchen door. The sun lovers will cope with the occasional drying out, others will need more regular watering and would benefit from some shade. Annuals can be protected from slug attack by a ring of copper tape around the pot.

Herb-lover's must grows

Grow basil (*Ocimum* spp.). Now basil is a bit more demanding than most herbs, but worth it for fresh leaves in salads and with pasta. An annual, it needs to be sown in late spring in a warm place. Basil loves hot, dry conditions so likes to be in a greenhouse or in a pot somewhere warm and bright. I know someone who has a pot growing in her car – perfect conditions and most people (not all) like the smell.

Grow Corsican mint (*Mentha requinii*). A good one for the smell. This mint has such tiny leaves it looks like a moss. It bears exquisite tiny pink flowers and is beautiful growing among paving or on shaped mounds of earth, near seats where you can run your hand over it.

Grow lemon balm (*Melissa officinalis*). Undemanding in nature but prefers damp conditions. It dies down each winter, then shoots up fresh and green in the spring with the most gorgeous-smelling leaves. Grow it for the smell, which is like breathing in happiness – and it is indeed said that a cup of lemon balm tea is good for alleviating melancholy.

Grow rosemary (*Rosmarinus officinalis*). An archetypal Mediterranean herb, rosemary has silvery aromatic leaves, grows to about 1.5 metres tall and likes it hot and dry. Bees love the blue flowers and the chopped leaves will grace your roasted veg. You don't need to do anything to it except cut bits off and eat them.

Above Rosemary (*Rosmarinus officinalis*) and sage (*Salvia officinalis*) varieties.
Left Mediterranean herbs are perfect for growing in pots.

This garden may contain nuts

One of the good things about nuts is that they grow on trees. One of the good things about trees is that they are big. This means that a) they produce a lot of nuts and b) they absorb a lot of carbon. All gardens should have trees. It's only fair to have a reasonable amount of biomass out back to soak up some of our emissions. Nut trees can also produce a lot of food per unit area due to their height. So not only are nut trees an up-and-coming garden tree, but are a possible agricultural crop for the UK.

Nut trees, like fruit, demand your time and enthusiasm in bursts. They need to be well chosen, well sited and well planted. They may require pruning and hopefully harvesting. They will of course require shelling! Nuts are a source of protein and beneficial fats. So if you are interested in novel crops, like to dedicate time to harvesting and processing your harvest, and appreciate plant proteins (which are good for veggies and vegans), then nuts are for you. Don't forget that they need both time and space. A hazel grows to 5m across, a walnut 12m. Most nut trees are not self-fertile so you will need space for two. Almonds begin to bear nuts at about four years old, a good variety of sweet chestnut or walnut will produce at about six years; modest crops at first, but increasing with age.

Nut-lover's must grows

Grow almonds (*Prunus dulcis*, pictured opposite). Best grown up against a sunny wall. They can be fan trained like peaches, and because they are also susceptible to peach leaf curl will benefit from a rain cover over winter. Don't grow them near peaches though, as cross fertilisation can make your almonds bitter.

Grow hazel (*Corylus* spp.). Varieties of hazel, often called filberts or cobnuts, have been cultivated for their nuts for hundreds of years. The trees bear male catkins, which glow yellow when lit by the low February sun, and tiny but incredibly beautiful female flowers. Take a look at one with a hand lens. The trees when left to grow as they please form a multi-stemmed bush, but they can be pruned into a standard tree on a clear stem. To maintain this shape you will need to remove suckers from the base as and when they appear. Squirrels are a huge pain because they take the nuts before they are ripe. There's not much that can be done about the little cute things. If you have squirrels, either joyously give your harvest to them, or try growing sweet chestnuts instead.

Grow sweet chestnuts (*Castanea sativa*, pictured right). Chestnuts have the advantage that we have an equal chance with the squirrels. The nuts have a spiny coating which prevents squirrels getting their paws in before the chestnuts ripen. Only when this opens can they get at them. They are richer in carbohydrates than other nuts and, more importantly, are very nice roasted on a bonfire.

Grow walnuts (*Juglans regia*). Large trees that like sun and grow well in places with warm summers such as Germany. But don't despair. Nurseries now offer us varieties with more cold tolerance. These also bear nuts at a younger age, so while once it was said that you planted a walnut for your children, now we can be a bit more demanding. If you've got a lot of space available, plant walnuts.

Well, that's a lot of stuff about growing food. If you've never grown food before then I hope it's given you some idea of how to get started. Growing food is fun. The only thing that sometimes makes me wish that I wasn't a professional gardener is that gardening must be the best ever hobby, and of course amateurs are much better at it than professionals.

Chapter five

Gardening for wildlife, ornament and fun

For some people gardening is just about the plants. To my mind, this is one-dimensional. If anything, I am probably more interested in the wildlife attracted by the plants and the whole cycle of life as it is played out in front of me. But wild things are not just for fun – they're doing a serious job in your garden too. In this chapter we look at what they do and why we need them to do what they do. Then there are suggestions for three other gardens – for cutting and decoration, children and fairies, and for the night.

A garden for wildlife

The key to all organic gardening is an appreciation of the role wildlife plays in creating balance in the garden. Wildlife gardening is not just a niche area of interest for people concerned with spending their free hours studying the native fauna and flora of their home country. It is an integral part of all gardening activity. In Chapter two I talked in depth about getting the right soil and micro-climate conditions for your garden, but it's important to talk here about wildlife. When you start to unravel the secrets of gardening you realise pretty quickly that without wildlife there is no gardening. There is no composting, no pollination, no pests and no predators of pests. Without composters there is no fertility. Without pollination there is no new life. Without pests and predators there are no checks and balances to keep natural systems alive. To my mind there is no such thing as 'a wildlife garden'. All gardens should be filled with wildlife. Of course, there are opportunities to tailor your garden to one particular group of species or another and this, I think, is what we mean by wildlife gardening. But to separate wildlife gardening as a niche interest negates the importance of gardening for wildlife in organic systems.

Through the story of *The Man Who Planted Trees* (see page 14) we can see that no one element of nature lives in isolation from any other. The soil is home to thousands of species of organisms which decompose living matter and cannot function without the food that trees provide (the leaves and the branches that fall ready to be decomposed), but trees need those soil organisms too. The soil organisms break down organic matter and free up nutrients for the trees to grow. Climate, soil and wildlife are inseparable parts of the same cycle of life that makes all gardening, and indeed all life on earth, possible. And we are part of that system too. We can help wildlife to flourish in our gardens by undertaking very simple acts of hospitality. Most of the rest of this section shows you what's good for wildlife, but let me spend a moment or two speaking about what's bad.

Pests, predators and pesticides

Every time you see an insect devour another you're witnessing evolution in action. We're lucky to be able to take in the trials and tribulations of the creatures in our garden. We should take the opportunity to learn from these activities and make the most of them.

Our plants may suffer from attack by pests at one time or another. This is a fairly inevitable part of all gardening and we have to accept it if we want to grow the plants we like, but these pests are also victimised by predators. If it wasn't so the world would not be the wonderful green place it is. Predators eat pests and we benefit.

Many gardeners never give predators the opportunity to do their bit. Someone using chemicals to kill pests will also kill any type of creature that is susceptible, including the predators. The fatal flaw of all chemical gardening is that it undermines the ability of wildlife to do the job it wants to do.

The first rule of gardening for wildlife is don't use chemicals. It seems a bit of an obvious thing to write so far into an organic gardening book but it's always worth remembering why organic gardening is different, and why it works in a different way. If you want to be a good organic gardener you need to know a little more about biology and ecology, and a little less about chemistry.

Pollinators and composters

An understanding of the wildlife in your garden should be incorporated into everything you do. Wildlife gardening is not an add on. It is the building block for all your activity. Soil, seedlings, shrubs, trees: every layer of the organic garden should be packed with wildlife. Otherwise the garden's not working properly.

When you go out to your garden you should feel like Darwin! Striding into a mysterious world you want to understand a bit better. Why does this creature like this flower? Why does that one like hiding here? What the hell is that? Some people spend a lifetime observing and counting up the creatures in their garden and never get to the bottom of the individual mysteries of their garden habitats. That's the whole fun of it. Whilst you learn about these creatures you also learn why they're good for the garden.

There is a tendency amongst first-time gardeners to panic when confronted with the sight of strange creatures in the garden, but we really shouldn't be alarmed: the chances are high that they are actually good guys. In fact, a fifteen-year study of a Leicestershire garden found that more than half of the 1,723 species of invertebrates discovered were predators or parasitoids (unlike parasites, which do not usually kill, parasitoids do!). Of the rest, a substantial number were creatures who subsist entirely on pollen and nectar or eat dead stuff for a living (i.e. rotting wood, fallen leaves and petals, other creatures, dung, and so on). Only a relatively small number were herbivores and of these a still smaller number bothered to eat our favourite crops.

It's impossible to talk about gardening for wildlife without mentioning Ken Thompson's book *No Nettles Required* and the study of fifty Sheffield gardens contained within it. Ken and his team of researchers set out to show what it took to be a wildlife gardener. They came up with some interesting results. Studying a range of gardens of various shapes, sizes and types, they found that most gardens were home to a large variety of wildlife without their gardeners having to do anything particularly special to attract them. It didn't matter whether the gardens were big or small, near the edge of the city or right at its heart. The study showed that you can increase the variety of wildlife in your garden by doing one or more of the following things: plant lots of different species of flowers; grow trees in a hedge or on their own; make a pond; make a mess; and make a compost heap. Let's take each of these in reverse order.

Wildlife essentials: the compost heap

It may seem an unlikely place to start a lifelong love of garden wildlife but the compost heap wins hands down in my book. Not only does it contain so many interesting things to look at, but all the creatures that live there – the decomposers – are doing an amazing job for us. Poke around in a compost heap for long enough and you'll find hundreds of little creatures scampering, crawling, jumping and otherwise loitering with intent. They're all there to eat the things you don't want (kitchen scraps and weeds); they're all doing a job you need doing (creating compost); and they are all food for someone else too. In my own compost I have several parts of the food chain going at each other tooth and claw. Slugs, snails, frogs, slowworms, toads, ants, worms, mice. Even the occasional bird will make an appearance to shovel up any lose pickings. Having a compost heap is a great way of learning about the perpetual cycle of life in action. Get hold of a microscope or even a little hand lens and you can see what creatures really rule the world (and have done so since before dinosaurs walked the earth): the springtails, the pseudo-scorpions and the nematodes. Once you see how many creatures live in a metre-square compost bin, you know instinctively that an organic approach to soil care is cleverer than any other. Why apply expensive chemicals that take a lot of energy to produce to provide nutrients for plants, when there are decomposers longing to do the job for us? A healthy soil packed with organic matter composted by compost creatures will provide your crops with a much better start. So start wildlife gardening by building a healthy soil and move on up from there. See Chapter two for more information on composting and soil care. If you start getting into observing the microscopic wildlife in your garden you'll need a hand glass, containers for collecting samples and a microscope. Check out www.watdon.com for supplies.

> Having a compost heap is a great way of learning about the perpetual cycle of life in action. Get hold of a microscope or even a little hand lens and you can see what creatures really rule the world...

Wildlife essentials: make a mess

Decomposers love mess. Compost heaps are a contained mess. But to get the full benefit of the decomposer community you need to organise mess around the garden. Now if the words 'organised mess' seem like a contradiction in terms, hear me out. A random scattering of logs across a lawn is a mess. A scattering of logs gathered together and placed in a fairly neat pile in a dark corner of a flower border is an organised mess. And if you're imagining big thick logs, the sort that go on a roaring fire in winter, then think again. A few sticks cut off a hedge and layered in a pile will work too.

Nests, shelters and feeders

If you want to go that extra mile for wildlife, you could consider making or buying shelter for them that recreates the sort of habitats they would occupy in the wild. In some cases, where natural environments have been destroyed, artificial habitats offer a lifeline helping to guarantee safe places for threatened wildlife to nest and breed. We tend to think of bird boxes when we think of shelters for wildlife but you can also make or buy homes for frogs, hedgehogs, lacewings, ladybirds and bees.

You can make many nests yourself with scrap materials and most wildlife organisations offer tips on how to do this. Many regular garden wildlife observers suggest that animals nest in unexpected places and leaving some mess around is one of the best ways to encourage wildlife to find its own nesting sites. Wild bees have been found to nest in discarded garden canes, disused locks in greenhouses, holes in large pieces of flint, nail holes in old fence posts and spaces amongst thatch and roofing tiles.

One sure-fire way to encourage wildlife in the garden is to provide them with food. Birds are very good predators. Encourage them into the garden and help to keep their numbers up by providing a range of bird food, including seeds, nuts and live worms. The RSPB provides good advice for gardeners who want to care for birds, including what sort of bird bath to provide and how to feed them the right food at the right time of year.

If you're buying a bird feeder or box, check where it was made. I've found some made in China (even in RSPB shops). It's hard to avoid ones made abroad, but there are some very nice UK-made bird feeders, made from Forest Stewardship Council timber by craftsmen and women. The bird feeders in my garden are handmade out of wood cut from locally felled timber by my Italian friend Luca (woodcataz@yahoo.co.uk). I also found some very nice FSC-approved feeders and nesting boxes at www.wildforms.co.uk, www.birdfood.co.uk and www.wigglywigglers.co.uk. CAT sells a variety of wildlife homes and feeders too. If you want something recycled, try www.bensbirdboxes.com. The boxes are made out of old estate agents' boards.

Every gardener has to trim their plants. Leave some back for wildlife. Frogs love ponds but they also like piles of damp sticks to hang out under too – probably because they find a ready supply of slugs to do away with under there. Also think about leaving fallen leaves on the surface of the soil. Decomposers and predators need shelter and fallen leaves are perfect cover for their activities. (For more on decomposers see page 99.)

Wildlife essentials: make a pond

If you think of beneficial animals as some sort of mercenary army recruited to the cause, a pond is the station ground for marine forces. As well as being the most beautiful training camp you could ever hope to see, it's packed full of deadly soldiers waiting to launch attacks on land-loving pests. Ponds are home to frogs, toads, dragonflies, newts and also many species of insects and other invertebrates that make a living knocking off pests.

Gardeners are looking for a natural balance of pest and predator in the garden. Finding that balance is not an exact science and there are always periods when the predators are playing catch up and numbers have to rise to meet the challenge. This is because predators like to occupy a space only when it is obvious there is enough food for them to eat. It makes sense for them to do this but the resultant 'predator-pest lag', as it is known, causes some concern for the gardener whose plants inevitably seem doomed. Nevertheless, as sure as day follows night, predators follow prey – provided the gardener creates the right set of circumstances. A pond is one whole load of right circumstances.

Making a pond

The best site for a pond is sunny during the morning with some shade in the afternoon. Avoid overhanging trees. When you've chosen the site, mark an outline with sand or string and dig contours with a spade. A pond should have shallows and a sloping shelf about 20–30cm in length. The shelf allows frogs and other pond animals to slip in and out of the water easily and the shallows are useful for plants that don't like deep waters. Hibernators need depths of at least 60cm in a pond to survive the winter, so make sure one part of the pond reaches at least that depth. You can use a ready-formed plastic pond, but a butyl rubber lining allows more flexibility, giving you the opportunity to shape the pond as you want it, as well as creating a bog garden area to complement it. Whichever material you use, you'll need to protect it from objects that may force a puncture. Remove any sharp objects like stones, and any roots from the soil. If you're using a butyl rubber lining put down a 6cm layer of sand followed by some old carpets, underlay or wet newspaper before the lining goes down. Then lay the lining on top. Be careful when you do this so that it doesn't rip. The amount of liner required is equal to the actual length plus twice the maximum depth, plus 50cm. Dig the pond liner under the soil around the edges. Once the pond liner is laid put a layer of soil over the flat parts and fill with a trickle of water. Not a deluge, as this will disturb the soil. Garden ponds will be naturally colonised quite quickly, but if you want to speed up the process, choose a variety of plants including a healthy selection of oxygenators, floating plants and shallow water species.

Tales of pond life

Another great thing about ponds is that they also provide a contained space within which we can watch wildlife. If we're feeling a bit bored there's always some sort of action going on in a pond. And even if it seems still and calm one moment, pretty soon something will happen to make life interesting again. This combination of calm and excitement is very rewarding. So many people don't bother putting a bench near a pond. Why not? It's the best seat in the house. Especially if you have a penchant for watching the cycle of life in all its noisy glory. There's nothing like a bit of frog's porn to wake you up on a spring morning.

There were fifty frogs mating in my pond this spring and as I write this I'm waiting for their progeny to emerge. The first morning I found them in my pond I startled them and they all disappeared beneath the surface – for a whole day. I felt a bit guilty about disturbing their pleasures. The next morning I crept up stealthily so as not to appear to be any threat to them. This worked and they seemed quite happy carrying on their orgy with me watching. I was, however, slightly unnerved when they all seemed to start watching me. There is a down side to all this romantic activity. Every year when the froglets leave the pond I have to stop strimming the lawn, tread gingerly on tippytoe and keep my fingers crossed as I make my way around the garden while they make their way to wherever it is they head to when they're done with my pond. Sometimes they end up in my kitchen. One morning I found a slowworm, a frog and a newt in there, staring at each other wondering what to do next. I ferried them all out together in an empty cereal box. Anyway, diversions aside, ponds are the frogs' bollocks (am I allowed to say this?) and everyone should have one.

Wildlife essentials: plant a tree (or two)

Trees, trees, trees – you might think I'm a bit obsessed with trees, but they really do add that extra dimension to a garden. Even the small ones are monumental. As gardeners we tend to concentrate our efforts on learning about smaller plants, but trees give shape and structure to a garden, as well as providing protection from the elements, boundaries to our space, resources to use (pea sticks, bean poles, barbecue charcoal, fruit, craft materials, etc.) and a home for wildlife. If felled locally in a way that isn't harmful to the environment they are the most sustainable, climate-friendly and ethical material we can use. As well as being the most beautiful.

In the UK the unsustainable felling of woodlands and hedgerows is endemic, and the effect is startling on our native wildlife. Moths, bats, butterflies, bees, owls and garden birds are all declining at an alarming rate. Some species have declined as much as 70 per cent in less than a decade. For a long time, gardens with their hedgerows, native trees and long flower borders have been a safe haven for declining species. These gardens are sheltered, prosperous and diverse; insects, birds, amphibians, mammals and all those invertebrate species that compost our garden waste can make a living in a garden, while they cannot in the agricultural and urban landscapes that surround us. But we are now losing gardens at an alarming rate too. Brownfield sites are very often the former back gardens of large Victorian homes. The government has hidden the fate of these gardens in statistics for several years and environmental groups are only now starting to identify the loss. The gardens are replaced with small blocks of flats with no gardens. It is a boon for developers, a loss for nature and a call to action for all wildlife gardeners.

> A tree like an elder can be part of the family or community calendar, reflecting the changes in the seasons

If I needed any more evidence for the value of trees the University of Sheffield's BUGS project came up with it (www.bugs.group.shef.ac.uk). As far as wildlife is concerned there were only two factors that significantly altered the number of varieties of species living in the gardens they studied. The first was altitude – Sheffield is very hilly and far fewer species lived in gardens on the tops of hills – and the second was trees. In every case gardens with trees were better for wildlife than those without. Trees provide a vertical layer for wildlife activity, playing host to caterpillars, for example, which birds will pick off ceaselessly to feed young chicks, and various other insects. Old trees are particularly valuable, full of nooks and crannies for birds to nest in and decomposing wood for insects to chew on.

Elder: the perfect garden tree

If you have room for only one tree, go for the elder (*Sambucus nigra*; pictured right): it's small enough to fit in any garden (although they can grow to six metres high and wide if unrestricted by space or human intervention); it's easily grown; it will reward you greatly with a bounty of goodies. The unopened flowers can be dipped in batter and fried, to make fritters or frizzets, or used to make elderflower 'champagne' or cordial, and the berries can be made into wine.

A tree like an elder can be part of the family or community calendar, reflecting the changes in the seasons and allowing you to form an association between the living world and the rest of your life – as well as encouraging you to learn other skills associated with the tree. In the winter the branches can be pruned to restrict growth and the cuttings used for decoration, kindling, or hollowed out to make a flute or a blow-pipe for children's games.

Plant trees when they are young (one to two years old) and always in the winter. You can also grow them from seeds gathered from local trees or from seed suppliers. Decide whether you want to let your tree grow to its natural height or cut back to keep as a low-growing shrub. If you are leaving it to grow you'll need plenty of space around it and to be tolerant or welcoming of the shade it will provide when mature. You'll also need to choose your spot carefully. Once a tree is planted and rooted you don't want to have to dig it up and move it. Buy *Sambucus nigra* (the Latin name is important to distinguish our native elder from other species) from a local nursery or from a specialist national supplier. Prices can vary enormously, so shop around. Follow any specific planting instructions provided.

The price of trees varies a lot but don't pay more than a few quid for a 'whip' (a tree about a metre tall); www.woodlandtrust.org.uk will send you a selection of four native trees for about £10. See also www. native-tree-shop.com and www. cooltemperate. co.uk for saplings. If you don't have room for trees in your garden but want to get involved in planting, check out charities such as The Woodland Trust, BTCV www.btcv.org.uk, Trees for Life www.treesforlife.org.uk or The Tree Council www.treecouncil.org.uk.

Collecting tree seeds

Most tree seeds should be collected and planted in September and October. Exceptions to this rule are wych elm (*Ulmus glabra*) (May–July); wild cherry (*Prunus avium*) (July); bird cherry (*Prunus padus*), black mulberry (*Morus nigra*) (July–August); birch (*Betula*) (August); elder (*Sambucus nigra*) (August–September); and hornbeam (*Carpinus betulus*) (November). If you go out collecting make sure seeds are ripe, pick straight from the tree if you can, or gather fresh from the ground. Don't pick up seeds that look like they're rotting. If collecting seeds from different species of tree, place in separate labelled paper bags. Don't collect in plastic bags – the seeds can get too moist and fail to germinate as a result.

Wildlife essentials: plant a variety of flowers

As if you needed any encouragement! Brightening up your garden with flowers really does work for wildlife. But don't just stick to one or two varieties, go for a wide range and make sure your predators and pollinators have something to interest them all year round. Even if you're just growing vegetables, make sure you plant some flowers in between your rows and all around your veggie patch. Predators such as lacewings, ladybirds and hoverflies will all be attracted to flowers and stick around to eat any pests they might find on your crops. Plants flower at different times in the year and as insects are vulnerable to starvation

in the early spring and late autumn and winter, it's good to come up with a flowering plan for the whole year. If you can get your insect population in the garden early and keep them interested all year, they'll have no reason to go elsewhere.

When you're planning a calendar of flowering times you can count in trees that produce great blooms too. I've already talked about elder, but blackthorn and hawthorn are good early flowerers too. Make sure your garden isn't filled with highly bred flowers with double blooms. They tend to have less nectar and some of them have such complicated floral structures that insects can't find their way to what little nectar there is. The BUGS survey (see page 173) found that it wasn't necessary to grow native plants to attract wildlife. It was more important to get a mix of open, flat flowers for beetles and hoverflies, and tubular flowers for large bees and long-tongued insects.

I find the mix of wild plants that come up naturally in my own garden, without me having to do anything to help them, provide just the right sort of variety insects need. These include herb Robert (*Geranium robertianum*), columbine (*Aquilegia vulgaris*), Cambrian poppies (*Meconopsis cambrica*), dandelion (*Taraxacum officinale*), cowslip (*Primula veris*), harebell (*Campanula rotundifolia*), foxglove (*Digitalis purpurea*) and red campion (*Silene dioica*); they're all beautiful and they all attract pollinators, particularly the last two. If you watch red campion during the evening, you can see the daytime pollinators (the bees) clock off and the night-time pollinators (the moths) clock on.

Choosing plants for wildlife

Any good plant reference book, nursery label or seed and plant catalogue will give you flowering times, but the best way to start to choose plants with flowers you like – trees and shrubs as well as those plants we commonly think of as flowers – is to spend a year looking around you, both in your own garden and in other people's, and also in parks, hedgerows, fields, woodlands and ponds, to see what flowers bloom when and where. Sometimes it's not that easy to identify a plant but if you have a digital camera, take a shot and match it up to a reference book back home. Create a plan for all-year flowering based on the information you've gathered. There are plenty of lists available for gardeners who would like recommendations. English Nature produces a list of plants for wildlife gardening in a leaflet and a guide, 'Help Save the Bumblebee'. Also check out www.wildaboutgardens.org and the excellent must-have book *Wildlife Gardening for Everyone* from Think Publishing. I've compiled a few lists from various sources including those mentioned above and the *HDRA Encyclopedia of Organic Gardening*. None of these lists is exhaustive. Observation is the best way to learn but those plants listed on pages 122–125 should give you a few suggestions if you just want to get on and plant something.

A garden for cutting and decoration

There are good environmental reasons for cutting your own flowers. Flower kilometres! Millions of roses and carnations arrive each year from Columbia (8,000 kilometres) and Kenya (6,500 kilometres), which are then packed with green leaves from Costa Rica or Israel. In 2004 cut flowers from Kenya were responsible for producing more than 30,000 tonnes of carbon dioxide. Most will have been grown with chemicals and by workers without access to Fairtrade agreements. You can buy European cut flowers, but how many of them are organic and grown outdoors without the aid of artificially heated glasshouses? Growing your own flowers or buying from a local grower cuts down on CO_2 emissions, adds extra interest to your home and gets you geared up to think about seasonality. Even in the middle of winter you can find hand-picked narcissi from the Isles of Scilly.

Cutting flowers for decoration allows you to appreciate which plants flower when. If you like to fill your house with cut blooms all year round, you should develop a flowering plan for four seasons and plant accordingly. You'd never cut all your garden flowers so there'll be some left over for the insects to feed upon. There's also a real sense of ceremony involved in cutting flowers, and of bringing the garden into the house. Each season is represented by a different set of plants and, if you're into decoration, different styles of arranging them. Christmas wreaths give way to Valentine posies to Easter bonnets to summer bouquets and harvest festival displays. Even in the depths of winter the dedicated flower gardener will find something to interest them.

Sue Harper (pictured right), owner of cut flower business Sweet Loving Flowers, recommends starting with what she considers to be the best summer annuals (see page 120 for some ideas). These are plants that produce a substantial number of flowers in one growing season, each flower lasting for several days in the vase after it's cut. She chooses old-fashioned varieties for their colours and scents, and stays clear of highly bred double blooms, so her flowers are also better for wildlife. Over the next few years she plans to grow bulbs and biennials (plants that live for no more than two years) for spring flowers, and a wide range of perennials for regular cropping. You could do the same in your garden. When planning a flower garden for cutting and decoration, include plants that produce interesting foliage to provide a variety of complementary colours, shapes and textures, and plants that produce attractive seed heads – they look great in displays, and birds, mice and other creatures will feed off any left over.

A garden for children and fairies

Young children seem to know instinctively that gardens are places in which to have fun. Stuffy adults seem to have lost their way by comparison. Children don't need everything to be perfect. Gardens are for treehouses and tipis, castles and dens, fairies and knights.

They are places where children can let their imagination and creativity go. It doesn't really matter what's real or not, all the action is going on in their heads. A handful of daisies tied together becomes a crown for a princess. An acorn becomes a kiss. The garden is Neverland or Narnia, an enchanted forest, a dangerous wolf-ridden wood – whatever they want it to be. Make a point of growing plants with fairytale names and get your children to make up stories that go with them. My editor Alastair suggested Dutchman's breeches (*Dicentra cucullaria*), but how about black-eyed Susan (*Rudbeckia fulgida*), fairy berry (Alpine strawberry), tiger lily (*Lilium lancifolium*) and Miss Go-to-bed-at-noon (chicory) - what a fantastic pirate story that might make! I already have a picture of black-eyed Susan in my head. She sails to sea in search of the magical Dutchman's breeches, which will bring great wealth to anyone who wears them. To find the trousers she has to eat a million fairy berries and put a terrible curse on Tiger Lily, the heroine of the story, who from that moment on shall forever go to bed at noon. Your children will do much better than me I'm sure.

Child's play

Of course, it's not just about make-believe. You will find children are keen to grow their own flowers and vegetables too, and they soon find they can do this activity just as well as the adults – what a feeling that is for a small child! You don't even need to force the idea of learning. In amongst all the hours spent in play, children will discover how a garden works, and how nature causes things to work. If they have grown the plants themselves they will start to take an interest in the strange creatures they find living amongst them, and with the guidance of an adult learn to identify which are good for the plants and which aren't. They will see how the cycle of life works. How some insects

A handful of daisies tied together becomes a crown for a princess. An acorn becomes a kiss.

grow from small eggs to baby larvae to fully grown adults. And how everything dies and returns to the soil. If they are lucky enough to live in a garden with a wormery they will learn all about worms and the soil and how compost creatures help their plants to grow. All these things can be learnt during or as a break from playtime. A love of nature will only help to get kids thinking about the environment (although as far as I can make out many are way ahead of the adults on that one already). Getting children involved with a garden at home or a community garden or allotment helps to give them a grounding in related science subjects they will encounter at school: biology, ecology, environmental studies and geography in particular.

CAT runs a theatre for children every summer that includes regular bug and slug hunts. The children parade around the CAT gardens looking for the good, the bad, the ugly – and usually find plenty of all three. The Fairyland Trust, **www.fairylandtrust.org**, aims to create a space for children to connect with nature away from the more traditional nature reserves, the emphasis being very much more on storytelling, adventure and, of course, fairies.

In a similar vein, The Woodcraft Folk, **www.woodcraft.org.uk**, was founded in 1925 to bring children into contact with natural spaces and is a bit like an eco-version of the Scouts and Guides. There are different groups for different ages (woodchips, elfins, pioneers and venturers) and the weekly meet includes games, drama, music, nature activities, crafts and dancing.

If you want to set up an organic garden at school, get in touch with Garden Organic (HDRA), who can help: **www.organicgardening.org.uk/schools_organic_network**.

Kid-friendly organics

Involving a child in organic gardening is a lot easier than involving them in gardening systems reliant on chemicals. Learning about composting, pests and predators and weeds is lots more fun for children than looking at rows of cans of chemicals in a superstore. Organics brings the whole subject of gardening alive. Of course, there are adult tasks and safety concerns in organic gardening too – e.g. laying a protective grid over a pond, keeping out poisonous plants, using power tools with caution – but nothing that is distinct to organic gardening. Not using chemicals is one less thing to worry about.

I was lucky enough to experience several different gardens when I was growing up – and although I lost interest when I was, in my eyes, too cool for old man's gardening (though I have to say I was never cool) – the experience has stayed with me and influenced me subconsciously throughout my life. If you don't connect with nature, how can you mourn it when it's damaged or gone? Even if children do eventually become too cool for gardening they will carry their early experiences through life and remember them fondly in adulthood, as I do now.

Above and right The vegetable plot in the children's garden at Garden Organic (HDRA), Yalding, designed to look like a pirate ship. The garden also features a living willow tunnel that's always a favourite with kids.

A garden for the night

I tried to capture the mood of a garden made for night in my book *Curious Incidents in the Garden at Night-time* and became more than usually obsessed with the subject matter. There's something I really love about being in a garden at night. I feel as though I can think more clearly. There are fewer visual and audible distractions both in the garden and in the world around. I can concentrate on enjoying the atmosphere of a garden in a way that quite often simply isn't possible during the day, especially as I live next to a main

road. Those sights and sounds I can see and hear are especially evocative, mysterious and pleasing. I like to light candles at night for atmosphere and a small contained fire for warmth. This burns in a fire pit I've dug into the bank next to my bench (see page 42). In it I burn all the hedgerow cuttings I can't find another use for. There are more than enough each year to last out the summer months. The candles are arranged around the garden to provide a low, unobtrusive glow. There are several ways to light a garden for atmosphere. Just enough to prevent stumbling, to illuminate key plants and objects, and to add to the drama of the garden, or a more intense light, which, though not as harsh as daylight, allows you to enjoy the garden almost as if it were day. I tend to avoid this bright, electric lighting, partly because it uses more energy and partly because I want to enjoy the mystery and intimacy of subdued lighting. Things look different in the dark and you see your garden in a different way. Our eyes can't detect colours at night. They can

only see the contrast between blacks and whites. White flowers really stand out amongst dark banks of foliage and any other colour simply disappears. It seems a shame to wipe out this difference between day and night with strong lighting.

Lighting choices

Whichever lighting option you choose, you need to decide whether you are going for permanent lighting, occasional, or a mixture of both. I've gone for occasional, which is why I use candles only. I've collected a number of recycled candle holders over the years – including a couple of tin cans punctured with hundreds of holes, an old chicken feeder, and two old paraffin cans, which I picked up

from the local tip, for larger candles. As for the candles themselves I have a confession to make. I have never sourced my candles ethically! I tend to use mass-produced night lights made out of paraffin, which of course is a by-product of the oil industry. I'd never really thought of candles as being that much of a problem until I started looking into it for this book, but the US Environmental Protection Agency say that lighting a candle releases almost as many toxins as a cigarette. So what are the green alternatives? Look out for soya- and vegetable oil-based candles. You can buy them from a wide range of sources including www.wwf.org.uk, www.timothyhan.com, www.ethical planet.com, www.mandala-aroma.com, www.thenatural store.co.uk and Selfridges. If you want handmade candles try www.ethicalwares.co.uk. For the ultimate eco option go for locally produced beeswax or vegetable oil-based candles. If you're looking for more permanent lighting check out the range of solar-powered lights on the CAT website, but before you invest in any electric lighting solution make a plan of exactly what you want to light, when and for what length of time. One advantage of solar energy is that it is free once purchased. There is no increase in your electricity bill. In my experience external lights get left on without thought, so for busy forgetful households solar is a good energy efficient option. Otherwise you can connect garden lighting to your home power supply but you will need an electrician. Before you take this option, work out how much power you can afford to use and plan accordingly, and make sure you switch to green electricity (see page 244).

Moth watching

When the moon is full there is no need for any lighting. I make the most of these evenings to check out the wildlife in my garden without disturbing anything with flashlights or candles. However full the moon, there is always plenty going on to make things interesting. I'm lucky enough to live near a colony of bats and they often fly overhead. There are owls about too. Unlike many urban garden owners, I've never seen a fox at night, or a hedgehog. My favourite night-time creature of all is one every gardener can enjoy – the moth. In most wildlife gardening books, butterflies get all the attention and if moths are featured at all they are a sideshow to the main attraction. But moths are more diverse, more important to wildlife ecology and in some cases far more beautiful and interesting to watch. (Ever seen the hummingbird hawk moth in action?) I guess butterflies get all the column inches because they are easier to see and identify, but if you've ever seen a moth trap opened in the first light of morning, you'll know that moths have got quite a lot going for them. Every year there's a national moth day. The month varies so watch out for it in the press and look for an event near you at a reserve or park. I went along to the local RSPB reserve at Ynys-Hir and marvelled along with (sadly) only a handful of other people as beautiful moth after beautiful moth was lifted from the light trap laid the night before. Dazed by the sunlight and not at all timid as you might expect, one large emerald moth fixed itself upon the front of a friend's belt like a great big jewelled buckle. Who needs to go to Africa for hidden gems?

You can 'trap' moths humanely to take a better look at them, by using either a light or a sugar trap. Moths are well known for liking light, but actually not all moths will come to a light trap. They vary from

For a proper recipe of how to make the right sort of sugar mixture for a moth trap, go to **www.butterfly-conservation.org**. For a free guide to moth trapping and to buy a commercially made light trap visit **www.angleps.btinternet.co.uk**. To make your own light trap visit **www.atropos. info**. For general information about night-time species contact The Bat Conservation Trust (**www.bats.org.uk**), **www.butterfly-conservation.org.uk** and **www.buglife. org.uk**.

If you want to get out of the garden and do a bit of moonwalking round your local neighbourhood, check out **www.themoonwalkers.org**. Website comes complete with all the full-moon dates for the next three years.

Some flowers only open at night. And at different times of the night. Stay up all night and you can mark the passage of time by watching them open and close.

species to species. If you want to see the moths in your garden, you could just suspend a light over a white sheet hung between two trees on a washing line. The moths will rest on the sheet and you can approach them and take your time looking at them. Alternatively, you can buy a solar insect theatre (from CAT and other suppliers). Made with FSC timber, this is basically an attractive wooden box with a glass front and a solar panel which powers a light that comes on at dusk. The insect theatre will attract a good deal of activity but for a more professional set up you could invest in a mercury vapour trap (mercury vapour describes the type of bulb used). This bulb is especially attractive to moths, which fly towards it and then into the wooden box trap beneath it. Sugar traps are simply sticky sugary liquids painted onto a tree or fence post. Moths are great nectar lovers so they'll eat anything sweet like this.

Flowers for the night

Many of the flowers I have already recommended for butterflies (see pages 122, 123) are good for moths too, but to appreciate the night-time more, think about using plants specifically meant to give their best at night. Some flowers only open at night. And at different times of the night. Stay up all night and you can mark the passage of time by watching them open and close. It reminds you how a seemingly still object like a plant is always busy doing something, even if only waiting for some special moment in the day. The RHS publishes a list of top ten plants for the night at www.rhs.org.uk/research/biodiversity/wildnightout_plants.asp, but I've put a few suggestions for night-time flowers on page 120.

Left Evening primrose (*Oenothera biennis*) opens in the evening or at night.
Above right Phlox is an evening and night-scented plant.

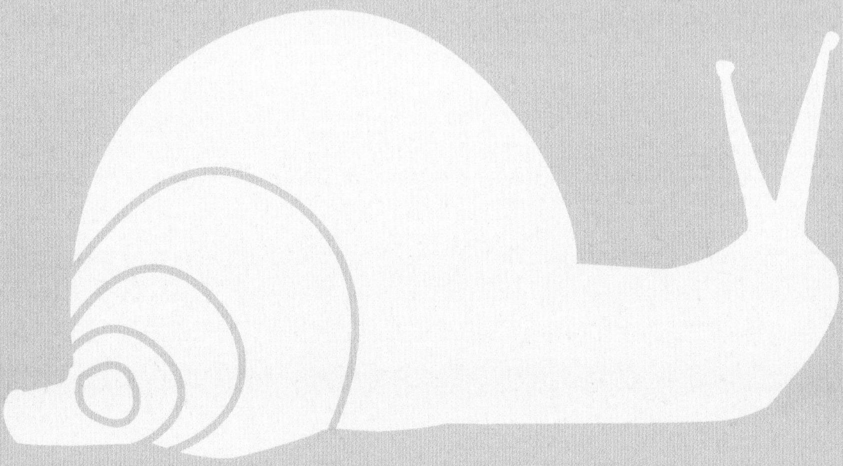

Chapter six

Weeds, pests, diseases and disorders

As the song goes, 'if they asked me, I could write a book...' about the way you grow and creep and look – but it would be an encyclopedia. And as we've only got one chapter, I've merely dipped my metaphoric toe into this stickly, prickly, bramble patch of a subject. But it will give you a feel of what to expect when you start tackling the problems that come up in your garden.

Dealing with weeds

I like to believe that somewhere in the petrified ruins of Pompeii stands the figure of a gardener locked forever in mortal struggle with a weed. While others spent their last moments in the doomed volcanic city making love, our hapless gardener is preserved for all eternity in a hideous contorted position, his muscles straining, his back bent over, his hands held in a strangler's pose, his face murderous as he lifts one more dock from his veggie patch. If there is one gardening struggle more titanic than the war against slugs it is the never-ending story of wrestling with weeds.

Of course it doesn't need to be like this. Weeds should never be left to become big, aggressive bullies. Even brambles were babies once. Deal with them small and you'll save yourself a lot of back pain later. This is a very quick guide to the types of weeds you will encounter in the average garden, the scenarios you can expect to have to deal with and the best organic ways to control them.

What's in a weed?

If there was a weed that characterised the early part of my life, it was mint. The garden I occupied before I arrived at that strange country known as adolescence (which incidentally coincided for me with a move from my beloved but barbaric moorland home in Lancashire to the soft, warm but altogether mysterious Lincolnshire fens) had a mint quarter, which one would visit for adventure now and then. Some people would say that mint is only a fast-growing herb best contained in a pot. But when is a weed a weed? In our garden mint had all the characteristics of a good old-fashioned weed:

• it wasn't wanted
• it took up growing space
• it stopped other plants growing.

To all intents and purposes mint in our garden was a weed. If you ask a horticultural scientist to say what a weed is they may tell you that weeds have a combination of some of the following attributes:

- an ability to colonise (move into and grow on) disturbed ground
- a drive for early growth – before the competition has even got started
- a capacity for rapid growth
- a knack of tolerating different environments and growing areas
- an ability (in some) to produce seed without the need for another plant to be involved
- mutually beneficial relationships with a whole range of pollinators that are not fussy about which plants they visit
- a capability to spread pollen using the wind
- a tendency to produce exceptionally large numbers of seeds that last a long time in the soil, and to spread them efficiently
- an ability to regenerate and spread without seeds (known as vegetative spread, more of which later).

Whichever way you look at it, a plant in the wrong place at the wrong time is a plant you have to deal with.

Right To encourage wildlife, this garden has been planted with a wildflower meadow, including plants such as wild carrot (*Daucus carota*), field scabious (*Knautia arvensis*) and ribwort plantain (*Plantago lanceolata*), which in other garden contexts could be considered weeds.

What's so bad about weeds, then?

The problem with weeds is that they are too successful at doing what nature intended them to do. They out-compete most other plants. They start growing earlier in the season, they grow quicker, they set more seed and faster, they attract more pollinating insects and their seed can lie dormant in the soil for longer. Weeds cramp other less vigorous plants. They use up water and nutrient reserves and shade slower plants, thus stopping them receiving the resources they need to grow. Because they provide a safe haven for nature they can also harbour slugs and harmful bugs that like to eat the non-weeds.

When we are battling against weeds we are battling against evolution and the natural order of things. But if we don't do it we won't get the results we want. The garden plants we want to grow are weeds compared to weeds. If we want to grow them we have to gang up on the weeds and make up for our plants' lack of natural competitiveness.

But then again weeds do have their redeeming features

Weeds are not all bad. Mint is only one of many edible weeds. Others include greater burdock (*Arctium lappa*), chickweed (*Stellaria media*), chicory (*Cichorium intybus*), dandelion (*Taraxacum officinale*), garlic mustard (*Alliaria petiolata*), Japanese honeysuckle (*Lonicera japonica*), Japanese knotweed (*Polygonum japonicum*), fat hen (*Chenopodium album*), wild roses (*Rosa canina*), wild carrot (*Daucus carota,* pictured left), shepherd's purse (*Capsella bursa-pastoris*), common sorrel (*Rumex acetosa*), stinging nettle (*Urtica dioica*), wild garlic (*Allium ursinum*), yellow sorrel (*Oxalis corniculata*), blackberry (*Rubus fruticosus*) and wild raspberry (*Rubus idaeus*). Then there are the therapeutic weeds, including the aptly named heal-all (*Prunella vulgaris*). And the weeds that can be turned into wine and beer – blackberry, coltsfoot (*Tussilago farfara*), daisy (*Bellis perennis*), dandelion and stinging nettle. You can also use weeds for crafts such as dried flower arrangements, botanical wall decorations, papercraft and pot pourri.

Some weeds are also very good at redistributing soil nutrients amongst other plants, in the same way that comfrey and the green manures do: chickweed and dock (*Rumex obtusifolius*) being the best. Nettles can be turned

I'm sure Elzéard Bouffier's forest would not have been so successful if it wasn't for the weeds. Weeds are pioneer species.

into a liquid feed, as I described before, and many weeds are extremely beneficial for wildlife – especially those that attract some of the predator insects that help to control pests. Some gardeners even like to grow a 'bank' of some of the less aggressive weeds (NOT big-rooted monsters like bramble and Japanese knotweed) to make a home for helpful wildlife such as foraging beetles and spiders, and larger creatures like frogs.

Any soil occupied by weeds will be more fertile than an empty soil. Beds that are left bare will soon lose soil fertility to rain and wind erosion. Weeds keep the soil structure intact, creating a good home for compost creatures. I've often lifted clumps of stray grass, only to find worms happily sheltering in their roots. Any plants will help to trap leaves as they fall and weeds are no exception. Once the leaves are trapped worms can get to work breaking them up and turning them into compost. I'm sure Elzéard Bouffier's forest would not have been so successful if it wasn't for the weeds (see page 14). Weeds are pioneer species.

Weed types

As with all plants, there are three basic types of weeds: perennial, biennial and annual. Perennial plants grow from the same root each year. Biennials grow from seed but take two years to flower. Annuals grow from seed but complete their life cycle in one year. Once they have sown their seed they die.

Within these broad groups you can categorise weeds as being easy, medium or hard to deal with. Usually the annual weeds are the easiest to tackle. And the perennials the hardest. But there are exceptions. The annual weeds black nightshade (*Solanum nigrum*) and yellow sorrel (*Oxalis corniculata*) are both considered hard to deal with.

Weeding

Before you pull up any weeds check in a weed identification book or chart that they are not harmful to the skin. Many weeds are perfectly fine to handle without gloves but some scratch, puncture or irritate; I try and wear gloves all the time when I am weeding – you never know what is lurking! And remember, some of the most poisonous plants are weeds so if you get into eating weeds make sure you pick the right ones. The following weeds should never be eaten: foxgloves (*Digitalis*), nightshade (*Solanum*), ragwort (*Senecio jacobaea*), various wild euphorbias and thorn apple (*Datura stramonium*).

Right Fat hen (*Chenopodium album*) is an annual weed that can be dealt with fairly easily by frequent hoeing or removing larger plants by hand.

Weeding scenarios

My childhood solution to our garden mint problem was, I think, quite entrepreneurial. Even if it wasn't quite horticulturally sound. Recruiting my much smaller but nonetheless willing neighbour, we hacked a great big path through the mint like Amazonian explorers. And then announced to our families a grand opening. When the moment arrived we walked them all in procession through the path – which seemed enormous to us, but was probably less than five or six paces of my adult stride – through to the lawn. Here we offered them mint for sale, and for some reason other bits of jumble we no longer wanted. The path opened, we planned to create small tributaries of activity into the rest of the jungle. It never happened. The mint re-grew and the path disappeared.

In any garden there are three or four potential weeding scenarios. The one I described from my childhood is the neglected plot scenario. The rumble in the jungle. My solution was basic. Chop the plants down at the base of the stem to deprive the roots of their solar collectors – their leaves. But this is not a knock-out move, as the mint will grow back up from the base. A weed is only disposed of when you remove leaf, stem and root complete. Even then, if it has already set seed, it may have left an invisible reminder of its presence.

The neglected plot

Most neglected plots will be dominated by perennial weeds such as bramble, couch grass (*Elytrigia repens*), coltsfoot, nettle, and so on. In between these will be a fair selection of annual weeds too. Any gardener should have a weed identification book. Weeds in a neglected plot will all be of different shapes, sizes and types. And they can look very different at different stages of their development. There's no easy way of removing them all. But there are several options.

Start by cutting down the growth to the stems. Always wear a good thick pair of gloves that still allow you a firm grip on whatever tools you are using. With a thin-stemmed weed like mint or nettle, cutting is relatively easy. You need a scythe, a strimmer or a pair of shears. A thick-stemmed weed like a bramble requires a little more care. Use a pair of secateurs and cut all large stems right down to the base. Sometimes it's hard to find the base. You have to get in amongst other weeds to do this, so wear long shirt sleeves to stop abrasions, cuts or stings.

Take your time doing this. Don't go at it like you're in any particular hurry. Clearing a neglected plot is tough on the back and physically demanding. Get to know

Right CAT gardener Roger MacLennan uses his wheeled hoe for quick weeding between rows.

Prickly sow thistle (*Sonchus asper*, **far left**) is a troublesome weed that should be dug out, root and all. Smaller annual weeds, such as stray grass plants, can be dislodged with a hoe **(left)**.

your weeds as you go along. If you come across anything edible, put it in a basket and serve it up that evening. See what wildlife you can find. Frogs, toads and hedgehogs like to hang out in places like this so beware of treading on them or, even worse, cutting them. If you're doing this job in winter be aware that you might disturb hibernating creatures. In a way, although more weeds are actively growing in the spring and summer, it's better to do this job when you can see exactly what you're dealing with.

Rooting around

Once all the weeds are cut to the base you have one of two options: total clearance of all roots or coverage with a thick mulch. Total clearance is the hard option but if you want to use your bed immediately, it is the only one. Do not use a Rotavator or any machinery that simply cuts the roots up and ploughs them back into the soil. Chopping weed roots up and leaving them in the soil is akin to the sorcerer's apprentice chopping up the broom. Weeds will only multiply and come at you with ever more persistence. This is one job best done by hand and will probably take a long time.

Each weed root is different and you need a different technique for removing each one. A dock has what's called a large tap root. This is a single long root that digs deep into the soil to get at nutrients. You can remove it with a special tool that levers the root out or do it with a fork. You have to coax a tap root out, rotating it in the soil gently whilst pushing the soil away from the root until it comes up freely. Don't tug at the root. It will snap. Try to get the root out whole – any tiny fragment will grow again.

Another type of common weed called couch (pronounced 'kooch') grass has thin, white roots that will also grow back again if they are left in the soil. These are particularly difficult to remove. They are numerous, long and break easily. Similarly, a bramble root goes off in all directions and depths under the soil and is almost impossible to remove whole once fully established.

Other roots are easier. I have lots of ferns in my garden. They are associated with wet plots. The root of the fern is like a big mop of tangled hair – for those of you who remember 70s' TV wrestling, like the hair on wrestler Giant Haystacks. A root like this, although big, is easy to remove because it comes up in one clump. Beware though, it is also extremely heavy when it comes out of the soil. Make sure you brush off as much soil as you can. There are also a whole load of weeds with tiny fibrous roots – such as groundsel (*Senecio vulgaris*) – these need nothing more than a quick dig with a trowel or a jerk of the hand.

Once you've cleared the plot of weeds, start to plant straight away or cover the soil with a mulch. Any unoccupied space will soon lose fertility.

Ethical choice: disposing of weeds

The top growth

You may be tempted to burn the weeds you've collected, but this is wasteful and actually not very environmentally sensitive. When you burn freshly cut, so-called green waste, you release a lot of particulates into the air, which can contribute to respiratory problems. It's much better to separate your waste as you go along. Nettle cuttings can be placed in a compost heap or allowed to rot into juice to use as a liquid feed. Likewise any wild comfrey (*Symphytum officinale*) you find. Most annual weeds can be composted so long as they haven't seeded. If there are seeds in the compost they will grow again when the compost is added back to the soil. Leaves from perennial weeds can also be composted. If you don't put the waste in a heap, let it wilt at the side of the bed, and then put it back on the soil as a mulch. Diseases can be a problem in a weed patch and any infected weeds should be burnt as a matter of course or disposed of through a council green waste collection scheme. Councils generally use hot composting techniques that kill off any latent weed seeds or diseases.

The roots

You can compost the roots of weeds in a black plastic bag. In his book *Weeds: An Earth-friendly Guide to their Identification, Use and Control*, John Walker suggests using an old potting compost bag, turning it inside out, puncturing it with holes and leaving the filled bag in a sunny place. The contents will rot in the heat, turning into rich, dark compost within a year. He also suggests drowning perennial weeds in a bucket. Starved of air they turn into a slurry-like liquid to be poured onto the garden.

Getting rid of weeds by mulching

If you don't like the idea of digging out roots there is an alternative. Like any other plants, weeds will not grow if they are starved of light. Most annual weed roots will rot in the soil if they are covered with a thick layer of mulch. This is the general term for a wide range of materials placed on the soil to deprive weeds of light. These could include wood chippings, bark, sawdust, cocoa shells, leaves, sheet plastic, pebbles, slate chippings, recycled glass pellets, seashells, and so on (see materials on page 41).

To deprive an area of weeds of light, you need to use a thick impermeable material like black plastic or cardboard. The best ecological option is cardboard that you've recycled from home. It's easy to handle and will naturally decompose in the soil after a year or so (pictured above). Layer the cardboard on thick – two or three layers is best – making sure each piece of cardboard overlaps another. Don't leave any gaps.

Layers of cardboard look unsightly and are liable to blow away in the wind if dry. Water it in thoroughly. If you don't want to leave your cardboard exposed, layer a second, more attractive, mulch on top. Chose an organic mulch, i.e. something that will

Japanese knotweed: a horror story

No mulch method is foolproof: some weeds will break through whatever barrier you place in their way. Japanese knotweed (*Polygonum japonicum*) is the most tenacious weed you may come across. Its shoots have been known to penetrate concrete. Its roots are almost impossible to remove. It grows over 2 metres tall. Fragments of root will travel in a gardener's fingernail and set up shop in whatever soil the fingernail touches next. It's a hideous monster of a plant. Given the risks of digging it up and moving it about, I nip the shoots as soon as I see them coming up. And keep on doing it all season. This is a fairly easy routine job. You can eat the tart shoots with apples or pears in fruit pies or puddings, but I've yet to try it. If shoots come up through your cardboard keep cutting them and in time the plant will lose strength. As for long-term eradication, dig the roots up either before or after mulching. As Japanese knotweed is a notifiable alien species, most councils will have a policy on its control, so ask for disposal advice.

Japanese knotweed is one of those weeds that spreads by sending out underground runners known as rhizomes. Ground elder (*Aegopodium podagraria*) is another. Vigorous weed roots suppressed by mulch will send off rhizomes to unmulched areas where they will surface like a U-boat in open seas. Watch out for weeds at the edge of your mulched area and dig up what you can.

The worst weeds

Weeds that need to be prioritised for removal if you want to grow anything else in the same bed.

Black nightshade (*Solanum nigrum*)

Bracken (*Pteridium aquilinum*)

Bramble (*Rubus fruticosus*)

Broad-leaved willow herb (*Epilobium montanum*)

Cinquefoil (*Potentilla reptans*)

Coltsfoot (*Tussilago farfara*)

Common field speedwell (*Veronica persica*)

Couch grass (*Elytrigia repens*)

Cow parsley (*Anthriscus sylvestris*)

Creeping thistle (*Cirsium repens*)

Field bindweed (*Convolvulus arvensis*)

Field horsetail (*Equisetum arvense*)

Giant hogweed (*Heracleum mantegazzianum*)

Great bindweed (*Calystegia silvatica*)

Great willow herb (*Epilobium hirsutum*)

Ground elder (*Aegopodium podagraria*)

Ground ivy (*Glechoma hederacea*)

Hairy bittercress (*Cardamine hirsuta*)

Japanese knotweed (*Polygonum japonica*)

Rosebay willow herb (*Epilobium angustifolium*)

Spear thistle (*Cirsium vulgare*)

Yellow sorrel (*Oxalis corniculata*)

rot – not stone or glass. You can buy in more attractive mulches (generally waste organic materials chipped for the purpose) or make your own. You could use straw, or if you wanted to get the bed ready for growing vegetables, a layer of manure. Whichever material serves your purpose.

There are two schools of thought about planting into an area of soil like this. Some people start to plant it up straight away, cutting holes in the cardboard and putting the plants in amongst the rotting roots of the weeds. I think it makes more sense to wait six months to a year and then do it. By this time most of the weed roots will be ineffective and the cardboard and the mulch will be starting to decompose and mix in with the topsoil. When you're ready to plant, you could clear the whole area of cardboard and mulch, rake over the soil and start planting; or just plant through what's left of the cardboard and mulch. It will be easy to put a shovel or a spade through.

If you don't want to use cardboard, the next best option is to buy or find some recycled sheet plastic, but this does not degrade naturally into the soil and takes a lot of energy to produce. You can also buy special plastic mulch systems using geo-textile permeable membrane with pegs to keep it in place. The greenest bought option is probably Hemcore Biomat (see page 41).

The cleared plot

As a scenario, the cleared plot is a much more tantalising and palatable prospect than the neglected plot. It is the one most gardeners hope to step into. A cleared plot is ready to work, without any visible sign of weed intrusion. 'All' you have to do is deal with weed problems as they arise.

And arise they will. Even if you've cleared a bed of all roots (probably an impossibility, even for the most careful of gardeners), your soil will be packed full of weed seeds ready to spring forth; some weed seeds stay dormant in the soil for decades, only growing when they are disturbed as the soil is forked over. You need to start managing the surface of the soil straight away. Have a plan of action ready the moment the bed is clear and ready for use.

As mentioned above, you could cover the entire bed with a permanent geo-textile mulch (a permeable, man-made fibre that lets water through but not light) topped off with a decorative hard (pebbles, slate, etc.) or soft (woodchip) mulch. This will stop the weeds and entomb the soil, effectively preventing the cycle of life carrying on. This sort of scenario is most appropriate for paths and for seating areas, where a low-maintenance alternative to grass, or a less intrusive alternative to decking, is required.

Left *Persicaria amplexicaulis* 'Firetail': a good weed suppressant and a great beauty – what more can you ask for?

Ground cover plants: eco-mulch

A living mulch of ground cover plants will do almost the same job as a geo-textile layer, but is more ecologically useful because it allows compost creatures, air and water to pass more naturally into the soil, and because it provides a habitat for beneficial garden creatures. This is an integral part of the forest garden system (see pages 145–147) where it's common to use *Rubus* species for effective ground cover and the added benefit of berries (pictured left). Ground cover plants form thick mats of leafy growth on the soil, effectively keeping light from the weed seeds. They are not impervious to weed growth but the number of weeds that can grow through them is much reduced. Those weeds that do get through can be removed in the usual ways. Ground cover plants are useful in large borders or beds in which the gardener requires a permanent low-maintenance feature. Although it is not common to use these groundcover plants as an alternative to grass, the low-growing herb camomile (*Chamomile nobile* 'Treneague') can be grown into an effective lawn.

Off to work we hoe...

Any gardener using an open bed – one not covered by a permanent mulch – will have to learn how to handle a hoe. Hoes are the best implement for dispatching tiny weed seedlings to weed heaven as they emerge from the soil. A hoe has two parts: a handle and a blade. Keep the blade sharp with a sharpening tool and the job will be much easier. When you want to clear a bed of weeds, hold the handle and push the blade of the hoe through the soil just under the surface, no more than 15mm deep. The weeds will fall easily and can be left on the surface of the soil to decompose naturally.

You need to be vigilant and regular with your hoe wielding. A hoe does not work on big weeds. If they get too big you will have to dig into the soil with a fork. As soon as you start doing this not only does the job get harder, you run the risk of disturbing other weed seeds and bringing them to the surface, where they are more likely to germinate. You also risk chopping up the roots of perennial weeds such as couch grass, dandelion and dock. It's best not to hoe after rain, but frankly this is a near impossibility in my garden, so that's one rule that I'm prepared to break. Some established weeds, such as the aptly named creeping buttercup (*Ranunculus repens*), send out runners in the same way that strawberries do, setting down plants wherever the runner meets the soil. These become particularly hard to remove with a hoe because they are all connected.

Hoeing is particularly useful when you are growing from seed, be they decorative plants or vegetables. Sow seeds in rows and mark the rows so you know where you planted them. Hoe anything that comes up in the gaps between the rows. Planted correctly, seeds will grow into plants, thicken out and take up all the space in the bed, keeping the sun off the surface of the soil and preventing any further weed germination. So long as you act early, the amount of weeding you have to do should decrease as the season continues. Most weeds are short-day plants (see page 115) and like to germinate, grow and set seed early. Once they've missed their growing season they are less likely to be a problem – at least that year if not the next.

If you've got a big plot you might consider investing in a wheeled hoe. They are particularly useful for hoeing vegetable plots and save valuable amounts of time.

Tricky weeding scenarios

It's quite easy to work out how to deal with weeds in a decorative bed or vegetable plot but it seems somehow trickier to go to work on lawns, paths, walls and water. Personally, I don't mind the odd weed in any of these situations, and mostly they add something to the character of the garden architecture, but like any other scenario they can get out of hand. Because of this I want to spend some time discussing the techniques available to reduce the risk of invasion by weeds and increase the possibility of their removal in all four of these situations.

Lawns

The debate about weeds in lawns is endless. Lawn purists want them all out and will more than likely use a chemical weedkiller to do the deed. Those with a more relaxed attitude will tolerate in small numbers some of the nicer tap-rooted weeds like the daisy and the dandelion, or friendly, bouncy, low-growing moss. But what if you want to be purist and organic? Or you've just decided that the lawn is in danger of being taken over by weeds if you don't do something about them? What are your options?

• Dandelions, daisies and other tap-rooted weeds can be 'grubbed' up using a tool called a daisy grubber or hand fork in the manner I described on page 198.

- Spreading weeds, such as speedwells (*Veronica* spp.), white clover (*Trifolium repens*), silverweed (*Potentilla anserina*) and sorrels (*Rumex* and *Oxalis* spp.), can be raked over.
- Weeds with shallow or fibrous roots, such as chickweed, buttercups and ground ivy, can be removed with a three-pronged weeder – a handheld device that has the appearance of a claw.
- Those weeds that prefer an acid soil can be deterred by liming the soil (50g per sq m applied in the winter).
- Severe patches of weed-infested lawn can be dug up and replaced with fresh grass seed.
- Lawns can be mowed at a higher setting (6–8cm instead of 3cm) to encourage taller grasses, which will shade the weed seeds and restrict seed germination.
- Lawns can be cut at the right time – before weeds have flowered, or at least before they have set seed.

Paths

Weed problems occur in paths when there are gaps or cracks in the surface cover. Removing them is not a problem. Under organic standards you can use a flame weeder – a mini flame-thrower that kills off weeds with a blast of ignited gas – but it all seems a bit over the top when we should be concerned with our carbon dioxide emissions. The gas comes in a little canister that has to be discarded after use so it's not reuse-friendly either. The other alternatives are all human powered.

- Any stray weeds in a gravel path can be disturbed with a rake or a hoe.
- Paving can be swept weekly to dislodge any seedlings growing in the cracks.
- Entrenched weeds can be removed with a butter knife or a weeding knife.
- Other weeds can be pinched out with finger and opposable thumb – we are human after all.

Walls

I have some very high-sided slate walls in my garden with lots of cracks in which weeds regularly nest. Most of them add to the wall rather than detract from it. I will, however, trim my weeds, preventing growth of unmanageable proportions and attempt to remove anything I don't want. I've tolerated a mass of ivy running down one wall, but I wouldn't want nettles, docks, trees (it happens regularly) and anything big in there that might damage the walls – Japanese knotweed is definitely out. Trimming isn't a very time-consuming job and I like looking at the spiders, snails and other fine garden fauna while I'm doing it. Removal is tricky, and can damage the wall if done hastily.

Weed seeds seem to get in the most awkward of crevices. I use a knife and a screwdriver to get in the difficult cracks and a pair of secateurs to trim anything that feels like it doesn't want to come out. Better to manage than to do nothing. In other types of walls, total elimination for aesthetic reasons may be more appropriate. As with all other weed scenarios, observation and prompt action are the key tools at your disposal. Nip the weeds out before they become a problem.

Ponds

Some pond weeds deserve less tolerance than others, the most common types being blanketweed (a type of algae) and duckweed (*Lemna minor*). If left unchecked both these weeds will choke other plants and (if you have them in your pond) restrict the movement of fish. They both thrive in bright light and love a pond with a high nutrient level. The RHS recommends allowing half the surface area of your pond to be covered with the leaves of water lilies to keep the light out and suggests regular removal of organic debris that might rot and increase the nutrient level of the pond.

Again, monitor the progress of your weeds and lift them out regularly. Blanketweed can be lifted with a stick or a rake; duckweed with a sieve, or by skimming the surface of the water with a small piece of board. Once you have removed the weeds let them dry out on the edge of the pond for a couple of days before putting them in the compost heap, or burying them in the ground. Whilst they are drying, all the creatures who want to be back in the pond will head back there.

There are plenty of other weeds that will arrive in your pond unexpectedly. If you are not sure whether a new arrival is a friendly visitor or an undesirable guest, identify it in a specialist pond book or simply remove it.

Above Ivy (*Hedera helix*) and Maidenhair spleenwort (*Asplenium trichomanes*) nesting in the author's slate wall.

Pests, diseases and disorders

Potato black leg, cucumber mosaic virus and privet thrips – just three of 500 complaints plants can be affected by. Pests, diseases and disorders sound pretty lurid when you start reading about them but, as Nick Ross used to say on *Crimewatch*, don't have nightmares – they don't happen every day. Of those complaints that do occur, most are preventable and curable without too much difficulty. Some are, of course, not so easy. The slug, for example, is a formidable opponent that most gardeners fear and hate in equal measure.

Pretty much any part of a plant can be affected by pests, diseases and disorders – from the root, bulb or tuber, right the way up through the stem and the leaf to the flower and the fruit. Any gardener has to learn to identify the signs of a problem and deal with it effectively. As there are hundreds of different plant ailments, I'm not going to be able to cover all of them in depth here. For that, I'd recommend *Pests, Diseases and Disorders of Garden Plants* by Buczacki and Harris, or *RHS Pests and Diseases*. What I want to do in this section is to provide a general overview of the different categories of problems you might expect to encounter.

Creating ambient conditions for growth and careful plant selection are the first two steps towards reducing damage caused by pests, diseases and disorders. Plants are more likely to suffer if they are planted in conditions that do not suit them, if they are watered too much or too little, fed too much or too little, strangled by weeds, neglected or left vulnerable to damage from wind, frost, drought or flood.

Pests

Good micro-climate control, soil care and weed management will reduce plant vulnerability and the risk of attack by some pests, but not all. A sheep, for example, is big and ugly enough to eat anything it likes. And quite often does in an unprotected Welsh garden (although it doesn't like azalea, rhododendron and bracken). This may sound quaintly rural, but mice, cats, dogs, rabbits, foxes and even the odd escaped tortoise are all urban pests who will graze, trample, scratch and urinate a garden into trouble. This section thus identifies the primary types of pest – from the minuscule to the mammalian – and explores some of the ways in which we can deal with them.

The nation's most hated pests

Each year the RHS receives thousands of enquiries from frustrated gardeners trying to find out how to deal with particular pests in the garden. Some of the RHS's most often cited pests include slugs and snails, red lily beetle, vine weevil, rosemary beetle, woolly beech aphid, leather jackets, chafer grubs in lawns, soft scale, cushion scale, ants, viburnum beetle, glasshouse red spider mite and mealybugs, rabbits and squirrels.

These are all insects except slugs, snails, rabbits, squirrels and red spider mites. And apart from rabbits and squirrels, all are what you might call creepy crawlies, mini-beasts or invertebrates. It makes sense then to start our bug hunt with them.

Left A line-up of garden goodies and baddies at CAT, from left to right: aphid and mole (baddies), ladybird and bumble bee (goodies – aphid predator and plant pollinator, respectively).

The invertebrates

The invertebrates are the number one species group on Earth, not just in number and sheer variety, but also in function. The world could happily go on without humans and mammals, but not so without invertebrates. They are the single most effective group of organisms on the planet and include amongst their number hundreds of thousands of composters, pollinators, munchers, suckers, cutters, killers and carriers of disease.

They include the arachnids (spiders and other eight-legged creatures like the red spider mite), the crustaceans (in the garden these include woodlice), the molluscs (single-footed gastropods like slugs and snails), the annelids (worms), the nematoda (nematodes), the chilopods and diplopods (centipedes and millipedes respectively) and the insects (the beetles, moths, butterflies, ants, aphids, weevils, scale insects, and so on).

Taken as a whole they represent a mass of activity of epic proportions. They are some of our most ancient creatures (dating back 500–600 million years in some cases) and are principal players in the life of a garden, or indeed almost any ecosystem. Invertebrates create life and balance in a garden. They turn the nutrients in decaying plant matter into food for living plants. They pollinate flowers. And, importantly for the gardener, they eat one another. If they did not, we would be overrun by gall-forming, sap-sucking, leaf-crunching, stem-twisting vegetarians. Not a pleasant thought.

The main predators

The chief invertebrate predators of invertebrate pests are ladybirds, hoverflies, lacewing larvae, parasitic wasps, Carabid (or ground) beetles, Straphilinid beetles, centipedes, Anthocorid bugs, assassin bugs, black-kneed capsid bugs, marsh flies, predatory mites, dragonflies, spiders and wasps. Then there are all the non-invertebrate predators: mammals such as hedgehogs, moles and mice (although these last two are also voracious pests to veggie growers and lawn lovers); amphibians such as frogs and toads; birds; and that confusingly named reptile the slow worm (which is not a worm at all!).

Without exception, all these species prefer to inhabit a garden that more closely resembles a natural ecosystem such as a woodland, meadow or wildlife pond (as distinct from the strictly formal ornamental kind you see in parks and gardens with pedalos or grand displays of water lillies). Predators of invertebrates do not like very formal clipped spaces with sparse planting schemes. They prefer areas that are planted with a diverse range of species. They like to feel secure, so they need hiding spaces. Some of them are composters as well as being predators and they like to find decaying matter in a garden, either to consume or to seek sanctuary within. Those that also feed on nectar search out flowers with high nectar content. In the winter when they hibernate they need nooks and

Above Unlike little children, caterpillars love to eat their greens and can inflict enormous damage on brassica crops.

crannies where they can stay undisturbed –
piles of rotting wood, hollow garden canes
within which to crawl, old tubs left upside
down, even bits of rubble.

Elements of wildlife gardening can
be incorporated into most gardening styles,
including straightforward veggie growing,
and there are lots of examples of how this
can be done in Chapter five. Incorporating these
features will encourage more predators and
reduce the number of pests operating on
your patch.

On its own though, this approach is
rarely enough to deal with all invertebrate pest
problems and should be supplemented with more
specific solutions targeted at particular pests.

Invertebrates create life and balance in a garden. They turn the nutrients in decaying plant matter into food for living plants. They pollinate flowers. And, importantly for the gardener, they eat one another.

Invertebrate pest control

The starting point for all hands-on pest control is observation. Take a tour of your
garden plants and see what's going on there. The principal pests operate by day and
night, so a nocturnal expedition with a torch is highly recommended. Sometimes when
you notice obvious damage on a plant it is quite clear what has caused it because no
other pest makes that sort of damage. Sometimes it is less clear. It is often difficult to tell
whether a pest or some other disorder is the cause. Again, a pest identification book will
give you lots of clues.

Aphids are one of the most common types of garden pests. They suck the sap
from the stems of plants, causing them to wilt and die. As they move from plant to
plant they spread infections around the garden. There are 500 different species in
Britain in all, the most well-known being greenfly and blackfly. Ladybirds, lacewing
larvae, earwigs, bats and birds all eat aphids but they are unlikely to deal with all
infestations on their own. Look under the leaves of plants for colonies, knock them off
with a fine jet of water or pinch them between your fingers. Ants love to eat an aphid
excretion rather coyly named honeydew. So enamoured of the honeydew are ants they
guard the aphids from ladybird predators in a kind of protection-racket farming
operation. It's easy to spot where this is happening because ants trail up and down the
stems of plants to get to their farm at the top.

Many pests can be brushed or picked off.
It's a very good targeted method of control. The slug is
a prime example. Slugs prefer to feed at night and it's
easy to catch them in the act. You need a stout heart, a
torch and a good pair of gloves when you go out on
patrol. Slugs excrete slime as a defensive reaction when
handled and the stuff sticks to your hands like glue.
I've got a woodland to throw slugs into but most people
devise some horrible end for their prisoners. CAT ran a
Bug-the-Slug campaign a few years back and people
described drowning, salting, freezing, cutting,
skewering and even eating slugs they had caught in
their patch. Sometimes it's hard to be a vegetarian
gardener.

Such is the obsession with slugs that gardeners
use every single preventative measure known to man to
stop them damaging plants. As well as encouraging
hedgehogs, frogs, Indian runner ducks (pictured top
right) and slow worms to eat them, they lay traps filled
with beer (pictured right); surround their plants with
barriers such as water-filled moats, copper rings
(pictured bottom right), woodchips, the shells of Brazil
nuts, walnuts and pistachios, eggshells and sea shells,
gravel chips, recycled glass chippings; and use biological
controls such as the commercially available Nemaslug
(see page 215). And then they, or their children in some
cases, hand pick the survivors just to make sure. Or they
give up and plant plants slugs don't like.

Organic vs. chemical controls
Traps, barriers, repellent devices and biological controls
are all acceptable tools for organic growers. Chemical
pesticides tend to be more indiscriminate. Used over the
whole garden they kill both the good and the bad.
This is not a sensible long-term strategy because pest
populations recover quicker than predators and more

and more chemicals need to be used to exercise the same level of control. Many pests also develop resistance to pesticides in their own evolutionary battle with the manufacturers of chemical products. This effect was noticed as far back as 1913 and manufacturers have to keep bringing out new products to keep up. These all have to be tested on animals and are dangerous if handled incorrectly.

Traps lure pests away from their intended goal by offering something much sweeter – usually a manufactured recreation of the pheromone scent of their mate, but also sweet food or liquid. For example, a jam jar filled with beer and topped off with a piece of paper with a small hole in it can be hung from an apple tree to lure wasps away from apple fruit. Pheromone traps are commercially available and are used to trap particular pests such as codling moth and plum moth. The moths fly into the trap and are caught on sticky sheets.

You can also hang sticky traps up in greenhouses to catch winged insects such as white flies, thrips and fungus gnats. These do not contain any scent and simply rely on accident: the unsuspecting insect lands by chance on the yellow sticky sheets and can't fly off again. You can also catch flea beetles by moving a sticky trap over infected plants (without actually touching them) and shaking the plants as you go. The beetles jump off the plant and land on the trap.

CAT's Bug-the-Slug campaign

'I was so angry at the state of the flowers being eaten alive, I went on a slug rampage. Equipped only with a pair of Marigolds and a bucket, I upturned everything that might be sheltering a slug! I'd collected a good amount but decided (being a vegetarian) I couldn't bring myself to kill them, so I put them on a bird table. Watching them slowly slime off, I thought, I'm not going to let them get the better of me! So I then poured salt all around the bird table, so they would have to stay and become bird food. I was horrified when they started to fizz, and realising what I'd done, quickly gathered them all back in the bucket and tried to rinse the salt off with a hosepipe! NEVER AGAIN! I throw them on the garden waste pile now. Frogs eat slugs, don't they? By the way my boyfriend's nickname is Slug!'

Elva Davies on the dilemmas of the vegetarian gardener, as featured in *The Little Book of Slugs* by CAT (and of course salt ingested in large quantities is bad for birds too!).

Barriers prevent insects getting to their intended victim. They include grease, which is applied to the trunks of fruit trees to prevent wingless female moths walking up and laying eggs on the twigs, and horticultural fleece. Horticultural fleece is highly spun lightweight material that can be laid over developing vegetable crops to exclude pests such as cabbage butterflies, carrot fly, flea beetles and cabbage root fly. Cabbage root fly can also be prevented by placing a collar around the base of the stem. These can be bought or made with old bits of carpet, underlay or cardboard. They are simply small circles or squares of material with a slit cut in one side to the centre to allow placement around the plant. Used as soon as brassica seedlings are transplanted, they prevent the eggs of the fly hatching at the base of the plants.

As well as creating the right conditions for encouraging general predators into your garden, you can buy specific biological controls to target individual pests. The most well known is probably the parasite Nemaslug, a nematode which burrows its way inside a slug, causing it to lose its appetite and die. Other biological controls do for whitefly, red spider mite, mealy bug, scale insect, chafer grub, leatherjacket, vine weevil and aphids (in the shape of ladybirds and lacewings). All are available through the post and from selected garden centres (www.just-green.com, www.organiccatalog.com, www.wigglywigglers.co.uk). They are extremely easy to use, safe to handle, and because they are targeted, do not harm other creatures.

The vertebrates

Beyond the small world of the invertebrate there are a number of pests that may warrant your attention: specifically birds and mammals (including mice, moles, squirrels, cats, foxes, deer and rabbits). The solutions to most of these problems are structural, rather than anything to do with the general culture of the garden – although in some cases it is possible to avoid growing plants that pests like.

Rabbits, badgers, deer and sheep

These blighters need to be fenced out. To keep out burrowers you need to dig a 2.5cm mesh wire fencing material 30cm under the ground, bending the lower 15cm outwards (i.e. away from the garden). To keep out deer you need 1.8m fencing, a tall hedge, or an electric fence. In her book *Common Garden Enemies*, Janet Thomson recommends using scare tactics to keep animals away. Most of these mammals hate sudden movement or noises and you can buy scarers that go off at intervals to keep them guessing.

Mice, moles, squirrels, foxes and cats

These cannot be fenced out so easily. They cause a wide variety of problems. Mice eat seeds before they have a chance to germinate (specifically peas and beans). Moles cause damage to lawns and flowerbeds by pushing up little hills of earth in inconvenient places. Squirrels dig up bulbs, eat flower buds, steal fruit and strip bark off trees. Foxes dig up plants and scorch leaves with their urine. Cats scrape holes in seed beds, spray plants with urine and generally mess up a garden through their day-to-day habits, although of course they also kill rabbits and mice. When we farmed Robert Plant's land, our two acres were fenced off underground and above ground with rabbit-proof fencing but baby rabbits still got through. Our cats loved it – they got regular fresh rabbit meat.

Keep mice out of seed trays by placing humane traps nearby. Alternatively, you can fence your seeds off with very fine wire mesh (mice can get through very small holes). If you're using traps in the garden, hide them under logs and bricks to keep them away from birds and pets. It's amazing how brutal you can get when it comes to mice. I killed one once with the edge of a rake – an instant sweeping kill that still surprises me now.

Moles can also be trapped or deterred with a sound scarer. You can buy electric devices, but some people recommend burying a bottle in a mole hill so the bottle top is level with the surface. Apparently moles don't like the sound of the wind as it whooshes through the open bottle and down into the little tunnel beneath.

Squirrels are best caged out of soft fruit areas with wire, but you can offer temporary protection to individual trees by placing netting over them when the fruit is nearly ready. Cats and foxes can be deterred by ultrasound, water sprinklers and other alarm systems, but you can also try dense planting arrangements, spiky plants and temporary protection for any vulnerable seed beds.

The birds

On the whole birds are a positive influence in the garden, eating their fair share of pests, but on some occasions they themselves can be a pest. Pigeons love to eat cabbages and although you can try and scare them off with fluttering tapes, CDs and glitter balls hung on string (pictured below), or intermittent sound devices, the best control measure is to cover your crops with a fleece or some other caging material. All fruit-loving garden birds will help themselves to your fruit, so keep bushes covered when a crop is due, or plant in a fruit cage for long-term protection.

Diseases and disorders

There are many, many different types of plant disease and disorder, although the chances of experiencing all of them in one garden are extremely slim. Nevertheless, it is important to have an identification book such as *RHS Pests and Diseases* on hand to make identification and cure possible.

Diseases are divided into three distinct areas: fungal diseases, bacterial infections and viruses. Fungi cannot photosynthesise. Most are saprophytic (feeding on dead and decaying tissue), but those that feed on living plant tissue cause problems in the garden. Most thrive in warm, damp conditions so control is limited to avoiding or preventing conditions in which they thrive. Good garden hygiene, adequate ventilation, avoidance of overwatering and the use of resistant cultivars can limit damage. Organic standards do allow the use of a few permitted fungicides but these should always be used as a last resort.

Bacterial infections enter plants through wounds, usually caused by pruning and pests, but also by wind damage and garden accidents. Following correct pruning techniques will help prevent problems. Use a sharp cutting device such as a pair of

secateurs, or if the stems are larger than the thickness of a pencil, a pair of loppers or a pruning saw. Cut the stem or branch cleanly at a slight angle (pictured left). After pruning a diseased plant, always wash your tools in boiling water before moving onto the next plant.

Viruses take over the cells of higher organisms and divert the cells' energy into producing masses of viral material that spreads to adjacent cells. This restricts the growth of the plant or causes malformations or malfunctions. Viruses usually rely on insects, especially sap suckers, or other animals to move from plant to plant, but they can also be passed via vegetative reproduction. Buy virus-free plants, use resistant varieties and keep sucking pests under control.

Disorders are caused by mineral deficiencies in the soil and climatic factors such as lack of water, and frost and wind damage. Use good horticultural practice as described throughout this chapter to reduce problems.

Sometimes it's hard to spot whether a problem is a disease or disorder. I recommend having a magnifying glass on hand for close inspection. Sometimes you can remedy disorders quite easily if your plant is suffering because it has simply been planted in the wrong place, or in the wrong soil. In these situations the plant should be removed, and if it is not too far gone, replanted in a more appropriate spot.

Permitted pesticides and fungicides

The following treatments are all permitted under organic standards, but should only be used as a last resort. Their use is constantly under review and copper products (such as Bordeaux mixture) and derris are likely to be banned in the next few years.

Derris – against greenfly, blackfly and other aphids; caterpillars, flea beetle, raspberry beetle, sawfly larvae
Pyrethrum – against greenfly, blackfly and other aphids
Insecticidal soap – against greenfly, blackfly and other aphids; whitefly; red spider mite; soft scale; rose slugworm
Rapeseed oil – against greenfly, blackfly and other aphids; whitefly; thrips; scale; red spider mites
Bordeaux mixture – against apple scab; peach leaf curl; potato blight
Sulphur – against powdery mildew; rose black spot
Bacillus thuringiensis – against cabbage caterpillars

If you decide to use any of the above, always follow these safety precautions:

• Don't use spray as a preventative measure
• Read the label and follow instructions precisely
• Use a good-quality sprayer
• Spray only when necessary
• Make up only as much spray as you need; never store made-up spray
• To avoid drift, spray only in still weather
• Never spray when bees are working – the evening is often safest
• Wear protection when spraying – rubber gloves, masks and goggles
• Always wash hands after spraying

Chapter seven

Gardening beyond the garden

A garden can be a window shelf or a box or a balcony. A garden can be a nature reserve, a forest that needs replanting, a raised bed on a concrete school yard, a woodland glade or a pebble beach. Friends of mine have spent years moving from one smallholding to another, travelling like itinerant farm labourers, learning to garden as they go. For them a garden was any place where someone needed help. Garden superheroes to the rescue.

For guerrilla gardeners a garden is any public space that needs to be made good. They head out at night to their clandestine gardens with cars full of plants to fill up urban soils left blank through neglect. Roundabouts, scraps of waste ground, neglected council planters. It's the reverse of vandalism. A positive statement against apathy.

Most of this book teaches the basics of the craft of gardening but you don't need to own a space to garden. The rules will apply to any garden you take on, be it back garden, allotment, community garden, roundabout, or an orchard in Japan.

Get organised

I like to encourage people to share ideas, resources and materials wherever they can. Even if it's just sharing your garden with others. We have a strong swapping culture in the Dyfi Valley and an excellent community organisation called Ecodyfi to offer community groups help and advice. What we have tried to do in the Dyfi Valley is provide a model of how local communities can work together to reduce their collective impact on the environment. The Ecodyfi project brings together renewable-energy makers, home gardeners, eco-builders, farmers and other local growers, school groups, health workers, tourism officials and other parts of our local economy. Together we create positive solutions that enhance living standards while creating a long-term strategic plan to ensure our local area can withstand the effects of climate change. Go to www.ecodyfi.org.uk for more information.

Because I've always learnt a huge amount from other gardeners I want to go through some of the options for learning from others. As I have a fairly liberal view of what constitutes a garden, I've included opportunities such as volunteering at nature reserves – actually very good places to learn essential skills like hedge laying, step making and so on. I haven't included lists of horticultural college qualifications; however, if you are thinking about hotfooting it off to college, check with the Institute of Horticulture for recognised organic gardening courses and the RHS for details of its certification programmes, see www.horticulture.org.uk and www.rhs.org.uk.

Diggers and dreamers: a short history of radical gardening in Britain

It was my history teacher at school who first told me about the Diggers, when I was seventeen. She had a natural love of words and she liked the word Digger. She also introduced me to Praisegod (an English Civil War Parliamentarian), the Barebones and the Rump Parliaments, and Gerrard Winstanley. Gerrard Winstanley sounds like a Rastafarian ska star but he was actually a cattle herdsman who, along with six helpers, dug up common land at St George's Hill, Weybridge, in 1649. A protest against serfdom and private property. Even though there were only seven of them, they were considered an affront on property serious enough for Cromwell's government to kick them off the land and burn all their houses. Thus ensuring the Diggers' place in the history of garden agitation.

William Cobbett took up the mantle in 1820 (see a garden celebrating his life at the Garden Organic (HDRA) garden at Yalding). Appalled by poverty in his rural rides around Britain, he described how the old rural culture of self-reliance was being destroyed by agricultural monocultures and industrialisation. Sound familiar? He was followed by a long list of rural radicals: John Ruskin, WB Yeats, William Morris, Henry David Thoreau, right up to GK Chesterton and latterly Robert Hart, inventor of the Forest Garden system, and John Seymour, author of the smallholders' bible *The Complete Book of Self-Sufficiency*, recently updated as *New Complete Self-Sufficiency: The Classic Guide for Realists and Dreamers*.

More recently the focus has moved back towards the city. In the 70s a nation audibly gasped at the sight of Tom Good ploughing up his suburban front lawn in the sitcom *The Good Life*. In the 90s a group of community-minded spirits set up a garden on the site of the old Guinness distillery in London and every Reclaim the Streets action included a symbolic tree planting through asphalt, www.rts. gn.apc.org. Now we have people like Richard Reynolds, a self-styled guerrilla gardener, www.guerrillagardening.org. He heads out in the dead of night with a group of friends and plants up barren wasted spaces. You can see his work at various locations around London and his example has inspired many similar green-fingered revolutionaries across the globe. Find a barren plot of land and sow some seeds. Resistance is fertile!

Above Fresh food, air and perspective. Allotments are back with a bang. Here in Machynlleth, allotmenteers look out to the foothills of Snowdonia.

Allotments

As I haven't until very recently had access to an allotment I've always been slightly envious of allotmenteers. Almost all of those I've spoken to say they get a lot of useful advice from fellow plot-holders. There are 330,000 allotments around the UK and demand for them is going up all the time. It's the easiest way to establish a permanent garden space if you don't have one at home. Renting an allotment is hit and miss. Some allotments are crying out for tenants and some have enormous waiting lists. Contact your local authority allotments officer and see what's available in your area. If you can't get an allotment near your house perhaps you'll find one a bit further afield. The rules governing allotments vary from plot to plot. Some are for veggie growing only. Some are chalet garden sites so think summerhouse rather than shed, and plants, flowers, shrubs and lawns instead of vegetables. Some allow permanent plants such as fruit trees, hedging and perennial ornamentals. Others don't. Some let you keep animals. Others not. Sometimes you can get the rules changed, but a radical campaign is probably not the best way to introduce yourself to your fellow allotmenteers. Most allotment holders are friendly and happy to offer advice and support.

Sometimes allotments are combined to make a community garden. At St Ann's Allotment Gardens in Nottingham one community group called Eco-works runs a not-for-profit operation spanning nine separate allotment plots. The group combines an interest in alternative technology, gardening and mental health issues. There's a café which uses an old range recycled from Nottingham Castle, and a market garden supplying organic fruit and vegetables to various cafés in town, and horticultural training for sixteen- to twenty-four-year-olds. Elsewhere in the country allotmenteers in Huddersfield have clubbed together and put up a polytunnel for wheelchair-using gardeners to grow their own food and contribute vegetables to a healthy-eating campaign aimed at pensioners in the local area.

> www.sharedgarden.co.uk is a really lovely and inspiring website for people wanting to share allotments. The National Society of Allotment and Leisure Gardeners is the main allotment organisation in the UK, www.nsalg.org.uk, and you can also try www.allotments-uk.com.

Community gardens and city farms

There are 10 million people in Britain today without access to a garden. The need for community gardens is huge. The Federation of City Farms and Community Gardens database holds details of more than 1,000 community gardening and farming groups (www.farmgarden.org.uk). Anyone looking to join an existing garden or start a new one should contact them first. They provide a range of information about volunteering, packs to start a garden yourself and several maps of city farms and community gardens around the country.

Community gardens do not have the same legal protection as allotments, despite the fact that 300,000 people use them regularly. Most are sited on previously derelict local authority land. As the demand for urban housing grows so does the threat to garden space. Community gardens are a great way to learn about veggie growing, wildlife gardening or looking after animals, and a great place to meet new people and

Food poverty is common in urban areas and community gardens play their part in reducing its impact.

Left Short on space? Make some. Cities are filled with empty rooftops waiting to be planted up. This garden was built on a community centre in Reading.

connect with those who share your interests. Most gardens are set up and run by volunteers: there's plenty of opportunity to get involved, not just in the gardening, but in helping run cafés, supporting people in care and providing training opportunities. Community gardens improve the health and mental wellbeing of the community, as well as providing sometimes the only source of fresh organic food for participants. Food poverty is common in urban areas and community gardens play their part in reducing its impact. Garden Organic (HDRA) runs the Organic Food For All programme (OFFA) to help provide the most basic gardening skills to get people growing their own food (www.organicgardening.org.uk/foodforall). You can see the OFFA garden at Garden Organic's garden at Yalding in Kent.

Conservation volunteers

If you want to learn some key natural gardening skills, such as hedge laying, dry-stone walling, step making, bridge building, tree planting, etc., there's probably no better place to start than volunteering for one of the conservation organisations, such as The National Trust (www.nationaltrust.org.uk), The Wildlife Trusts (www.wildlifetrusts.org), RSPB (www.rspb.org.uk) and The British Trust for Conservation Volunteers (BTCV, www.btcv.org.uk). The BTCV provides a whole series of opportunities with different levels of commitment required – from the low commitment Green Gym sessions (three hours a week complete with warm up, muscle toning and practical gardening), and the day and weekend sessions working on a project close to home, through to working holidays in the UK and abroad.

Volunteer gardening

Some of our most well-known gardens provide volunteer opportunities for would-be gardeners, including the Royal Botanic Gardens at Kew. Garden Organic (HDRA) needs volunteers and volunteer tour guides. CAT runs a one-week or a six-month volunteer programme for gardeners (as well as ones for engineers, biologists, builders and office-based staff). Many local organisations need volunteers to tend the gardens of elderly people who are no longer able to manage their own and those of people with disabilities. Contact local voluntary work agencies and look for requests for help on the bulletin boards of local libraries; also look at www.volunteering.org.uk. You need a garden – somebody somewhere needs you.

Above No garden? No problem. Volunteer. Get experience. Have fun. Hannah worked as a volunteer at CAT.

Holiday gardening

If you want to see a whole country go organic Cuba is the place to visit (although you'll have to feel guilty about your air miles). When the communist bloc fell apart Cuba had no option but to go organic. Russia used to supply it with cut-price chemicals for agricultural production but this all ended about ten years ago. Since then it has had to develop its own brand of sustainable organic urban and rural agriculture and some of the lessons learnt could be really helpful for the rest of us. They are also one of the great recycling nations. Denied access to new goods by the United States, who have enforced a trade embargo on Cuba for forty years, they have had to make do and mend. It's a low-tech approach to life that isn't ideal for the people of Cuba, the kind of life many people in the UK would associate with wartime austerity, but to a certain extent it does work. Cuba has one of the highest literacy rates in the world, and probably the best free health care service. Contact the Cuban Solidarity Campaign (**www.cuba-solidarity.org.uk**) for details of their gardening tours. Most include a work element as well as touring the gardens themselves. For something slightly less exotic you should consider WWOOFING (see below) or conservation volunteering (see page 227).

WWOOFING

WWOOF is short for World Wide Opportunities on Organic Farms. It's a volunteering scheme for people who want to travel and learn how to grow organic food. In the UK it's usually a weekend activity. You get a list of places to stay from the WWOOF organisation, make a booking and head down to the farm or smallholding of your choice on a Friday evening. It's a mini break with a big difference – you work.

The type and amount of work you do varies from place to place. Some WWOOF hosts just ask you to do a long morning on each day. The rest of the time you can explore the local area, socialise with your hosts or just hang out in the garden. Some expect you to work the whole day. In return you get top-notch organic food and an opportunity to learn about gardening. The great thing about the WWOOF scheme is that you can just do it for a weekend and never again if you don't

> The first time I went on a WWOOF weekend I found myself helping my host to assist an old boar mating with a sow. That's when you know you've gone organic.

Julie meets Little Fuwa and Wara,
the most gorgeous apple-dumpling pixie ever

Sometimes I feel like a bit of a fraggle compared to my adventurous friend Julie. She sends me email dispatches from the far corners of the globe. This one came after she'd been WWOOFing in Japan. It's such a lovely email I wanted to include it here.

I am well wedged into my spring holiday, and it fits nicely! I've been WWOOFing with a lovely family on an orchard in the Japanese alps. It was a proper WWOOF house: draughty nooks and cosy crannies, good compost toilet, baskets of cabbages and apples in every room, laundry drying over the wood stove, and random people popping in to talk about tomatoes. Little Fuwa wasn't sure about me and kept growling, but he loved the windpower badges I brought because they looked like ninja stars. His baby sister Wara is THE most gorgeous apple-dumpling pixie ever. I spent most of the time collecting pruned branches in the orchard, breathing in the crispy white mountains. Bird song, wheeling hawks, smell of woodsmoke, clean cold air, warm sun. The region is old and wise. Elderly people up ladders in bonnets. Spent one day in a big steaming community kitchen, making miso paste with jolly ladies. Lots of trading of homemade tofu or apple juice; people stopping by with newspaper parcels of spinach they couldn't sell at the market. A postman who likes to talk about bio-diesel, and an onsen [hot spring] on a hill with a slide down to the bottom (surreal alone in the dark!).

enjoy it, or, like some people I know, travel all over the world, moving from farm to farm. The type of experience you can expect to have on a WWOOF farm can vary enormously and there are safeguards to make sure the host is reputable. If WWOOF receives complaints about farms they will investigate and, if need be, take them off the list. Some people treat it as a working alternative to horticultural college (although you don't get a qualification); others just as a way of travelling cheaply. The amount and quality of teaching also varies, as does the type of farm. If you're veggie or vegan, look out for the farms that specify no animals. See www.wwoof.org/wwoof_uk and www.wwoof.org for international visits.

    The first time I went on a WWOOF weekend I found myself helping my host to assist an old boar mating with a sow. Thankfully I only had to hold the torch. I won't tell you what the WWOOF host had to do. That's when you know you've gone organic.

Courses

Leisure courses in gardening range from the more expensive day and weekend sessions taught by celebrities (Bob Flowerdew and Sarah Raven, to name but two) through to the amazingly good value one-day events at organic gardens, such as those hosted by Garden Organic (HDRA), through to residential weekend courses based at one of the many organic, permaculture and wildlife farms around the country. CAT offers a wide range of weekend courses in green crafts, renewable energy, environmental building and ecological sewage treatment, as well as one titled Organic Gardening Weekend. One of the most inspiring courses I've ever participated in is The Permaculture Association's 72-hour permaculture design course. Permaculture stands for permanent culture or permanent agriculture. There's a whole range of permaculture courses and activities to get involved with but the 72-hour permaculture design course is the best practical introduction to organic growing I can imagine. Lasting two weeks, the course is jam-packed with interesting classes, practical activities and inspiring site visits. You learn how natural cycles work and how we can more easily fit in with our ecology. I hardly slept the two weeks I took my course. We spent all the days learning and all the evenings talking. I remember going down to my friend's 25th birthday party in Hertfordshire the day after the course finished, travelling through the cities of central England on the train. After two weeks of inspiring organic living I felt a real culture shock. For me I think that was the point of no return.

For more information about permaculture, including courses, check out the inspiring Permaculture Magazine, www.permaculture.co.uk. This website will also give you access to a wide range of useful books, including the introductory guide *Permaculture in A Nutshell*. Also try www.permaculture.org.uk – the website of The Permaculture Association.

Above Peter Harper who teaches at CAT.

Enjoy the hard work of fellow gardeners

Take a day off from the garden and visit somebody else's. This is a great way to pick up ideas, chat to other gardeners and find plants and books. There are some nationally and internationally renowned gardens to visit in Britain, including the Royal Botanic Gardens at Kew in London, www.rbgkew.org.uk; all four RHS gardens in Essex, Devon, Surrey and North Yorkshire, www.rhs.org.uk; the three Garden Organic (HDRA) gardens at Yalding, Ryton and Audley End, www.gardenorganic.org.uk; and individual gardens such as that belonging to the late TV gardener Geoff Hamilton at Barnsdale, www.barnsdalegardens.co.uk. If you come to CAT's visitor centre in the summer you can join expert organic gardener Roger MacLennan or another member of staff on a one-hour tour of the gardens.

Garden Organic organises gardening weekends where organic gardens around the country open their gardens to visitors for a small fee. There are also the many private gardens opened for odd days under the auspices of the National Gardens Scheme (www.ngs.org.uk). Though not specifically organic, they are a valuable source of inspiration and information. The gardeners are probably some of the most well-informed 'amateurs' in the country – not to mention experts in the art of garden hospitality. An open day isn't complete without a slice of homemade cake or a cream tea. There are also various regional events, such as the private London parks open days, which give people the chance to visit gardens that are normally closed to the public.

Above You can walk through this recycled bottle dome at CAT and see the colours of sunlight refracted a thousand different ways.

Chapter eight

Climate change and gardening:

the elephant in the room

The elephant in the room – an enormous problem wilfully overlooked by some, even though it is obvious to everyone else. Climate change is an elephant that's wandered out of the house through the patio windows and made itself at home in the garden. There is no single bigger threat to our ability to create the kind of successful caring, beautiful, inspiring gardens we want than climate change. In the next two decades gardeners will not only have to learn what it means to garden in an era of climatic instability, they will have to change their idea of what a garden can be. We need a new style of climate-friendly gardening that allows us to reduce the carbon cost of our gardens and helps protect them from bad weather.

Why climate matters

Humans are an incredible and incredibly lucky species. We have evolved to enjoy, appreciate and materially benefit from a vast biodiversity of life – we could not hope to be born into a richer world. And yet we are only the product and the beneficiaries of a blessedly secure and stable climate. Look back 20,000 years to the last ice age to see how humans fared in an unfavourable climate. We were a ragtag species, disparate and marginal. Not doing particularly well. Okay, even then we were blessed with a unique creative ingenuity, but without the right climate in which to exercise it, we must have been a haunted species.

Gardeners will have to learn what it means to garden in an era of climatic instability, and change their idea of what a garden can be.

Only when the earth started to warm again, and stayed warm, could we start to fulfil our potential. What we actually did with our favourable climate was remarkable: something that none of the other members of our *Hominidae* family had been capable of doing before, something that allowed everything else that followed to happen – we settled down and invented gardening.

Actually it's more accurate to say that some of us settled down and invented gardening. Millions of people around the world continued the same hunter-gatherer lifestyles that had gone before. These people lived with whatever nature offered. They did not try to shape it. Why these people remained true to nature while others rushed headlong through agriculture, civilisation, colonisation, industrialisation, globalisation, to where we are now – gardeners on the verge of a climate breakdown – remains an eternal mystery. If climates have changed before, why do we think that the climate change we are experiencing now is anything other than a natural phenomenon?

Why climate changes

There are two sets of reasons why the Earth experiences such extreme climatic changes. The first set is to do with the movement of our planet: how it orbits the sun, and the way it revolves around its own axis and the angle at which it tilts. These movements exist as part of a natural cycle that lasts for millennia and raises and lowers temperatures on Earth by changing our position in relation to the sun. Scientists have been able to pinpoint them with some accuracy. For example:

- Every 95,800 years the Earth's orbit around the sun changes from being roughly circular to elliptical, a switch that sparks off ice ages.

- Every 41,000 years a change in the inclination of the tilt of the Earth from 21.39 to 24.36 degrees and back makes for hotter summers and colder winters.

- And every 21,700 years the Earth wobbles on its axis of rotation. If this happens when the Earth is relatively close to the sun the winters will be short and warm.

The second set of reasons is much harder to pin down. These could best be described as changes to the balance of natural systems within the Earth's atmosphere. For example, changes in oceanic and atmospheric currents, the build-up of greenhouse gases like carbon dioxide and the growth of ice sheets (which reflect sunlight away from the planet as they increase in size). Scientists generally believe that changes in shape, tilt and wobble are insufficient in themselves to account for the immense magnitude and speed of recent climate change – the second set of forces make the difference.

Britain's climate

The climate in Britain is influenced by the Gulf Stream and its northern extension, the North Atlantic Drift – a great movement of water that flows continuously through the Atlantic between the Gulf of Mexico and the Arctic and then back again. These two ocean currents have power equivalent to one hundred Amazon rivers (check out the children's movie *Finding Nemo* for a cartoon visualisation of what it feels like to be in the flow). They push warm water from Mexico into our seas, which warm the climate in Britain.

The last time the Atlantic conveyor belt ceased to function, northern Europe was plunged into a mini ice age. It happened because fresh water from a massive lake in Canada found its way into the Atlantic. Brian Fagan, author of *The Long Summer:*

Left Caused by too much carbon dioxide in the atmosphere, the greenhouse effect is warming the planet – and giving the garden equivalent a bad name.

How Climate Changed Civilisation, described what happened next: 'The Netherlands saw winter temperatures plunge regularly below -20°C. Snow might fall any time from September to May, while summers were cool, averaging between 13° and 14°C. Throughout much of Europe tree cover retreated, to be replaced by artemesia and other shrubs typical of severe, cold conditions. Dramatic temperature fluctuations, wide annual climate swings, and severe winter storms pummelled Europe. The cold endured for ten centuries.'

That was 12,000 years ago. As higher 21st-century temperatures cause ice to melt in the Arctic, and as fresh water pours into the sea, we could see the same thing happen again.

But why are temperatures going up now?

None of this explains why the temperature is going up now. We cannot blame the planetary cycle. It's the wrong time of the aeon. We cannot blame changes in the movement of air and water, or an increase or decrease in the amount of ice on the surface of the earth. These changes have all been triggered by something else. And that something else is CO_2 or carbon dioxide.

Carbon dioxide is the fundamental agent of climate change. When heat from the sun arrives on the Earth's surface some of it is absorbed into earth or water. That which cannot be absorbed bounces back into the atmosphere. If our atmosphere contained no carbon dioxide at all the heat would disappear into space. Our planet would not be the fun-loving place it is. In fact it would probably be dead, like all the other planets in our solar system. As it is, carbon dioxide traps heat and allows our planet, and consequently the species that live upon it, to be warm – even the penguins. If there is too much carbon dioxide in the atmosphere the world heats up. Too little and it cools down. Without it we would have no climate at all. I don't know, carbon dioxide: can't live with it, can't live without it.

It is possible to measure the amount of carbon dioxide in the atmosphere in parts per million and track that figure against rising temperatures. Temperatures go up when the amount of CO_2 in the atmosphere increases. Since the industrial revolution global atmospheric concentrations of CO_2 have increased from 220 parts per million to 370 parts per million. The burning of fossil fuels is to blame. If current trends continue we will reach a figure of 450 parts per million by the year 2050. When we reach this point the Earth's average temperatures will have risen by 2°C. Many scientists view this figure as a threshold. The last time the temperature of the planet rose by not much more than this it took 60,000 years for the climate to recover.

What does climate change mean for gardeners?

In the long term no scientist can predict exactly what will happen to our climate and the best thing any gardener can do is to reduce his or her personal CO_2 emissions by adopting some of the ideas below. This will help to ensure the climate remains as close as possible to the one we know and enjoy now.

In the short term scientists predict that temperatures will rise and the weather will get more and more bad-tempered. We have already seen an increase in the frequency of record-breaking temperatures and freak weather events and this looks set to continue. This will throw up all kinds of practical problems gardeners will have to consider. We will have to create a new style of climate-friendly gardening.

Freak weather is like a rude uncle who descends on a happy household every now and again to disturb the balance of family life. We may be used to his occasional visits. We might even enjoy the drama he brings with him. But we could never imagine what life would be like if he became a more regular visitor.

As the seasons change it will become harder to judge when to plant crops that are not frost tolerant. As temperatures increase, some plants that are used to certain temperatures will become more susceptible to disease. As bad weather becomes more frequent, plants are more likely to suffer damage through flood, drought and storm.

The short-term change may not be so noticeable. If there are certain plants that we cannot grow, because the climate no longer suits them, we will find others we can. Already some adventurous farmers are growing olives and avocado in Britain. However, the perceived benefits will only ever be temporary. We cannot imagine that the climate will change to suit our desire for Mediterranean sun and just stop there (although I'm one of those people who quite like our climate as it is). Even if it did, our understanding of pests, diseases, weeds and soil fertility will have to be continually refreshed as climatic changes affect how our gardens perform. A recent RHS report on climate change says that the variety and number of outbreaks of diseases are likely to increase under conditions of climate change (www.rhs.org.uk/news/climate_change/climate_reports.asp). For example, oak wilt (*Ceratocystis fagacearum*), a major disease in North America, is transmitted by an insect that cannot survive under current UK climate conditions. When these change, accidental introduction of this insect could be a serious threat to oaks.

Conditions for weeds will be more favourable too as the climate changes. Though not for soil. Evaporation will increase in hot summers, and waterlogging and

As temperatures rise and summer drought becomes a regular fixture for the growing year, gardeners will need to adapt their planting to cope. Some beautiful succulent plants adapted to dry conditions include *Aeonium* 'Schwarzkopf' (**left**), and *Echeveria,* (**below**).

the leaching of nutrients will become a problem as winters become wetter. Soil fertility will decrease more quickly and we will have to be careful to add more organic matter to our soils to keep soil conditions good (see pages 93–110). It is also believed that plants will grow quicker when there is more CO_2 in the atmosphere and that the length of season will extend because of warmer temperatures. This could be a benefit to some plants but not to others. Light-loving woodland species such as bluebells, which flower before other plants have come into leaf, might find themselves disadvantaged as the leaves of taller plants appear earlier and shade their view of the sun. Normal evolutionary principles suggest that the bluebell would adapt to these changes if they happened over thousands of years – but in a few decades? That seems unlikely. Although climate change does bring some opportunities to gardening, it is hard to remain confident that these opportunities will outweigh the things we will lose.

What can we do about it?

Gardeners have three special roles to play in the fight against global climate change.

First of all they can help to monitor the change of seasons through observation of plant and animal behaviour in the garden. Under conditions of climate change it is likely that spring will start earlier, that flowers will fruit quicker and winter events such as the first frost occur later. Watching events in your garden really helps you keep in touch with what's going on there. Are your flowers opening earlier than usual? Are the swallows coming home earlier? Have your blackberries ripened quicker? There's a name given to the study of the times of recurring natural phenomena: phenology. You can do it informally for your own interest, but the information you gather is more useful when combined with other people's. The UK Phenology Network (www.natures calendar.org.uk) combines information from 100,000 people to create a huge databank of climate-change indicators. The network will give you all the information you need to study events and make notes correctly. You might also want to start studying rainfall and temperature variations. Check out www.ukweathershop.co.uk and www.metoffice.gov.uk for weather-related kit and information respectively.

Above As temperatures start to go up, it will be more important for gardeners to monitor the shifting seasons. This picture was taken at the CAT gardens and records the hottest ever day in Wales. At least for now.

Secondly, gardeners can change their buying habits (see Making Ethical Decisions on page 26). Many plants, tools and materials are produced outside the UK. Some are even flown in. Others take an awful lot of energy to grow because they are not meant to be grown in Britain. Garden centres continue to grow potted plants in peat, even though a peat bog can help to absorb methane, another global warming gas. As consumers we need to get savvy as to what's climate friendly. Home-grown, locally produced plants and seeds grown in compost made from recycled waste is a much better option. Buying tools made in Britain, or ones that are reclaimed or recycled, is not only better for the climate, it is better for the people who make them (see page 30).

Thirdly, gardeners can create gardens that sustain themselves without artificial fertilisers and pesticides, protect themselves against climate change, provide some home-grown food and give a little extra space for nature. In short they can make exactly the sort of gardens we've described in this book.

How climate change will mark the end of evolution as we know it

As temperatures go up we won't be the only ones to suffer the consequence. Thousands of species of plants and animals will become extinct. An increase in the ferocity of freak weather events will lead to some delicate species being wiped out by storms, but there is a much more worrying scenario for all plants and animals under conditions of climate change. One that is written into the evolutionary code of all species. A set of species-specific needs you could call climate criteria. A kind of checklist for survival. Right range of temperature. Check. Nice humidity. Check. Good rainfall. Check. And so on. Plants and animals evolve into their climates over millions of years. They have genetic expectations. If the climate changes they can't suddenly decide to be something they are not. The great 18th-century biologist Linnaeus found this out to his cost three centuries ago. He had a great scheme to turn his native Sweden into an economic powerhouse by introducing plants from all over the world. He thought he could fool warm-loving plants to adapt to a cold climate by starting them off in the warmer southern parts of his country and moving them further north as the years went by. It didn't work. Plants, and animals can't adapt that quickly.

There are fossil records of the final part of the last ice age that show the rate at which the ice flow receded. It worked out at about 190 kilometres a century. The only trees that could fill the gap the ice flow left were a couple of species of spruce. Everything else could only extend its range by 40 kilometres every century. The same kind of temperature shifts are happening now. As the planet warms, most temperature zones will move north, or south in the southern hemisphere. To survive, species will have to follow their temperature zone. But not all species can. They may be surrounded by ocean or mountains or some man-made obstacle like a city. One report has already suggested that 37 per cent of all species could be wiped out by global climate change because they will be unable to move fast enough to reach areas with the ideal temperature range. In Britain this could result in the loss of some of our most treasured wild plants and animals. Already eight out of ten species have started to move north. The RSPB is concerned about the future of some of the colonies of sea birds it protects. The birds are no longer breeding, because the fish stocks they rely on have gone north. In the Antarctic, where temperatures have risen by 9°C in some places, the change is already having a startling effect.

Eating and heating

One of my favourite gardening columnists is John Walker in *Organic Gardening* magazine. An erudite writer not afraid to get stuck into important issues, he's taken up the challenge of global warming by taking a close look at seemingly innocent ordinary objects of desire, such as the soon-to-be ubiquitous patio heater. There are 630,000 garden patio heaters being used in Britain, each one capable of releasing 5.2kg of carbon dioxide (CO_2) in a two-hour session. They have already increased our CO_2 emissions by 380,000 tonnes a year. To quote John: 'The patio heater has to be the most un-green beacon of the outdoor living phenomenon.'

So what's the green alternative? Open fires of any description are inefficient at keeping us warm. All the heat disappears into the atmosphere. A contained space will keep warm longer. A chiminea (a pot stove) will radiate heat for longer and doubles up as a cooker for grilling barbecue food or baking potatoes. Wood is carbon neutral as long as it is replaced by new growth. I use the trimmings from my hedge in a couple of small open fires around the garden. I don't light that many fires so there's always enough for garden fires and winter kindling for the wood stove in the house.

If you want to make your own outdoor cooker try www.lowimpact .org or www.traditionaloven.com. I especially like www.barrel-barbecue.co.uk – barbecues made from recycled oil barrels.

Stack whatever you cut for a year and it will burn better, being free of sap and moisture. If you haven't got a hedge to trim, find fallen wood in parks and common ground – collect stuff that breaks easily. Alternatively, ask around builders' yards, mills and carpenters for scrap wood. Most of them will be happy to get rid of it. But make sure it is untreated and not contaminated with bits of metal or plastic. Burning treated and contaminated wood in fires is bad for the environment and may lead to respiratory problems. Also check in skips and in recycling yards. If you buy firewood, make sure it's local from a sustainable source.

If you really enjoy outdoor cooking you could think about building a wood-fired bread oven. Once the fire kicks in you can use the oven all day, baking huge quantities of bread, pizzas, cakes, and so on – a great way to feed a lot of people.

What should I cook on the barbecue?

Research by *Farmers' Weekly* found that an average basket of barbecue food (labelled as such by supermarkets), including chicken from Brazil, had travelled 77,000 kilometres. One of the big issues facing the ethical food lover at the moment is whether to buy local or organic. Of course, the ideal is to buy local and organic, but most people don't have the opportunity to do so, especially as 70 per cent of organic food sold in supermarkets comes from overseas. Organic food production reduces chemical use, saves energy and helps to encourage wildlife. Buying local is a good way of reducing the pollution caused by road and air haulage – so-called food miles. As environmental organisation Sustain points out, organic produce imported from New Zealand by plane consumes 235 times more energy than the amount of energy saved through organic farming.

When *Ethical Consumer* magazine asked Friends of the Earth which they preferred (non-organic local vs. organic imported) they replied: 'In a perfect world we would like there to be organic food available for everyone in every locality. Realistically this isn't the case and the next best environmental choice would be to buy local where possible.' Many people also prefer to boycott foods brought from what are considered to be oppressive regimes – states that suppress the people or have corrupt and undemocratic governments (Kenya, Israel, Mexico, Egypt, Thailand, Zimbabwe and Guatemala have all been singled out by *Ethical Consumer* magazine). Still more prefer to buy Fairtrade, which not only provides workers with a fair wage, acceptable living conditions and freedom to join trade unions, but also encourages farmers to go organic. And as *Ethical Consumer* points out, there are no criteria for acceptable wages and working conditions in overseas organic production.

Ethical choice: the case for charcoal

Barbecue charcoal should be bought with caution. Just 3 per cent of charcoal used in Britain is 'sustainable' – out of 40–50,000 tonnes consumed every year. The rest comes from rainforests and other deforested areas. If you buy charcoal make sure it's made in the UK from managed coppiced woodlands. Coppiced trees grow back every time they are cut and can keep living for hundreds of years. The charcoal is prepared in small batches by craftspeople. You can get BioRegional charcoal (www.bioregional.com) from B&Q and other major retailers, but many garden estates, wildlife trusts and small woodlands now make their own, so you can probably buy a very local supply. Look out for White Dog Charcoal in Suffolk, Cornwall Wildlife Trust charcoal, the Dorset Charcoal Company, Malvern Biofuels and Graig Farm in Wales (amongst others), as well as farmers' markets and agricultural shows. Because charcoal is made from burnt wood it's quite inefficient. Liquid petroleum gas is said to emit around 100 times less CO_2 than the average charcoal briquette doused in petroleum solvents but it is questionable as to which is better. Soundly managed wood can be replaced and gas can't. Gas also needs a huge industrial infrastructure to get it to us, while coppicing supports wildlife.

Doing your bit for climate change beyond the garden

Each person living in Britain produces about 10 tonnes of carbon dioxide per year. Our fair share of carbon emissions is 2.6 tonnes each. If you want to work out how much you produce, you can calculate your own carbon spend on a carbon calculator. Try the one at www.cat.org.uk. CAT's Carbon Gym, as it is known, asks you questions about your lifestyle. For example, how many miles do you travel each day? How many foreign holidays do you take? What sort of food do you eat? How many people do you live with? It then gives you the total amount of carbon dioxide you produce in a year and tells you how to reduce it to the 2.6 figure you need to get down to.

The best ways to do this are to:

- Buy your electricity from a supplier that supports renewable energy. This is a simple procedure that takes about an hour of your time. Most companies offer you green electricity at the same price. Check out www.foe.co.uk for details.

- Carry out an energy audit in your home. Home energy use accounts for 25 per cent of all CO_2 emissions, but you can save energy through clever design and conservation measures. Check out the Energy Saving Trust, www.est.org.uk.

- Change the way you travel. Avoid single-occupancy car journeys. Take public transport. Ride a bike. Join a car share scheme. There are lots of options.

- Don't fly. Go by train or boat. Holiday in Britain, or take 'within reach' holidays. Go to a local health spa, or ecological retreat, or just spend the time relaxing in your garden or someone else's – like me (pictured right)!

Ethical choice: carbon offsetting

There's been a lot of talk about carbon offsetting in recent years – the process of paying off your carbon debt by planting trees to soak up the carbon you've used – but does it really work? The idea is fairly simple. Trees soak up carbon as they grow so it makes sense to assume that if you plant them they'll help to reduce global climate change. But according to *Ethical Consumer* magazine many of the trees planted in offset schemes are fast-growing plantation trees such as eucalyptus, which are harvested well before they soak up enough carbon to make planting them as carbon sinks worthwhile. Burning fossil fuels also releases many other pollutants, and carbon offsetting does not take these into account, or 'the damaging effects of exploration, extraction, refining and use of fossil fuels, which include rainforest destruction, land right abuses and oil spills'.

The conclusion the magazine comes to is that it is better to support an organisation that invests in long-term tree-planting schemes such as The Woodland Trust, The Tree Council, British Trust for Conservation Volunteers, or those companies who put the carbon offset money into developing renewable energy and other technologies and lifestyles that reduce dependence on fossil fuels. Have your own carbon offsetting strategy in the home and garden. Make a list of what you would like to prioritise and set aside some money each week to create your own carbon offset fund. Invest in energy conservation before you do anything else. It's not as sexy as tree planting or buying your own wind turbine, but it does more immediate good and provides a long-term pay-back on your investment equivalent to any savings account (see CAT's *Energy Saving House* book for details).

Right Looking through the hub of a large wind farm turbine you can see a smaller domestic wind turbine (though not the sort some people misguidedly attach to their houses). To the right stands a prairie wind pump for raising water.

Further reading

Published by Centre for Alternative Technology (CAT) Publications

By the author

Curious Incidents in the Garden at Night-time, Allan Shepherd (CAT Publications, 2005)

How to Make Soil and Save Earth, Allan Shepherd (CAT Publications, 2003)

The Little Book of Garden Heroes, Allan Shepherd (CAT Publications, 2004)

The Little Book of Garden Villains, Allan Shepherd (CAT Publications, 2006)

The Little Book of Slugs, Allan Shepherd and Suzanne Gallant (CAT Publications, 2002)

52 Weeks to Change Your World, Allan Shepherd and Caroline Oakley (CAT Publications, 2004)

Other titles

Cool Composting, Peter Harper (CAT Publications, 1998)

Choosing Windpower, Hugh Piggott (CAT Publications, 2006)

Crazy Idealists? The CAT story (CAT Publications, 1995)

Home Heating with Wood, Chris Laughton (CAT Publications, 2006)

How to Build a Yurt, Steve Place (CAT Publications, 1997)

How to Build with Straw Bales, Kevin Beale (CAT Publications, 1998)

Lifting the Lid: An ecological approach to toilet systems, Peter Harper and Louise Halestrap (CAT Publications, 1999)

Sewage Solutions: Answering the Call of Nature, Grant, Moodie and Weedon (CAT Publications, 2005)

Solar Water Heating: A DIY Guide, Paul Trimby (CAT Publications, 2006)

Tapping the Sun: A guide to solar water heating (CAT Publications, 2006)

The Water Book: Find it, move it, store it, clean it...use it, Judith Thornton (CAT Publications, 2005)

The Whole House Book, Cindy Harris and Pat Borer (CAT Publications, 2005)

General gardening

Garden Problem Solver, Pippa Greenwood (Dorling Kindersley, 2001)

Growing Green, Jenny Hall and Iain Tolhurst (Vegan Organic Network, 2006)

HDRA: Encyclopedia of Organic Gardening, Anna Kruger (Editor) (Dorling Kindersley, 2005)

Organic Gardening, Geoff Hamilton (Dorling Kindersley, 2004)

Perfect Plant, Perfect Place, Roy Lancaster (Dorling Kindersley, 2002)

RHS Encyclopedia of Gardening, Christopher Brickell (Editor in Chief) (Dorling Kindersley, 2002)

RHS Encyclopedia of Plants and Flowers, Christopher Brickell (Editor in Chief) (Dorling Kindersley, 2006)

RHS Pruning and Training, Christopher Brickell and David Joyce (Dorling Kindersley, 2003)

Food and flowers

The Allotment Book, Andi Clevely (Collins, 2006)

The Complete Book of Vegetables, Herbs and Fruit, Matthew Biggs, Jekka McVicar and Bob Flowerdew (Kyle Cathie, 2002)

Eco-friendly House Plants, BC Wolverton (Weidenfeld and Nicolson, 1996)

Grow Your Own Cut Flowers, Sarah Raven (BBC, 2002)

Vegetables for Small Gardens, Joy Larkcom (Hamlyn, 1995)

Wildlife

British Wildlife (Collins, 2005)

How to Make A Wildlife Garden, Chris Baines (Frances Lincoln, 2000)

No Nettles Required: The Reassuring Truth About Wildlife Gardening, Ken Thompson (Eden Books, 2006)

Wildlife Gardening for Everyone, Malcolm Tait (Think Books, 2006)

Forest Gardening

Forest Gardening, Robert Hart (Green Books, 1991)

How to Make a Forest Garden, Patrick Whitefield (Permanent Publications, 1997)

Plants for a Future, Ken Fern (Permanent Publications, 1997)

Gardening for children and the night

The Evening Garden, Peter Loewer (Timber Press, 2002; out of print)

Sunflower Houses: A book for children and their grown ups, Sharon Lovejoy (Workman, 2001)

Growing from seed

Back Garden Seed Saving, Sue Stickland (Eco-Logic Books, 2001)
Seeds: The Definitive Guide to Growing, History, and Lore, Peter Loewer (Timber Press, 2005)
Seeds: The ultimate guide to growing successfully from seed, Jekka McVicar (Kyle Cathie, 2001)

Soil and composting

Compost, Clare Foster (Cassell, 2005)
Create Compost, Pauline Pears (Impact Publishing, 2004)
Start with the Soil, Grace Gershuny (Rodale, 1993)
Worms Eat My Garbage, Mary Applehof (Eco-Logic Books, 2003)

Weeds, pests and diseases

The "Daily Telegraph" Weeds: An earth friendly guide to their identification, use and control, John Walker (Cassell, 2003)
The Gardener's Guide to Common Sense Pest Control, Olkowski, Olkowski and Daar (The Taunton Press, 1995)
How to Enjoy Your Weeds, Audrey Wynne Hatfield (Plum Tree Publishing, 1999)
Natural Enemies Handbook: The Illustrated Guide to Biological Pest Control, Mary Louise Flint (University of California Press, 1999)
Pests, Diseases and Disorders of Garden Plants, Stefan Buczacki and Keith Harris (Collins, 2005)
RHS Pests and Diseases, Pippa Greenwood and Andrew Halstead (Dorling Kindersley, 2003)
Weeds: Friend or Foe?, Sally Roth (Carroll and Brown, 2001)

Sheds, DIY and woodcraft

Building a Shed, Joseph Truini (Taunton Press, 2003)
Green Woodworking Pattern Book, Ray Tabor (Batsford, 2005)

Ecology and plant science

An Ear to the Ground: Garden Science for Ordinary Mortals, Ken Thompson (Eden Books, 2003)
Ecology for Gardeners, Carroll and Salt (Timber Press, 2004)

Environment

The Future of Life, Edward O.Wilson (Abacus, 2002)
High Tide: News from a Warming World, Mark Lynas (HarperCollins, 2005)
How we can Save the Planet, Mayer Hillman (Penguin, 2004)
The Man Who Planted Trees, Jean Giono (various editions; also available as audiobook and animation on DVD)

No-nonsense Guide to Climate Change, Dinyar Godrej (New Internationalist, 2003)
Save Cash and Save the Planet, Andrea Smith and Nicola Baird (Collins, 2005)
Silent Spring, Rachel Carson (Penguin, 2000)

For a complete list of all the books referenced in this book and further suggestions, see the Deeper Digging page on www.allanshepherd.com.

Essential magazines

Organic Gardening
Minehead
TA24 6YY
+44 (0)1643 707 339
subscriptions@ organicgardeningmagazine.co.uk
www.organicgardeningmagazine.co.uk

Gardening Which?
Castlemead
Gascoyne Way
Hertford SG14 1LH
+44 (0)845 307 4000
gardening@which.co.uk
www.which.co.uk/gardeningwhich

Ethical Consumer
Unit 21
41 Old Birley Street
Manchester M15 5RF
+44 (0)161 226 2929
mail@ethicalconsumer.org
www.ethicalconsumer.org

The Ecologist
www.theecologist.org

Permaculture Magazine
Permanent Publications
Freepost (SCE8120)
Petersfield GU32 1HR
+ 44 (0)1730 823 311
orders@permaculture.co.uk
www.permaculture.co.uk

www.allanshepherd.com

If you want to contact me or post comments on my blog go to my website, www.allanshepherd.com. You'll also find links to CAT, CAT's information service and Collins.

Directory

Featured organisations

Agroforestry Research Trust
46 Hunters Moon
Dartington
Totnes
Devon TQ9 6JT
+44 (0)1803 840 776
mail@ agroforestry.co.uk
www.agroforestry.co.uk

Barnsdale Gardens
The Avenue
Exton
Oakham
Rutland LE15 8AH
+44 (0)1572 813 200
office@ barnsdalegardens.co.uk
www.barnsdalegardens.co.uk

Centre for Alternative Technology (CAT)
Machynlleth
Powys SY20 9AZ
+44 (0)1654 705 950
www.cat.org.uk

Garden Organic (HDRA) Yalding
Benover Road
Yalding
Nr Maidstone
Kent ME18 6EX
+44 (0)1622 814 650
www.gardenorganic.org.uk

Jenny and Mehdi
jennyandmehdi@yahoo.com
www.jennyandmehdi.org

Reading Rooftop Garden
RISC
35–39 London Street
Reading RG1 4PS
+44 (0)118 958 6692
admin@risc.org.uk
www.risc.org.uk

Sweet Loving Flowers
sweetlovingflowers@hotmail.co.uk
www.sweetlovingflowers.co.uk

Gardening organisations

Biodiversity in Urban Gardens in Sheffield (BUGS)
Prof. Kevin Gaston
Dept Animal & Plant Sciences
University of Sheffield
Sheffield S10 2TN
+44 (0)114 2220 030
www.bugs.group.shef.ac.uk

Cool Temperate (nursery)
Trinity Farm
Awsworth Lane
Cossall
Nottinghamshire NG16 2RZ
+44 (0)115 916 2673
phil.corbett@cooltemperate.co.uk
www.cooltemperate.co.uk

Federation of City Farms and Community Gardens
The GreenHouse
Hereford Street
Bristol BS3 4NA
+44 (0)117 923 1800
www.farmgarden.org.uk

Garden Organic (HDRA)
Ryton Organic Gardens
Coventry
Warwickshire CV8 3LG
+44 (0)24 7630 3517
enquiry@hdra.org.uk
www.gardenorganic.org.uk

The Heritage Seed Library (HSL)
Details as for Garden Organic (HDRA)

National Society of Allotment and Leisure Gardeners Ltd
O'Dell House
Hunters Road
Corby
Northants NN17 5JE
+44 (0)1536 266 576
natsoc@nsalg.org.uk
www.nsalg.org.uk

Permaculture Association
BCM Permaculture Association
London WC1N 3XX
+44 (0)845 458 1805
office@permaculture.org.uk
www.permaculture.org.uk

Plants for A Future
1 Lerryn View
Lerryn, Lostwithiel
Cornwall PL22 0QJ
+44 (0)1208 872 963
www.pfaf.org

Ragman's Lane Farm
Lydbrook
Gloucestershire GL17 9PA
+44 (0)1594 860 244
info@ragmans.co.uk
www.ragmans.co.uk

Royal Botanic Gardens Kew
Kew, Richmond
Surrey TW9 3AB
+44 (0)20 8332 5655
info@kew.org
www.rbgkew.org.uk

Royal Horticultural Society (RHS)
80 Vincent Square
London SW1P 2PE
+44 (0)845 260 5000
info@rhs.org.uk
www.rhs.org.uk

The National Gardens Scheme (NGS)
Hatchlands Park
East Clandon, Guildford
Surrey GU4 7RT
+44 (0)1483 211 535
ngs@ngs.org.uk
www.ngs.org.uk

Thrive (formerly Horticultural Therapy)
The Geoffrey Udall Centre
Beech Hill
Reading
Berkshire RG7 2AT
+44 (0)118 988 5688
Blind gardeners' helpline:
+44 (0)118 988 6668
www.thrive.org.uk

WWOOF UK
PO Box 2675

Lewes
East Sussex BN7 1RB
+44 (0)1273 476 286
www.wwoof.org/wwoof_uk

Organic organisations

Elm Farm
Hamstead Marshall
Newbury
Berkshire RG20 0HR
+44 (0)1488 658 298
elmfarm@efrc.com
www.efrc.com

Soil Association
South Plaza
Marlborough Street
Bristol BS1 3NX
+44 (0)117 314 5000
info@soilassociation.org
www.soilassociation.org

Vegan Organic Network
Anandavan
58 High Lane
Chorlton cum Hardy
Manchester M21 9DZ
+44 (0)845 223 5232
www.veganorganic.net

Environmental organisations

The Big Green Gathering
The Big Green Gathering Co Ltd
P.O. Box 3423
Glastonbury BA6 9ZN
+44 (0)1458 834 629
info@big-green-gathering.com
www.big-green-gathering.com

BioRegional Development Group
BedZED Centre
24 Helios Road
Wallington
Surrey SM6 7BZ
+44 (0)20 8404 4880
info@bioregional.com
www.bioregional.com

Cuban Solidarity Campaign (for
details of eco- and organic holidays)
The Red Rose Club
129 Seven Sisters Road
London N7 7QG

+44 (0)20 7263 6452
office@cuba-solidarity.org.uk
www.cuba-solidarity.org

Ecodyfi
Ty Bro Ddyfi
52 Heol Maengwyn
Machynlleth
Powys SY20 8DT
+44 (0)1654 703965
info@ecodyfi.org.uk
www.ecodyfi.org.uk

Environment Agency
www.environment-agency.gov.uk
check website or your phone book for
regional addresses and telephone contacts

Greenpeace
Canonbury Villas
London N1 2PN
+44 (0)20 7865 8100
info@uk.greenpeace.org
www.greenpeace.org.uk

Friends of the Earth
26-28 Underwood Street
London N1 7JQ
+44 (0)20 7490 1555
www.foe.co.uk

Low-Impact Living Initiative (LILI)
Redfield Community, Winslow
Bucks MK18 3LZ
+44 (0)1296 714 184
lili@lowimpact.org
www.lowimpact.org

Pesticide Action Network
Development House
56-64 Leonard Street
London EC2A 4JX
+44 (0)20 7065 0905
admin@pan-uk.org
www.pan-uk.org

Conservation and wildlife organisations

Bat Conservation Trust
Unit 2
15 Cloisters House
8 Battersea Park Road
London SW8 4BG

+44 (0)20 7627 2629
enquiries@bats.org.uk
www.bats.org.uk

**The British Hedgehog Preservation
Society (BHPS)**
Hedgehog House
Dhustone, Ludlow
Shropshire SY8 3PL
+44 (0)1584 890 801
info@britishhedgehogs.org.uk
www.britishhedgehogs.org.uk

British Trust for Ornithology (BTO)
The Nunnery
Thetford
Norfolk IP24 2PU
+44 (0)1842 750 050
info@bto.org
www.bto.org

**Buglife - The Invertebrate
Conservation Trust**
170a Park Road
Peterborough
Cambridgeshire PE1 2UF
+44 (0)1733 201 210
info@buglife.org.uk
www.buglife.org.uk

Butterfly Conservation
Manor Yard
East Lulworth
Wareham
Dorset BH20 5QP
+44 (0)870 774 430
info@butterfly-conservation.org
www.butterfly-conservation.org

English Nature
Northminster House
Peterborough PE1 1UA
+44 (0)1733 455 000
enquiries@english-nature.org.uk
www.english-nature.org.uk

Froglife
White Lodge
London Road
Peterborough PE7 0LG
+44 (0)1733 558 844
info@froglife.org
www.froglife.org

The National Trust
PO Box 39
Warrington WA5 7WD
+44 (0)870 458 400
enquiries@thenationaltrust.org.uk
www.nationaltrust.org.uk

Pond Conservation
School of Life Sciences
Oxford Brookes University
Gipsy Lane, Headington
Oxford OX3 0BP
+44 (0)1865 483 249
info@pondconservation.org.uk
www.pondstrust.org.uk

**Plantlife International
The Wild-Plant Conservation
Charity**
14 Rollestone Street
Salisbury
Wiltshire SP1 1DX
+44 (0)1722 342 730
enquiries@plantlife.org.uk
www.plantlife.org.uk

**Royal Society for the Protection of
Birds (RSPB)**
The Lodge, Sandy
Bedfordshire SG19 2DL
+44 (0)1767 680 551
www.rspb.org.uk

The Wildlife Trusts
The Kiln
Waterside
Mather Road, Newark
Nottinghamshire NG24 1WT
+44 (0)870 036 7711
enquiry@wildlifetrusts.org
www.wildlifetrusts.org

**WWF – the global environment
network**
Panda House
Weyside Park, Godalming
Surrey GU7 1XR
+44 (0)1483 426 444
www.wwf.org.uk

Trees and woodland

**British Trust for Conservation
Volunteers** (BTCV)
Sedum House, Mallard Way

Potteric Carr
Doncaster DN4 8DB
+44 (0)1302 388 888
information@btcv.org.uk
www2.btcv.org.uk

**Brogdale Horticultural
Trust/National Apple Collection
at Brogdale**
Brogdale Road
Faversham
ME13 8XZ
01795 535286
www.brogdale.org.uk

Forestry Commission
Great Eastern House
Tenison Road
Cambridge CB1 2DU
+44 (0)1223 314 546
www.forestry.gov.uk

Forest Stewardship Council
11–13 Great Oak Street
Llanidloes
Powys SY18 6BU
+44 (0)1686 413 916
info@fsc-uk.org
www.fsc-uk.org

Green Wood Trust
Green Wood Centre
Station Road
Coalbrookdale, Telford
Shropshire TF8 7DR
+44 (0)1952 432 769
www.greenwoodcentre.org.uk

**Movement for Compassionate
Living (MCL)**
105 Cyfyng Road
Ystalyfera
Swansea SA9 2BT
www.mclveganway.org.uk

Rainforest Alliance
665 Broadway, Suite 500
New York
NY 10012 USA
+1 (212) 677 1900
info@ra.org
www.rainforest-alliance.org

Reforesting Scotland
62–66 Newhaven Road

Edinburgh EH6 5QB
+44 (0)131 554 4321
info@reforestingscotland.org
www.reforestingscotland.org

The Tree Council
71 Newcomen Street
London SE1 1YT
+44 (0)20 7407 9992
Info@treecouncil.org.uk
www.treecouncil.org.uk

Trees for Life
The Park
Findhorn Bay
Forres IV36 3TZ
+44 (0)1309 691 292
trees@findhorn.org
www.treesforlife.org.uk

The Woodland Trust
Autumn Park
Dysart Road, Grantham
Lincolnshire NG31 6LL
+44 (0)1476 581 111
www.woodland-trust.org.uk

Eco-sheds

**Association for Environment
Conscious Building**
PO Box 32
LLandysul SA44 5ZA
+44 (0)845 456 9773
graigoffice@aecb.net
www.aecb.net

**Straw Bale Building Association
(WISE)**
Hollinroyd Farm, Butts Lane
Todmorden. OL14 8RJ
+44 (0)1442 825 421
www.strawbalebuildingassociation.
org.uk

Tools for Self Reliance
Southampton
Hampshire SO40 7GY
+44 (0)2380 869 697
info@tfsr.org
www.tfsr.org

**The Waste and Resources Action
Programme (WRAP)**
The Old Academy

21 Horse Fair
Banbury OX16 0AH
+44 (0)808 100 2040
www.wrap.org.uk

Walter Segal Self Build Trust
info@segalselfbuild.co.uk
www.segalselfbuild.co.uk

Children

The Fairyland Trust
PO Box 14
Wells-Next-The-Sea
Norfolk NR23 1WB
+44 (0)1328 710 165
sarah@fairylandtrust.org
www.fairylandtrust.org

Schools Organic Network
Garden Organic (HDRA)
Ryton Organic Gardens
Coventry
Warwickshire CV8 3LG
+44 (0)24 7630 3517
www.gardenorganic.org.uk/schools_org
anic_network/index.php

The Woodcraft Folk
13 Ritherdon Road
London SW17 8QE
+44 (0)20 8672 6031
info@woodcraft.org.uk
www.woodcraft.org.uk

Accreditation organisations

British Union for the Abolition of Vivisection (BUAV)
16a Crane Grove
London N7 8NN
+44 (0)20 7700 4888
info@buav.org
www.buav.org

Defra (Department for Environment, Food & Rural Affairs)
Customer Contact Unit
Eastbury House
30–34 Albert Embankment
London SE1 7TL
+44 (0)8459 33 55 77
helpline@defra.gsi.gov.uk
www.defra.gov.uk

Energy Saving Trust
21 Dartmouth Street
London SW1H 9BP
+44 (0)20 7222 0101
www.est.org.uk

Fairtrade Foundation
Room 204
16 Baldwin's Gardens
London EC1N 7RJ
+44 (0)20 7405 5942
mail@fairtrade.org.uk
www.fairtrade.org.uk

Marine Stewardship Council
3rd floor, Mountbarrow House
6–20 Elizabeth Street
London SW1W 9RB
+44 (0)20 7811 3300
www.msc.org

Organic Farmers and Growers
Elim Centre
Lancaster Road
Shrewsbury
Shropshire SY1 3LE
+44 (0)845 330 5122
www.organicfarmers.org.uk

The Vegan Society
Donald Watson House
7 Battle Road
St Leonards-on-Sea
East Sussex TN37 7AA
+44 (0)1424 427 393
info@vegansociety.com
www.vegansociety.com

Vegetarian Society
Parkdale
Dunham Road
Altrincham
Cheshire WA14 4QG
+44 (0)161 925 2000
info@vegsoc.org
www.vegsoc.org

Climate organisations

Climate Action Network (Europe)
asbl
Rue de la Charité, 48
1210
Brussels, Belgium
+32 (0) 2 229 52 20

info@climnet.org
www.climatenetwork.org

IPCC (Intergovernmental Panel on Climate Change)
IPCC Secretariat
c/o World Meteorological Organization
7bis Avenue de la Paix
C.P. 2300
CH-1211 Geneva 2, Switzerland
+41 22 730 8208
IPCC-Sec@wmo.int
www.ipcc.ch

UK Phenology Network
Woodland Trust
Autumn Park
Grantham NG31 6L
+44 (0)1476 584 878
phenology@woodland-trust.org.uk
www.naturescalendar.org.uk

Fencing

www.grange-fencing.com
If you want homemade and recycled, check out:
www.summervillenovascotia.com/PalletFence for their fence made out of old pallets. For hurdles look at www.coppice-products.co.uk.

Seed and plant suppliers

There are many good seed and plant suppliers, here are a few:
www.wildflowers.co.uk
www.wildflower.org.uk
www.organiccatalogue.com
www.tamarorganics.co.uk
www.wigglywigglers.org.uk
www.thompson-morgan.com
www.nickys-nursery.co.uk.

Organic food suppliers

Search the web for your local organic food suppliers. Sites include:
www.bigbarn.co.uk
www.alotoforganics.co.uk
www.ethicalfoods.co.uk
www.organic-supermarket.co.uk
www.farmers-markets.net.
www.freerangemag.co.uk
www.organic.aber.ac.uk.

Index

Acknowledgements

This book has taken the best part of a year of my life. During that time I have missed a million moments with my friends and family. I would like to thank all of the people close to me for being there and understanding that I could not be there, in particular my mum Lesley and my sister Hazel. I would like to thank Chloë (who contributed the sections on growing food as well as offering much help and advice throughout) and Sue, Jenny and Mehdi. Thank you for making *The Organic Garden* rich and beautiful. I would like to thank Caroline, Graham, Hele, Christian, Bethan, Joan, Hazel, Sally, Deirdre, Jenny, Thea, Jessa, Roger and Peter and everyone else at The Centre for Alternative Technology who have supported and encouraged me not only in this year but also in the past – the names are too numerous to mention in full. Outside of CAT, in the valleys and villages of the Dyfi Valley I would like to thank the following gardeners for allowing *The Organic Garden* on to their hallowed turf – Pete of Sweet Loving Flowers, Petra and Hussam, Kay, Tom and Liza, Duncan and Heather, Dave and Liz, Jo and Tony, Luca and Tom. I would also like to thank Darren and Marly, Luca and Hala, Hannah and Kestral for allowing themselves to be photographed. I would like to thank Iona for helping me when I most needed help and Julie for her exquisite ramblings. Imogen and the Dyfi Valley Seed Savers. Andy and Teresa at Eco-Dyfi. I would like to thank everyone in the valley for their friendly hellos and small conversations that make life so much easier and more rewarding.

Away from Wales now: Thank you Jenny, Alastair and Lizzy at Collins, my amazing photographer Cristian Barnett and his assistants, editor Barbara Dixon and designers Lisa and Emma. It has been a pleasure to work with all of you. I would like to thank Sharon Amos for her editorial suggestions and corrections. Thank you for lavishing so much care and attention on *The Organic Garden*, for giving me the opportunity to write this book and for creating such a wonderful finished product.

Cristian photographed several gardens in various locations across Britain and I would like to thank the following people and organisations for their time and helpful assistance: Martin Crawford and the Agroforestry Research Trust; Bob Sherman of Garden Organic (HDRA) and all the staff and volunteers at Garden Organic's garden at Yalding. In particular Chloë would like to thank Nicola, Sally, Aileen, Mary and Alan, who have directly inspired in the writing of this book. Thanks also to Steve Jones and The Reading Roof Top project at RISC, and the staff at Geoff Hamilton's gardens at Barnsdale. Lastly I would like to pay homage to all the writers, the scientists and the gardeners who have enabled me to understand the world a little better and inspire me to know it a whole lot more.